Responses to the book

Christine Thornton has followed up her excellent previous book on Group and Team Coaching with this new edited book showing how psychoanalytic and systemic theories and approaches can be applied to work with groups, teams and whole organizations. A rich panoply of theories, case examples and dialogue between different perspectives, offering much to all of us who work with the challenges of enabling change in organisations and wider systems.

Professor Peter Hawkins, author of *Leadership Team Coaching*
and *Leadership Team Coaching in Practice*

This collection of essays richly describes the work of consultants and leaders in group analysis in a number of diverse settings from the NHS to monasteries and more. It poses questions and offers theoretical frameworks for the consultant to hold in mind in the process of creating dialogue in order to capture the complexity in the work of leaders and followers, in teams and organizations. To quote the editor, 'Every team is threaded through, like a stick of rock, with the qualities of the organization and its purpose'.

The Editor has achieved a balance between theory and practice, art and science, that makes this an important book for all those wishing to understand more about their role as organizational consultant. This is a great book!

Frances Griffiths, Chair of the Board of Trustees,
Institute of Group Analysis, UK

This book offers profound and revealing insights into how we humans work and live together in the groups we form and leave. Our development as a species has enabled us to trace the origins of the universe, to unravel the structure of our life forms, to understand something of the functioning of quantum particles and black holes. We have done this in groups and teams over more than 300,000 years and evolved an ability and inclination to work and live in groups. This book is unique in enabling us to make wiser sense of the complexity and beauty of these interactions, predicated as they are on dialogue. It offers a richer understanding than many of the easy and superficial management books on teamworking and group functioning and enables us to begin to imagine how we can overcome some of the profound challenges of working within and across groups that we face.

Michael West, Professor of Organizational Psychology Lancaster University Management School

The current era is plagued by over-simplification, when it needs simplexity – the art of making things simple (i.e. understandable) but not simplistic. Group analysis is one of the most powerful tools we have to cope with growing complexity. This book is a major contribution into this growing field of insight and practice.

Professor David Clutterbuck, David Clutterbuck Partnership

This thoughtful book adds to the growing literature on managing group processes in teams and contemporary workplaces. Written by leading scholarly practitioners in the field of group analysis, it provides both important insights and techniques for intervening in the complex emotions, politics and interactions that typify organisational group dynamics. Here is a well-grounded riposte to those who see group dynamics as marginal to the effective leadership of contemporary organizations.

Michael Fischer, Professor of Organisational Behaviour and Leadership at Australian Catholic University. Visiting Scholar, University of Oxford

Christine's previous book, *Group and Team Coaching*, outlined what goes on in groups – key driving processes which are usually outside conscious awareness. In this latest book on group analysis she again lifts the veil to reveal the deeper factors at play. With the help of chapter authors many different perspectives of group analysis are explored. A distinction is drawn between group analysis in therapeutic work and organizational work. The book is extremely thorough and includes discussion about previous writing on the theory and praxis of group analysis. It will be invaluable to anyone already working in the field of group analysis and should be read by anyone working systemically with organizations, in order to increase their awareness and understanding of what is happening beneath the surface.

Gill Smith, Former Chair, Association for Coaching, and author, *Because I Can*

This book is a rich resource for consultants and managers looking for alternative ways of thinking about organizations. It brings together insights from a wide variety of highly skilled group analysts with many years' experience successfully supporting organisations to function better, and who point to the importance of paying attention to what is usually least discussable in contemporary organisations: feelings, anxiety, and seemingly 'irrational' group behaviour. It serves as a refreshing antidote to the current managerial preoccupation with metrics, targets, and positivity.

Chris Mowles, Professor of Complexity and Management, Director of the Doctor of Management, Research Theme Leader Managing Complex Change, Hertfordshire Business School

Group Analytic thinking has much to offer to the understanding of organizations. This book presents a rich compilation of papers from the organizational experience of talented Group Analysts and Group Analytic Practitioners. The chapters are accessible and offer an excellent insight into the complexities of organizational life, clearly outlining the dilemmas, struggles, competing pressures and conflicts for those working in and with organizations. The generous use of vignettes helps illustrate how group analytic thinking provides an in depth understanding of problematic dynamics emerging in various organizational contexts, and the potential traps awaiting the inexperienced or unsuspecting practitioner.

This book is an important must read for managers, organizational consultants or anyone wanting to understand what emerges in and between individuals, teams and organizations. It is the kind of book I wish had been available when I started my own journey in organizations.

Marion Brown, Former Chair of the Institute of Group Analysis, and organizational consultant

If leadership and management in organizations means anything it has to do with dealing with people and the often difficult relation between them as they do their work. Yet education and development progress do very little to help people acquire the skills required to understand group dynamics and so deal with people. This book fulfils a very important function of providing group analytic insights into these matters.

Ralph Stacey, Professor of Management, Hertfordshire Business School, University of Hertfordshire

The Art and Science of Working Together

The Art and Science of Working Together: Practising Group Analysis in Teams and Organizations is a primary resource for anyone wishing to learn more about the complex unconscious dynamics of organizations, providing a practical guide for organizational work, a guide to how to improve things, and a strong theoretical foundation in the group analytic concept of the 'tripartite matrix'.

Group analysis is a highly developed science of group relationships, which allows complexity and systems perspectives to be held in mind alongside organizational psychology, strategic development and business wisdom. Organized into eight sections, the book describes the essence of organizational group analysis, including the art of conversation, leadership, ethical issues in team working, and working with whole organizations. It addresses issues such as 'us-and-them' dynamics, the nature of systems boundaries, and the relationship between an organization and its context.

Leaders and leading consultants give case studies, describing their thinking as they work, to illustrate the theory in action. This essential new resource will allow clinically trained practitioners to extend their scope into organizational work, and all coaches and leaders to benefit from knowledge of the group analytic discipline. It is essential reading for consultants and coaches working with teams and organizations, and for leaders within organizations.

Christine Thornton is a group analyst, organizational consultant, and author of the best-selling *Group and Team Coaching*. She was Founding Director of the IGA RPiO organizational training and has been honored for contributions to the coaching profession. Christine works with organizational leaders and coaches, enabling better understanding of complex, perhaps unconscious systemic and relationship dynamics.

The New International Library of Group Analysis (NILGA)
Series Editor: Earl Hopper

Drawing on the seminal ideas of British, European and American group analysts, psychoanalysts, social psychologists and social scientists, the books in this series focus on the study of small and large groups, organisations and other social systems, and on the study of the transpersonal and transgenerational sociality of human nature. NILGA books will be required reading for the members of professional organisations in the field of group analysis, psychoanalysis, and related social sciences. They will be indispensable for the "formation" of students of psychotherapy, whether they are mainly interested in clinical work with patients or in consultancy to teams and organisational clients within the private and public sectors.

Recent titles in the series include:

The Art and Science of Working Together: Practising Group Analysis in Teams and Organizations
Edited by Christine Thornton

Dream Telling, Relations, and Large Groups: New Developments in Group Analysis
By Robi Friedman

Group Analysis: Working with Staff, Teams and Organizations
Edited by David Vincent and Aleksandra Novakovic

The Social Unconscious in Persons, Groups, and Societies: Volume 3: The Foundation Matrix Extended and Re-configured
Edited by Earl Hopper

Fairy Tales and the Social Unconscious: The Hidden Language
By Ravit Raufman and Haim Weinberg

Group Analysis in the Land of Milk and Honey
Edited by Yael Doron

For a full list of titles in this series, please visit www.routledge.com

The Art and Science of Working Together

Practising Group Analysis in Teams and Organizations

Edited by Christine Thornton

Routledge
Taylor & Francis Group

LONDON AND NEW YORK

First published 2019
by Routledge
2 Park Square, Milton Park, Abingdon, Oxon OX14 4RN

and by Routledge
52 Vanderbilt Avenue, New York, NY 10017

Routledge is an imprint of the Taylor & Francis Group, an informa business

British Library Cataloguing-in-Publication Data
A catalogue record for this book is available from the British Library

Library of Congress Cataloging-in-Publication Data
A catalog record for this book has been requested

ISBN: 9780367182564 (hbk)
ISBN: 9780367182588 (pbk)
ISBN: 9780429060359 (ebk)

Typeset in Palatino
by Apex CoVantage, LLC

Contents

Series editor's foreword

Writing a foreword to a new book in the New International Library of Group Analysis always gives me a sense of satisfaction, especially when I have been very involved in editing the book. However, writing the foreword to this study of group analytic consultation to teams and organizations has reminded me of how much I have also enjoyed working with Christine Thornton and her authors and consultants. Christine is an experienced organizational consultant who latterly trained as a clinical group analyst. She founded and chaired the Diploma in Reflective Practice in Organizations at the Institute of Group Analysis from 2015 to 2018 and has many publications to her credit.

For this book Christine has conceived, authored, co-authored, and edited a set of linked discussions and written contributions from a network of colleagues who share her commitment to the practice of reflecting together, or 'dialogue', as the essence of organizational consultation informed by the theory of Group Analysis. The chapters are based on consultations to organizations in virtually each *situs* of the occupational structures of contemporary societies, ranging from health care to government to education to manufacturing. Although focused on the dialectical tension between theory and experience, the chapters convey the healthy curiosity which seasoned consultants bring to their work. Small, median, and large groups are discussed, as are those patterns of leadership, followership, and bystandership associated with basic assumption processes.

The consultant authors are fascinated by the connections among the personal, dynamic, and foundational matrices of the social systems of organizations. Although organizations have the power to be effective in delivering goods and services, a sense of accomplishment, and wealth, they can also be inefficient, causing frustration, emotional pain, hatred, and destruction. What is the purpose of a consultation to an organization which (or who) has been brought to see the 'doctor' by those members/participants in the organization who have the power and resources to authorize the consultation? In fact, the organization is more likely to be troubled than it is to be ill. Therefore, from the very start of the process, the consultant must become a kind of healer who wants to engage in a special kind of conversation regarding what are perceived to be the obstacles to the growth and development of the organization.

Consultants informed by Group Analysis are aware of the rituals which characterize all forms of healing. They are protective of the liminal processes through which new spaces might be discovered, and they are oriented towards integration and wholeness. Imbued with knowledge from the social sciences, the study of group dynamics, and depth psychology – if not psychoanalysis itself, such consultants are sensitive to unconscious processes. If the participants in a troubled organization are good people who are trying to do the best they can with limited resources, so too are the consultants. They can only encourage people to take as 'problematic' the social, cultural, and communicational dimensions of the matrices by which they are restrained and constrained.

Keenly aware of the vicissitudes of organizational trauma, and the consequent regression in the dynamics of large groups, the authors are sensitive to the restraints and constraints of what has come to be called the social unconscious. This involves an appreciation of the sociality of human nature and the dimensions of the tripartite matrix. Their goal is to broaden and deepen their understanding of the organization in order to be better able to change it, but not always as they would please.

The authors of this book include both men and women, which is unusual in consultation to organizations outside the field of healthcare. There is a feminine sensibility in their descriptions of the consultative process. Their special conversations are oriented towards the mutual and relational discovery of the nature of the problem, which is often invisible except in its affects throughout the system.

This very personal book illustrates the steady development of a group analytic approach to organizational consultation, with its own identity, strengths, and weaknesses. It is the fourth volume in the sub-series of NILGA concerned with the study of organizations, which are not groups as such, but very special kinds of groupings which are managed in the service of achieving the most effective and efficient completion of primary and secondary tasks, as well as providing rewards for doing so. This will always require an appreciation of the dynamics of power as well as the dynamics of personal charisma and relational creativity.

I am sure that all readers of this book will enjoy the conversations of which it is comprised and be tempted to engage in them. They are likely to become aware of a body of knowledge and experience from which they can draw and to which they can contribute.

Earl Hopper,
Series Editor

Preface and acknowledgments

When my book on *Group and team coaching* (2010, 2016) was met with such interest and appreciation, the seed for this book began to form in my mind. My ideas, how group analytic insights help organizational leaders and team consultants, are developed here but now they sit alongside the ideas of other highly skilled and experienced colleagues. Group analysis is a discipline based in the value of diverse perspectives in any system, and therefore this book is itself a group analytic offering. On 9 December 2017, most of us contributors met together for a day's conversation. In the book are fragments of the conversation from that day, illustrating the rich, non-linear nature of group analytic dialogue.

The book is informed by innumerable relationships and interactions, mine and those of the other contributors, too many to list here, but for which we are nevertheless grateful. I wish to distinguish one person in particular. In 2014, I met and began to work with Gerhard Wilke, whom I am honored to count as a professional friend. As we talked, we discovered considerable overlap in our thinking about organizations, rooted both in our group analytic training, and a shared pragmatism in praxis based in long experience: a nuanced understanding of boundaries, central to effective organizational work.

Gerhard has been a staunch supporter and diligent colleague in the development of the book, and has made a substantial contribution himself, particularly in the final two sections of the book. Our jointly written chapters (22, 23, and 24) are the fruit of our conversations, particularly about 'translucent boundaries' and the necessary flexibility of the organizational consultant, and leader, in working with them.

Finally, I should like to thank Gabrielle Rowan for her careful work on the graphic on the next page.

Christine Thornton
March 2019

Contributors

Gwen Adshead FRCPsych is a group analyst and consultant forensic psychiatrist, for many years at Broadmoor Hospital. Qualified in medicine in 1983, she holds two masters' degrees reflecting her interests, one in medical law and ethics, and the other in mindfulness-based cognitive therapy. She is Visiting Professor of Psychiatry at Gresham College, previously Visiting Professor at Yale School of Law and Psychiatry and was the castaway on Desert Island Discs on 1 July 2010. Gwen has written more than a hundred academic papers; in 2012 she received a Jerwood Award to write *A Short Book About Evil*, published 2015.

Dick Blackwell is a group analyst, family therapist, and organizational consultant in private practice, an Associate Editor of *Group Analysis*, Director of the Centre for Psychotherapy and Human Rights, and former Chair of the IGA. With a background in business management, education, and alternative community work, he has supervised and taught at the Institute of Family Therapy, London Marriage Guidance, Westminster Pastoral Foundation, and the IGA. His family work combines systemic and psychoanalytic thinking in a human rights context, with clients predominantly from the 'third world'. He is particularly interested in power, culture, and communication in the context of trauma.

Farideh Dizadji M. Inst. G.A., MSc is a group analyst, psychotherapist, and organizational consultant, formerly clinical director of Kids Company's principal London Centre and NAFSIYAT, with previous posts at the Women's Therapy Centre, Hertfordshire University, and the Medical Foundation for the Care of Victims of Torture. Farideh holds a BA in Political Science from Tehran University and an MBA from UCLA. While a systems analyst in Iran, she trained as a lawyer and was involved in international socio-political/feminist movements. After 1979 she was forced to leave Iran as a political refugee, living in Berlin before settling in London.

Clare Gerada trained in psychiatry and general practice, with a special interest in linking mental health, addiction, and primary care. She has held numerous senior national policy roles with the Department of Health and Royal College of General Physicians (RCGP), becoming the high profile second female Chair of the RCGP between 2011–2013. Clare, an avid tweeter, is often called upon by mainstream media to make sense of current health news. She established and leads the award-winning Practitioner Health Service and is proud still to do the 'day job' as a South London GP, in the same surgery since 1992.

Earl Hopper is a psychoanalyst, group analyst, training analyst, and organizational consultant based in London. A Fellow of the British Psychoanalytical Society and a Distinguished Fellow of the American Group Psychotherapy Association, he is a former President of the International Association for Group Psychotherapy, and a former Chair of the Association of Independent Psychoanalysts of the British Psychoanalytical Society. Earl is particularly well-known for his theory of the fourth basic assumption, 'Incohesion: Massification/Aggregation or (ba) I:A/M', especially relevant to trauma and organizations. He edited *Trauma and Organisations* in the New International Library of Group Analysis (NILGA) of which he is the General Editor.

Raman Kapur is Chief Executive and Consultant Clinical Psychologist with Threshold, running therapeutic communities/atmospheres for people with severe mental illness within Northern Ireland. He was Course Director of the Masters in Psychoanalytic Psychotherapy at Queens University Belfast, previously working in the NHS in Blackburn and London. He was awarded an MBE in 2012 for his work in Northern Ireland and regularly contributes to television and radio programs. With over 35 papers on psychotherapy, mental health, and trauma and books on 'The Troubled Mind of Northern Ireland', and his recently published 'Psychiatric Rehabilitation: A Psychoanalytic Approach to Recovery'.

Vincent Leahy MA, MSc, Fellow of the Chartered Institute of Personnel and Development, and Trustee of the Institute of Group Analysis. An independent analytic team coach and organization development facilitator working with individuals and teams in education and various business sectors in the Middle East, North Africa, and the UK. Associate lecturer with the Open University Faculty of Business and Law and Winchester University Faculty of Education, Health and Social Care. Academic focus is on ways of helping groups to work together through complex change and facilitating them in sustaining communication and relationships.

Abdullah Mia is a Principal Clinical Psychologist and Clinical Lead for a partnership service between the NHS and Her Majesty's Prison and Probation Service (HMPPS) working with complex trauma and persistent offending in young male adults. He also works in private practice as a therapist, trainer, and facilitator within teams and organizations focusing on equality, diversity, and inclusion. He has written about the individual and group experiences of difference and the impact this has on the mental health of people within their communities. Abdullah has an interest in men's mental health and the impact of social discourses on communities.

Morris Nitsun is a consultant psychologist in group psychotherapy in Camden and Islington NHS Mental Health Trust: a training group analyst at IGA London, and founder member of the Fitzrovia Group Analytic Practice. His publications include 'The Anti-group: destructive forces in the group and their creative potential' (1996) and 'Beyond the Anti-group: survival and transformation' (2015).

Christine Oliver PhD is Consultant Family Therapist and Group Analyst for East London Foundation Trust and a psychotherapist, supervisor, and organizational consultant in private practice. She is especially interested in methodologies for structuring dialogue to engender reflexive practice at work. She co-directs the Diploma in Systemic Leadership and Consulting Practice, accredited by the Institute of Group Analysis, and provides systemic leadership training and consultancy locally and globally. She has contributed to the development of systemic theory and practice through many published papers and two books: *Reflexive Inquiry*, Karnac, London (2005) and *Complexity, Relationships and Strange Loops*, MHA Institute, Canada (2003).

Chris Powell is a group analyst and organizational consultant. Formerly Head of Psychological Therapies at The Retreat, York he now works independently in Leeds. He has extensive experience as a psychotherapist in NHS and independent services, and as a consultant to national organizations, university departments, boards of charities, NHS teams, GP partnerships, and businesses. He practises as a clinician, runs organizational consultation and supervision groups, and mentors senior staff. He is the founder of Café Psychologique which takes psychological thinking out of consulting rooms and into public spaces. His Room to Breathe group does the same in the outdoors.

Christopher Rance is a group analyst who started his consultancy career with what is now PwC and has been running his own Project Management firm for the last 40 years. He is a senior member of the British Computer Society, specializing in Artificial Intelligence. He has been a senior lecturer and group conductor on the Judge Institute of

Management's MBA course at Cambridge University and on the Complexity Faculty of Hertfordshire University's IGA-sponsored MA and Doctorate of Management programs. Active in both the IGA and GASI over the years, he has written and taught extensively on Group Analytic Organizational Consultancy.

Cynthia Rogers explores how Group Analytic theory and practice can inform work with institutional and colleague relationships. She is an experienced group analyst, supervisor, researcher, organizational consultant, and company director. Her organizational work is informed by her research interest in professional identity, published as 'Psychotherapy and Counselling a Professional Business'. Wiley (2004). Cynthia has a particular interest in the contribution of median dialogue groups to organizational consultancy and was a key speaker at the first international congress on Median Groups in Bolzano, Italy. She has consulted to the voluntary and public services, the business community, and individuals.

Christopher Scanlon DPhil is an Independent Psycho-socialist Researcher and Consultant, Training Analyst at the Institute of Group Analysis (London), member of the Irish Group Analytic Society, Associate at the Tavistock Institute of Human Relations, and Founder member of the Association for Psychosocial Studies (APS). Previously a Consultant Adult and Forensic Psychotherapist and Reflective Practice Team Development (RPTD) Consultant he worked in a range of health, social care, and social justice settings, has published widely in the field, has acted as expert adviser to various Government Departments and NGOs and currently sits of the NHS *Social Care Research Ethics Committee.*

Ian Simpson is a group analyst and was Head of Psychotherapy Services at a major London teaching hospital for 20 years. He retired from the NHS five years ago and continues to have a small private practice offering individual and group psychotherapy, supervision, and reflective practice for staff teams. He has written several papers and book chapters on group dynamics, containment and contextual safety in the workplace.

Margaret Smith is a Psychodynamic Psychotherapist, Supervisor, Group Analyst and role consultant. Her background is work with young people with emotional and behavioral difficulties, first in London then in Liverpool. She set up and managed a Staff Support Service for NHS Staff in Liverpool, including staff counseling, group psychotherapy, post trauma support, workplace mediation, training, supervision, and organizational consultancy. She led and taught on the Liverpool University Diploma in Psychotherapy, was a visiting lecturer at the

Tavistock Institute, teaching on D10, and co-led the IGA supervision training, 'Using the Group as the Medium for Supervision' between 2008 and 2017.

Marlene Spero PhD (contributors' dialogue pieces only) is a group analyst, psychoanalytic psychotherapist, and organizational consultant. She has consulted to private and public organizations in diverse fields including retail, insurance, security, banking, education, social services, the NHS, and the religious, and has published in the field. Founding Chair of the IGA Organisational Section, she formerly developed courses facilitating understanding of group analysis and organizations. Vice-President of EATGA, she has directed and staffed group analytic and leadership courses in Europe; she continues as a tutor and teacher at the IGA. Her particular interest is in transitions, change, leadership development, and coaching.

Christine Thornton is a group analyst, supervisor, and consultant, author of the best-selling *Group and team coaching* [Routledge 2010, 2016], and many other books and papers. Christine works with leaders and coaches enabling better understanding of complex unconscious dynamics in organizational relationships. She has applied group analysis in organizational consultation, team coaching, large groups, action learning, supervision, and professional development groups, in thirty years' consulting; she has been honored for her contributions to coaching. As a senior leader, most recently she was national clinical director at icap. Christine was Founding Director of the IGA organizational training, *Reflective Practice in Organisations*.

Gerhard Wilke studied anthropology at King's College, Cambridge before training as a group analyst. For 25 years he has consulted across Europe in many industries and public sector organizations, combining group analytic insights with ethnographic ways of studying and working with clients, and building up an international reputation as a Large Group conductor. An Associate of Ashridge Business School, he has developed leadership skills for ten years with the UK National Institute of Health Research; he teaches group analysis in the UK and Germany. Gerhard is widely published in English and German, including *Living Leadership* and *Breaking free of Bonkers*.

Ewa Wojciechowska is a training group analyst, psychotherapist, supervisor and organizational consultant in private practice. She is a member of the Institute of Group Analysis and Group Analytic Society international. Her career in the mental health field began as a psychiatric social worker in the pioneering therapeutic community, Henderson Hospital, where she first learnt the importance of clear boundaries and boundary management. She consults to organisations in healthcare services, group analytic training institutes in the UK and Eastern Europe, the voluntary sector, and tertiary education.

David Wood FRCPsych is a group analyst and family therapist at the Fitzrovia Group Analytic Practice, seeing individuals, couples, and families. He was a GP for six years before choosing psychiatry, qualifying as a group analyst in 1985, then as a child and adolescent psychiatrist and family therapist at the Tavistock Clinic, London. He specialized for 20 years in treating young people with severe eating disorders, setting up his own in-patient service with milieu therapy at its center. He has published many papers and chapters on group analysis, family therapy, and psychotherapy, and presented papers and workshops at numerous conferences.

Section I

Editor's introduction

What group analysis can offer in organizational work

Section I gives my editor's introduction to group analytic praxis. The material in these chapters has been expanded from two papers originally published in Group Analysis, in vols 50(4) and 51(1), December 2017 and March 2018, entitled *Towards a group analytic praxis for working with teams in organizations I and II*. The reprinted material is by permission of SAGE Publications, Ltd.

Chapter one gives an account of what drew me, as an organizational practitioner, to group analysis; shares a fragment of conversation which sheds light on what brought some of the other contributors; reviews group analytic organizational literature; and gives a brief introduction to each chapter.

Chapter two sets out six aspects of group analysis that render it a valuable basis for organizational work: attention to the individual in the group, nuanced understanding of interpersonal communication, attention to context, tolerance and value of multiple perspectives, creative incorporation of difference, and a flexible developmental approach to managing anxiety and leadership projections. It also highlights key differences between clinical and organizational group analysis and ends with a focus on two group analytic concepts, *communication* and *translation*, including a fragment of group analytic conversation on these themes among the book's contributors.

Chapter three, *Persecutor, victim, rescuer: imperfect consulting in an imperfect world* offers an extended vignette in illustration, explored through the use of 'five questions' I have developed as an aid to making praxis decisions; Margaret Smith takes this analysis further from a systemic perspective in chapter 15.

Chapter four analyzes the vignette from the perspective of the six characteristics set out in chapter two.

Chapter 1

Coming to group analysis and this book

Christine Thornton

Adapted from Thornton, C. Towards a group analytic praxis for working with teams in organizations. Group Analysis 50(4), pp. 519–536. Copyright © 2017 by the Author. Reprinted by permission of SAGE Publications, Ltd.

Group analysis is above all the art of conversation, or 'dialogue' (De Mare, Piper and Thompson, 1991). Dialogue, the sharing of differing perspectives through conversation, is central. I feel profound gratitude for the time, care, and thought invested by the group analytic colleagues who have shared their perspectives in this volume. We have very different routes to and uses of group analysis, and yet share common threads in the way we think and practice that go beyond work in organizations; they reflect a desire and commitment to using our discipline to increase dialogue and so humane behavior in the world. We hope that this book will bring group analytic principles to a wider audience.

In this introductory chapter I give an account of what drew me, as an organizational practitioner, to group analysis; share a fragment of conversation which sheds light on what brought some of the other contributors; review group analytic organizational literature; and give a brief introduction to each chapter.

Background: coming to group analysis

In the late 1980s, I began working with organizations and teams. I was usually hired to improve strategic thinking and/or the ability to work together. There were several 'models' purporting to help with these undertakings, but they were almost all rational, addressed to conscious, relatively controllable aspects of people's experience at work. However, most teams' difficulties, especially the intractable ones, lay in the realm of the *irrational*. Psychoanalytic and systems

This chapter contains

theories seemed to offer more useful perspectives, and so I attended a number of experiential educational events; these helped me help clients understand and change a broader range of problems.

A little later, sitting in a group in the Tavistock Institute, London, I heard that there was an Institute of Group Analysis (IGA) next door. Intrigued, in 1993 I joined the IGA Foundation Course and engaged a group analyst, Dick Blackwell, as a supervisor. I enjoyed Dick's insights and his engagement with the contexts and politics of organizations. I liked the strong emphasis in the Course on experience and praxis, and the theory, more like a framework than a blueprint. I particularly enjoyed the large groups, dialogue among many people, and the experienced validity of many different views of a single topic. I experienced 'koinonia' – the 'impersonal fellowship . . . in which people can speak, hear, see and think freely, a form of togetherness and amity that brings a pooling of resources' (De Mare, Piper and Thompson, 1991). I particularly remember profoundly shared mourning for John Smith[1] in May 1994.

Group analysis had been developed as a psychotherapy, and I chose to train, qualifying as a therapist. I became excited by what I observed in my now bifurcated practice: that the processes in my therapeutic groups were identical to those in the organizational groups with which I had worked for over a decade. I hoped to integrate group analytic principles in my 'day job' as an organizational consultant, or coach, as we were by then beginning to be called. Since then this has been my work, and this book ultimately results from the greater realization of that ambition.

Fragment of contributors' dialogue: what drew us to group analysis?

CHRISTINE T – *We practice in the way that we are. You practice as an anthropologist, Gerhard. We use the experience that we've had because we are using our selves.*

CYNTHIA – *I always feel at disadvantage being a scientist. It's just such a different paradigm.*

CHRISTINE T – *I didn't know that. It explains to me how you teach and write so clearly, because you are breaking it down.*

GERHARD – *Explain?*

CYNTHIA – *Ask me about DNA, enzymes and I'm away. Particle theory versus wave theory. Complexity theory – fractals. That was the first time I understood group analysis. Once I understood it as a mathematical thing I could understand why you just let it flow and I could explain it to people. If I am doing some work, a large part of it will be teaching and explaining.*

MARLENE – *I never thought group analysis was enough because it never dealt with roles, structure, authority, the task is always internal to the group rather than external. The wider context is not just politics or culture but legal systems and accountancy impacting on a particular group within the firm that may be going wrong. If we don't hold the task in mind, we tend to get caught up with the process and perhaps individual members.*

SOMEONE – *When I talk about transitional thinking it's Winnicott pure and simple.*

GERHARD – *What other experience do you carry inside that helps you do the work?*

MARLENE – *The people I've worked with have been in different roles, structures, and contexts, in transition and change. I suppose I hold a lot in my mind, both theoretically and practically – that is what is group analytical – it is sitting back and thinking about what is going on.*

CHRISTINE T – *You are holding so many different perspectives in your mind and I think that is group analysis.*

MARLENE – *I disagree. For me group analysis was always about clinical practice. If we start introducing too many different perspectives we might dilute it.*

CHRISTINE T – *That's the fear.*

CYNTHIA – *But Group analysis started off in so many different fields, sociology like Elias for example. Because psychiatry was the most prestigious it got located there but it must be relocated.*

MARLENE – *Foulkes' understanding of culture and its impact, and his links with the Frankfurt School of sociology, as well as the holistic approach of Goldstein influenced his thinking.*

GERHARD – *I come from a society where science is not only created by natural science. Science is systematic study in a university. From ancient tombs to DNA.*

CHRISTINE O – *Group analysis is both a model and way of thinking. For me, it is a way of thinking.*

ABDULLAH – *I am confused in this in discussion – are we talking about ownership of knowledge? Is it ours to own? Can we draw on multiple knowledges? When I do reflexive practice, it is not just my neuro-scientific or psychological background, it's my life experience. I like to share my knowledge. Not own it.*

MARLENE – *Something is linked to experience. You don't learn things unless you experience it.*

IAN – *Developing a psychotherapy service in the NHS needed a group analytic understanding – enormously helpful because it took into account what happened to the individual as well as what happened to the group. The whole thing seen as community based on group. The problem for me in that was how it fitted into the wider organizational structure. I don't know how it would apply in a business – I am talking about a social care organization.*

MARLENE – *You cannot talk about what an organization is in the way that you used to. They are too big and too interconnected with wider systems, both internal and external.*

CHRISTINE O – *Can we not think of group analysis as a living community?*

GERHARD – *I think it is a generational thing. Things have changed. Things have to change, be adapted and handed on with each generational shift.*

CHRISTINE T – *I'm seeking to change something. I came to group analysis as someone who had worked with organizations then learned to be a clinician . . . . I found that it was the most coherent intellectual framework for what I was doing with organizations, because it could take in so many perspectives. I don't think that's at odds with there being many ways of practising group analysis. There is no one group analysis, it's a very catholic institution. If we manage to make a contribution to group analytic organizational theory in this book, it will likely also turn out to be catholic.*

VINCE – *My background is human resources. Talking to people I work closely with in HR – they do use group analytic concepts. They don't all know that but they do use them. I've never worked in a clinical setting but in FMCGs such as dairy companies and also schools, going in and talking about community – not gatekeeping group analysis as a little self-referencing group. Applicability is so vast and so profound. Gatekeeping/owning does not do it justice.*

GERHARD – *How do you talk to people using these group analytic ideas without the language?*

VINCE – *You translate. Using different perspectives to look at an organization. If you go in with particular perspective you will see different things – new science – group analysis or HR will see different things.*

EARL – *What you just said is the very essence of the group analytic perspective – that it is a matter of abstraction and perception. Perception and the need to translate from one to the other is a highly political undertaking.*

VINCE – *Organizations are highly political.*

CHRISTINE T – *And value-led.*

VINCE – *I suspect that is what people like us to do – to take a deeper perspective on what they are already doing but aren't confident to give a name to. . . . using group analysis to understand what people are already doing and making deeper connections. But there is a danger of being a self-referential community – when I first went to the IGA, it felt like a dentist's in the 1960's. (Laughter)*

CHRISTINE O – *But practice can also develop theory, that's something I am very interested in.*

CHRISTINE T – *That's also what Lewin said – nothing so practical as a good theory.*

GWEN – *The idea of process is important and drew me to group analysis. The training has allowed me to occupy both positions – to be there as a person, and to see people in context. The group analytic view is essential for people who have offended – without figure and ground of context you cannot think about offenders. Is deviance individual or broader than individual? I wouldn't have been able to work in a secure institution without this perspective. This*

> *notion of personhood and a person who is continually constructed but also has a personal story, narrative. This is fundamental. It doesn't make much difference whether persons come together in a group to try to understand why they have done something wrong, or to understand how to do a good job.*

The matrix: core of group analytic thinking and praxis

The group processes articulated first by Foulkes[2] seem to be universal, no matter how different the people, purposes, or depth of those groups. This observation was the kernel around which *Group and team coaching* (2010, 2016) formed, and the response to that book confirmed my sense that here was a discipline with much to offer the organizational practitioner in complex modern environments.

Group analysis is not a single theory. Foulkes (1948, 1990b) sketched profound principles, but theory has been and still is being developed. It is deeply rooted in praxis and in group experience, both as members and 'conductors' (Foulkes' musical metaphor for facilitators, still the term we use today).

Foulkes' concept of the 'matrix' is central, describing the interpenetration of person, group, and society, the radical proposition that people are fundamentally social beings, and that the lived experience of being a person is dynamic, that is, changing all the time:

> In group analytic theory we do not orient ourselves by discerning "intrapsychic", "interpersonal" and "group dynamic" processes. We believe and can show they are the same processes which can and must be described from different standpoints according to the task which we pursue. "Society" is *inside* the individual, just as well as outside him, and what is "intrapsychic" is at the same time shared by the group, unconsciously most of the time in either sphere, except in the group-analytic group. The borderline of what is "in" or "outside" is constantly moving, and the experience of these changes is of particular significance
> Foulkes (1990a)

This mind-blowing proposition allows the organizational practitioner to re-position her/his perspective as the task requires. Based on Foulkes, Bhurruth (2008) proposed the 'tripartite matrix', and this area of theory is still being elaborated, for example by Nitzgen and Hopper (2017):

> The matrix should be conceptualized in terms of multi-relational processes. From the Foulkesian group analytical point of view, the matrix of any group can be analyzed in terms of patterns of relations, values

and norms, verbal and non-verbal communication, styles of thinking
and feeling, etc., depending on what is taken as problematic

(Hopper and Weinberg, 2017)

The matrix is thus the foundation for becoming aware of many perspectives on/in a given situation, together building a rich picture. It focuses on
patterns of relating, occurring through conversation, a process in which
we co-construct experience and learning. Conversation is the group analytic method (Stacey, 2005). This applies in praxis, between the people
we are working with, in the way we conceptualize the organization as
a whole, and simultaneously in the mind of the practitioner, who is considering many possible explanations (theories) about 'what is happening
now'. It has profound implications for leaders and for working with relationships between divisions within organizations, see further chapters 22
and 23. Conversation is the goal, the method, and if things go well, the
substantive outcome of our work.

The matrix makes group analysis a highly advantageous mindset for
work with complex modern organizations. It derives from the same
mid-twentieth century intellectual paradigm as quantum theory in physics and systems theory in biology (Bohm, 1951; Von Bertalanffy, 1951),
advances emphasizing the interconnectedness of everything, ultimately
bearing fruit in contingency, complexity, and chaos thinking. Sociology is
central: the sociologist Norbert Elias (2000), an 'elder' of group analysis,
shows how context is fundamental. Foulkes' concept of the matrix, with
its emphasis on multiple perspectives, meshes readily with systems and
complexity theories so that group analysis offers a coherent intellectual
framework for understanding and working with interplaying processes
from individual, through team, departmental and organizational, to societal and global levels.

Theory and praxis in group analysis are continuously intertwined. While
for the average practitioner[3] the concept 'matrix' is quite enough to be
thinking about, further down the page the ever practice-oriented Foulkes
adds 'Ours is a creative task. The group analyst should be flexible, natural,
spontaneous, follow the group's lead and learn from them'. The key praxis
message is to adapt one's practice and interventions to the needs of the
specific group; to 'translate' (see chapters two, three and 18) the perspectives into the right language for these particular people. 'Putting it into
words' (Rogers, 1987) is an art as well as a science. Group-analytic conversation (or 'free-floating discussion') reflects the complexity of reality.

Group analytic organizational literature

Group analysts have developed a sophisticated literature for the clinical applications of group analysis, but a relatively sparse analysis of its

application in work settings. What exists is largely geared to the specialized need to understand the dynamics of organizations providing services for traumatized individuals/people with severe mental health issues. While this is valuable, and often generalizable, the theoretical framework of group analysis has value for a far wider range of organizational dynamics. Group analytic training too is mostly geared to clinical practice (Heinskou, 2002), and I found it not immediately illuminating as to how to apply learning in both my organizational and clinical groups. My ideas have developed from the relatively unusual position of starting as a specialist in organizational work and only later becoming a clinician.

Foulkes' comments on organizational work are also (characteristically) sparse, but apart from founding the scientific society GASI,[4] he gives an account of his work of Northfield Military Hospital (1948, 1964) and refers to organizational applications of group analysis in various late papers (1990b) including the important *The group as matrix of the individual's mental life*.

In two short early pieces, Rance (1987, 1989) proposes the use of group analysis in consulting as 'an instrument for radical individual and organizational change' with small stranger-group experience as the mechanism of group-analytic consulting (1989).

Dorothy Stock Whitaker's Foulkes Lecture[5] *Transposing Learnings from Group Psychotherapy to Work Groups* (Whitaker, 1992) is the first substantive attempt to address similarities and differences in theory and praxis as between conducting therapeutic groups and work groups. Whitaker traces important phenomena and dynamics in common, notes the importance in both settings of monitoring group phenomena, and moves on to emphasize the difference in purpose of the two kinds of group. Whitaker advocates caution in praxis: 'a prudent group therapist, a prudent group leader, takes into account the norms and expectations of group members in intervening, and does not push too far beyond them'. She makes the important distinction between *understanding* and *intervening*, and acknowledges the need at times to reframe and to 'name the unnamable'. Noting the additional group phenomena arising from being embedded in a larger system, such as rivalry, competition, and the forming of alliances, she adds 'it follows that some additional understanding and skills, over and above those normally developed by group therapists, are required to understand and manage work groups'.

Blackwell's contributions, while rarely explicitly addressing questions of praxis, demonstrate a willingness to engage authoritatively with the reality of experience in organizations, and to design humane interventions to support those within them. His (1998) piece on 'bounded instability' offers an account of how groups can be useful in institutional situations of rapid change and uncertainty by promoting dialogue so that anxiety is expressed and channeled creatively rather than destructively. He places the encounter with difference (Thornton, 2004) front and center: 'the important elements of the matrix are the reflexivity, the playfulness, and the humor of its dialogue and communication'. Blackwell is also very good on context, and many of his ideas about organizations are expressed in the context of writing about the impact of power and political violence on culture and communication (2003, 2005, 2011a and b, 2014).

Nitsun (1998a and b) describes the 'organizational mirror', outlining how some group analytic concepts can be used to understand organizational dynamics, though again with little attention to praxis; Rance (1998a, 2019 this volume) elaborates the 'conversational' aspect of group analysis, a strong thread in Stacey's work.

Stacey's (2005) contribution over many years sets out the case for understanding organizations as complex responsive processes between people, requiring the practitioners to engage with the particularity and complexity of each situation. His influence, particularly with regards to conversational processes and the informal organization, can be traced through several of the writers represented in this volume. He has explored (2012) the limitations of the dominant management discourse of tools and techniques to 'fix' organizations, finding in favor of 'practical judgment', the experience-honed choices of the practitioner in the complexity of any given situation. My own thirty years' consulting to organizations persuades me of the merit of this approach; Stacey's group analysis has strong sociological foundations, an emphasis on conversation, and a group-based educational praxis (Pennycook-Greaves, 2003; Rance, 2003).

The question of whether group analysis alone is adequate for an understanding of organizational life is tackled head-on by Spero in her (2003) paper about the management-educational conferences she ran for several years with Harold Bridger of the Tavistock Institute, staffed both by group analysts and Tavistock consultants. Spero posits that Foulkes was uninterested in organizational issues – a position refuted by Rance (2003) and contradicting Foulkes (1964) (Nichol, 2000; Campbell, 2010b) – and that many group analysts do not fully appreciate issues of leadership, authority, and hierarchy in conducting work groups; I think this latter challenge withstands examination today. Fortunately, group analytic theory is a 'holey cheese' (Wilke, 2016, personal communication) which allows us to make use of a multiplicity of perspectives not necessarily published in *Group Analysis*.[6] Pennycook-Greaves' response (2003) brings forward the important question of the location of the consultant: part of the group or outside it? Spero identified the need for a 'new working paradigm' and succeeded in provoking discussion of some important questions; her focus is however not on consultants' practice in organizations. She is represented in this book by her contributions to the dialogue fragments.

In a collection of papers on praxis in 'the helping professions' (Hartley and Kennard, 2009) Powell (2009) makes a useful contribution on the complexity of working as an internal consultant, Wojciechowska (2009) on the subtle interplay of the personal and the professional, and Maher (2009) on the links between group analysis and the work of Yvonne Agazarian (Agazarian and Peters, 1995).

In the sub-field of 'Trauma and Organizations', Hopper's collection (2012b) includes a particularly clear exposition of the fourth basic assumption. Like Blackwell, even when Hopper's writing is not explicitly directed to organizational praxis, his thinking provides an important underpinning, since the fourth basic assumption (1997, 2012a) elaborates the most basic tension in a group: that between individual identity and group identity; this concept is essential to understanding the dynamics of any work group. His recent work with Nitzgen (Nitzgen and Hopper, 2017) elaborating the tripartite matrix is an important clarification for both clinical and organizational group analysis. Wilke (2014) and Scanlon and Adlam (2011a and b, 2012) have also made substantial contributions to the study of traumatized organizations.

Schermer's (2012a and b) two-part paper considers group psychology alongside complexity theory, critiquing Bion, Foulkesian Group Analysis and Agazarian-style systems theory. He proposes that group psychology derived from the paradigm of Enlightenment science. This is inaccurate, at least in relation to Foulkes and group analysis, which arose at the same time and as part of the same new paradigm (Nitsun, 1996; Spero, 2003; Thornton, 2010, 2016) with quantum physics, general systems theory in biology, and a host of other mid-twentieth century technologies emphasizing interconnectedness. What Foulkes has to say about the group processes and individual/group nexus hardly reflects Enlightenment thinking:

> (of Cartesian dualism) Its strict subject-object dualism is still responsible for many pseudo-problems of our time
>
> (1990b, p. 152)

> (group processes) pass through the individual, though each individual elaborates them and contributes to them and moderates them in his own way. Nevertheless, they go through all the individuals – similar to X-rays in the physical sphere . . . Psychology is thus neither "individual" nor "group" except by abstraction. We cannot speak about the individual without reference to the group, nor about a human group that does not consist of individuals
>
> (1990a, pp. 229–230)

It is therefore no great struggle to incorporate complexity thinking into group analysis, since it derives from the same origins; Schermer acknowledges that Foulkes' 'intellectual frame allows for integration of diverse intellectual and scientific currents' and that 'some elements of complexity theory are already implicit in group analysis', which is not surprising if his thesis as to its origins is discounted. Unfortunately, Schermer ends by endorsing the fallacy that Foulkes was too optimistic about groups and ignored their destructive potential; whereas attention to what Foulkes actually wrote tends to contradict that view. For example, from 'My philosophy in psychotherapy':

> Why do we fail? The strongest factors are two. One is the enormous resistance in people to change, to learn or to unlearn. The other factor is the need for self-damage, self-destruction. This is also universal, and one could say that it is the amount and nature of unnecessary suffering that people add to that inevitable suffering which is part of human life. It may help if we conduct our analyses with the conviction that life contains great and deep pleasure and satisfaction, but inevitably is weighted on the side of suffering
>
> (1990b)

Foulkes' emphasis on strengthening the positive capacities of groups was not the result of myopia, but a deliberate moral and praxis choice, made in the shadow of the second world war and personal loss.

Corina Grace describes merger/acquisition dynamics (2016), with a thoughtful response from Christine Oliver (2016). It is interesting that in applying group analysis to organizations, the contribution of women group analysts has been so strong.

Seeking to integrate thinking from group analysis and critical management scholarship, Chris Mowles (2017) reviews some group analytical reflections on organizational consultancy, including Prodgers, Nitsun, and in particular Blackwell, Spero, and Wilke. Mowles himself states that

> Group analytic thinking can help better frame enduring problems in organizational life, can work against the tendency to rush to action without reflection, and can address the profound feelings which are often provoked by being in relation with others, often in conditions of uncertainty.

However, he observes that group analysts are insufficiently engaged with and critical of the dominant discourse of managerialism, resulting from a weak analysis of power relations within organizations (Spero, 2003).

In the last decade a couple of successful management and coaching books have brought group analytic thinking and concepts to a far wider readership (Binney, Wilke and Williams, 2012; Thornton, 2016), now in their third and second editions respectively. Wilke's more recent volume (2014) celebrates group analysis as a basis for flexible praxis and makes a particularly strong contribution to the understanding of using large groups in organizations.

The reference/bibliography list starting on page 257 provides a further resource of relevant material.

Introducing this book

The book illustrates the rich diversity of group analysis practised in organizations, bringing together the best thinking by talented group analysts working in the field. It is a long book of short chapters, suitable for 'dipping into' and coming back to for reference. This is deliberate; the value of multiple perspectives is a core concept in group analysis, and a 'matrix' of thinking held in common, with individual variations on the themes, can be traced through the different voices in the book. The multi-faceted perspective of group analytic thinking will hopefully provide enduring illumination on organizational perplexities. The cross-references between chapters aim to identify some of the strongest links between ideas, and more may be found through the index.

Group analysis may be used as a praxis with teams in organizations, and also as a way of thinking about whole organizations. This is implicit in every chapter in the book, although some focus more explicitly on team praxis and some more explicitly on whole-organization praxis, the latter especially in chapters 19–23.

Section I gives my introduction to group analytic praxis, comprising this introductory chapter and three others. The material in these chapters has been expanded from two papers originally published in Group Analysis, in vols 50(4) and 51(1), December 2017 and March 2018, entitled *Towards a group analytic praxis for working with teams in organizations I and II*. The reprinted material is by permission of SAGE Publications, Ltd.

Chapter two sets out six aspects of group analysis that render it a valuable basis for organizational work: attention to the individual in the group, nuanced understanding of interpersonal communication, attention to context, tolerance and value of multiple perspectives, creative incorporation of difference, and a flexible developmental approach to managing anxiety and leadership projections. It also highlights key differences between clinical and organizational group analysis and ends with a focus on two group analytic concepts, *communication* and *translation*, including a fragment of group analytic conversation on these themes among the book's contributors.

Chapter three, *Persecutor, victim, rescuer: imperfect consulting in an imperfect world* offers an extended vignette in illustration, explored through the use of 'five questions' I have developed as an aid to making praxis decisions; Margaret Smith takes this analysis further from a systemic perspective in chapter 15.

Chapter four analyzes the vignette from the perspective of the six characteristics set out in chapter two.

Praxis based on complexity and chaos thinking is a thread running through the book, and the focus of section II. In chapter five, Christopher Rance deconstructs communication and the art of conversation which is the core of group analytic praxis. Following the work of G.H. Mead, he explains how meaning is made between people through gesture and response, listening as well as speaking. He gives us the benefit of his mature thinking about many years of organizational practice in handling common difficulties.

'Parallel process' (see also the reflection process, isomorphism, equivalence, and refracted countertransference) is a concept much used but little examined. David Wood's erudite chapter six gives a scientific account of how it works. David traverses several fields, including physics, biology, evolutionary theory, genetics, cognitive science, and computational neuroscience. He links these processes to Foulkes' core concept, the group matrix, highlighting its far-sighted accuracy, and proposes a more accurate re-definition of 'parallel process'. Along the way he sheds light on the anatomy of learning.

There follow in section III two passionate chapters on the place of group analysis in the wider world. Dick Blackwell traces the global economic and societal context(s) within which organizations now function, highlighting the ubiquitous anxiety and reactive control which deaden so many workplaces in all sectors. Chapter seven is a plea to create work environments for creativity and job satisfaction, and an indispensable critique of the managerialism which stifles them.

Not all 'organizations' are formally constituted; organizations working for social change usually begin with the 'organizing' of activists. Christopher Scanlon develops his work on *disappointment* in a societal context, describing some 'organizings' which use group analytic principles in seeking to address global/local challenges. Chapter eight challenges us to 'get out more'.

Leadership can only occur in a group. It can be understood as a function rather than a characteristic located in one person: a leader is someone whom the group is willing to entrust with leadership; effective leaders create thinking spaces, share their real perceptions, seek help and enable others in their groups to 'take a lead' when needed. In section IV, three leaders describe how group analytic thinking helped them manage in highly pressurized situations, and a fourth comments.

In chapter nine, Dr Clare Gerada gives a moving account of being a leading doctor who became nationally prominent for her courageous opposition to the Lansley NHS changes, which passed into law in 2012. She describes the leader's internal process and the sense she made of it through experiences in group analytic groups. Clare, always a leader who acts on her convictions, has now incorporated groups into care packages for traumatized doctors.

For 18 years Raman Kapur has led a residential and support service for mainly psychotic people in Northern Ireland, a context where madness is intensified by 'the Troubles'. In chapter 10 he takes us through an incident, highlighting how psychoanalytic and group analytic thinking contain him, describing his use of intense experiences of projective identification as a daily tool in understanding and fulfilling his role as CEO, to hold and contain the inevitable mess in this important, difficult work.

In chapter 11, Morris Nitsun comments on Raman's chapter, linking it with his own experience leading NHS mental health services. He raises an important topic: the appropriate style of group leadership, on a spectrum from active/authoritative to understated/enabling – a debate he has done much to stimulate.

Farideh Dizadji focuses in chapter 12 on the leader's role in containing chaos to create a situation for creative therapeutic work. She draws on her experience as clinical director at Kids Company's main Centre and at two other community agencies. In services where members bring chaos, holding boundaries is a creative and flexible process (Thornton and Corbett, 2014) simultaneously allowing members to flex those boundaries, which is crucial in their development of increased agency and control.

In section V, we gain insight into the mind of the practitioner as s/he works. Chris Powell engages us with a witty and self-deprecating 'real-life' account of the lived experience of consulting in chapter 13, using the experience of the self to help teams make sense of things. His 'three questions' encapsulate some of the most commonly encountered organizational dynamics.

In chapter 14, Christine Oliver treats us to another thoughtful dissection of a consultancy intervention, focusing on the *communications* within the process, both within the community and within the consultants. *Communication* is a core group analytic idea, meaning any event which may communicate a meaning. Like Chris Powell, she gives us a clear sense of how she uses her self in making sense of communications made simultaneously at many levels, and how she makes praxis decisions.

Frankly bringing to bear her own experience of consulting in equivocal circumstances, in chapter 15 Margaret Smith gives us a commentary on the work described in *Persecutor, victim, rescuer* (chapter three). She draws in further useful perspectives such as systemic family therapy, exploring more fully the 'five questions' which structure the vignette in chapter three. This chapter was also originally published in *Group Analysis vol 51(1)* and the reprinted material is by permission of SAGE Publications, Ltd.

Section VI on ethical issues continues to give insight into practitioner thinking processes, and focuses on the dynamics of power in organizations.

Ewa Wojciechowska opens it with a 'social dream' (Lawrence, 2004) linked to the turning of blind eyes, a constant pressure on the reflective practitioner in human services. Exploring the dynamics of power and associated inhibition, her exploration of boundaries in chapter 16 shows us how taking the risk of opening our eyes and refraining from 'managing' responses can be richly productive for the quality of mental health services, and the well-being of professionals.

Gwen Adshead and Ian Simpson bring their many years of experience leading departments and consulting to mental health services to a consideration of the contextual politics, ethics, and values of this work today. Their chapter 17 highlights the boundaries of the work and some of the dilemmas facing practitioners; their dialogue reflects both common analysis and differing strategies.

The validity of differing experiences and perceptions is a central tenet of group analysis, and in chapter 18 Vincent Leahy and Abdullah Mia share their experiences of working with difference and power dynamics in many organizational settings. They face the difficulties and limitations squarely, offering real-life descriptions of dilemmas and impasses, alongside analysis offering sage advice.

In section VII we turn to work with and between groups within a whole organization. Chapter 19, opening the section on working with whole organizations, records a conversation with Earl Hopper about his insights linking consulting to organizations with group analytic theory. It introduces some important ideas, providing a more informal commentary to be read alongside his substantive contributions to theory.

Cynthia Rogers gives us a richly illustrated description of the internal process of the consultant as s/he enters an organization, and clear and astute advice on how to create the best possible conditions for change. Her chapter 20 explores the 'how' of the group analytic concept 'dynamic administration', particularly with regards to 'median' groups of up to 70 people.

Gerhard Wilke, one of our finest conductors of large groups, has written a concise and practical account of the core processes in large groups, and the key tasks of the large group conductor in chapter 21. It is illustrated with a story which underlines the broader societal value of a group analytic approach to dialogue.

In chapter 22 Gerhard and I discuss the relationship between the matrix, the systemic concept autopoiesis, and the formation of organizational identities, which regulate the behavior of the people within. We focus particularly on the dynamics of mergers in this chapter, with case stories suggesting practical ways to work with the challenges.

In chapter 23, we consider the impact of insider/outsider or 'us-and-them' dynamics between parts of organizations. Through the chapter we offer examples of how these can be successfully worked with. We close the chapter with ten key points for leaders and consultants seeking to 'tweak' an organization in the direction of greater coherence and mutual loyalty.

Section VIII consists of the single chapter 24, bringing together some of my reflections on endings with those of Gerhard Wilke. It underlines the real world non-ideal character of many endings in organizational work. It offers questions, not answers. 'The end is in the beginning' is our watchword, and the ambiguities and complexities of 'good enough' endings are explored.

Section IX rounds off the book, a combined list of references for all chapters which provides the curious reader with bibliographical leads, and an index to help the reader navigate and make sense of the 'matrix' of the book.

Notes

1 John Smith was the 'lost leader' of the British Labour Party, in whom much faith and hope had been placed by many left-of-center people following years of Conservative government; he died unexpectedly in May 1994. A discussion can be found at www.independent.co.uk/news/uk/politics/remembering-john-smith-20-years-on-what-would-his-government-have-looked-like-9357017.html
2 Throughout the book you will find references to 'Foulkes', the founder of Group Analysis. S.H. Foulkes was a German Jewish psychoanalyst who sought refuge in the UK in the 1930s, where he developed Group Analysis and articulated its key concepts, including matrix, 'communication' and 'translation'. Group Analysis has been further elaborated by many others in the 70 years since Foulkes' first book, 'Introduction to group analytic psychotherapy' (1948).
3 In the book several terms are used more-or-less interchangeably for the 'practitioner', or person who works 'into' the organization – group analyst, consultant, coach, reflective practitioner for example.
4 The Group Analytic Society International (GASI).
5 An annual GASI event held in London each May, bringing together group analysts from around the world.
6 GASI's journal, in which new theory developments are published, as indeed was much of the material in the opening four chapters of this book.

Chapter 2

Group analytic praxis in teams and organizations

Christine Thornton

Introduction

Group analysis is a highly useful discipline for consulting to organizations and working with teams in complex post-modern environments because its concepts, particularly '*matrix*', can accommodate a high degree of complexity. The importance assigned to context, and the value placed on multiple perspectives as holding elements of reality, mesh with systems and complexity theories so that group analysis offers a coherent intellectual framework for understanding interplaying processes in the system, from individual, through team, departmental and organizational, to societal and global levels.

This chapter articulates some core contextual differences between clinical and organizational applications and identifies the characteristics of group analysis that make it a valuable discipline in organizational work. Lewin (1951) said, 'There is nothing so practical as a good theory' and in group analysis, theory developed alongside praxis. Six aspects of this praxis make it an effective discipline with organizations: attention to the individual in the group, sophisticated grasp of the nuances of interpersonal communication, attention to context, tolerance and value of multiple perspectives, creative incorporation of difference, and a flexible developmental approach to managing anxiety and leadership projections.

I highlight the importance of the group analytic concepts *communication* and *translation* through which unconscious aspects of the matrix are accessed in organizational work, closing with a fragment of conversation among the book's contributors exploring these themes and their links to meaning and identity.

Organizational group analysis

The group analyst's praxis in organizational work is fundamentally different from that of the clinician. Perhaps the most basic difference is that whereas in clinical work we bring patients into the 'world' of the group, created by the group analyst as therapist, the group analyst as organizational practitioner must instead enter the world of the organization with which s/he is working. The group analyst is no longer an originator and powerful authority figure, but instead arrives as the stranger.

In organizations the group analyst may work with an individual, a group of people who usually work together, that is, one or more teams,[1] a whole department, or whole organization, or any combination of these. Every team is threaded through, like a stick of rock, with the qualities of the organization and its purpose; when working with the team that leads the organization, the 'top team', this is even more marked.

The team is a serviceable focus for several reasons: first, because in effect we always consult to a leader and their immediate cohort even within a very large organization; a whole-organization commission will usually begin with the chief executive and her/his senior team. Second, every team assignment is an organizational intervention. Third, group analysis, focused first on small groups, has its most developed praxis at team scale. It nevertheless includes articulation of the differing dynamics of small, median, and larger groups.

We explore the dynamics of working with whole organizations in chapters 19–23.

How is working with an intact team different?

Group analysis in organizations is different in purpose from working with therapy groups. Group analysis was originally developed as a therapy of the individual in a stranger group context. By contrast, in work with teams, we focus on the effectiveness of this group of people in carrying out their shared work, rather than the health and development of individuals, though there is a paradox here (see below).

The group analyst in a clinical setting is an influential figure. A stranger group meeting for therapy (or learning, such as an action learning set) starts with relatively simple power dynamics: members do not know each other, the group has not existed before, and the purpose is to collaborate to help each other. It is the therapist's group, into which s/he invites chosen members; they are strangers, developing their network of relationships – the group matrix – always in the practitioner's presence. Group members consciously and unconsciously look to her/him for the group's 'rules', its norms and expectations, and s/he influences these by example and at an implicit level (Foulkes, 1975; Waldhoff, 2007b.[2] This is particularly true at the beginning of a group; over time these projections pass to the group itself, and it comes to represent the mother in whose presence the members play; the nature of this 'mother' will however always be strongly influenced by the nature of the clinician.

The group analyst working with a team has a far different experience. The team already exists when s/he arrives and will likely continue when s/he leaves. The members are not strangers. They already have a complex web of working relationships that continue to develop between members when they are *not* meeting with the group analyst. Here the group analyst is the stranger. S/he may have 'expert' status and standing, but no direct power. As in clinical work, her role is mediated through influencing, but in organizational work her/his presence is by invitation, usually from the team leader. S/he must forge a relationship with that leader, as well as with the team as a whole, if the work is to have any longevity of impact.

Further, here the group analyst will be working within a given time frame and usually with some specific objectives, or desires. S/he must seek to influence a world with existing dynamics, relationships and history. The organizational system *shared* by the team members is a pervasive influence, far more powerful than the *differing* familial matrices of clinical group members; which are of course *also* present. From Foulkes we learn that the differences between patients in a group enable them to help each other. In a team, personal and role differences may be overshadowed by the power of established norms and expectations, influenced by the needs and habits of its members and end users[3] and the context (the service, department, organization, industry, and society).

I am sitting alone in a group room, waiting for the ward team to arrive. No message. I close the door at the time the group was to start. Have I got the wrong day? No. I feel confused. Where are they? Minutes pass. I feel completely worthless, without value. Then I feel disrespected, and so, gradually, angry. More minutes pass as I sit.

After about 10 minutes I hear a few voices in the corridor, and a little later three ward staff enter the room. The ward manager is not among them. It is explained that there has been a crisis in the ward.

This was my third meeting with this adult psychiatric ward team. I had worked hard to build an alliance with the (ambivalent) ward manager and emphasized the importance of consistent time and venue and attendance as consistent as possible. We had a carefully negotiated contract to provide a reflective space in which they could think about their work.

The feeling of being useless and disregarded pervaded all my arrivals to work with this team, whether or not the sessions were well-attended or appeared to be useful; I would arrive to find that the room had been unbooked, or to be forbidden entrance by the melodramatic hand gesture of a therapist working with a patient group. We would find some room, one time a grand former ballroom where staff feared that a litigious patient was lurking outside the open windows, to hear what they would say about him.

Conversations were all dominated by fear:

- Fear that patients would break loose and throw themselves into the sea or the middle of the nearby main road
- Fear for the chronically ill eating disordered patient discharged into the community without support or further treatment
- Fear of what would happen if they challenged the demands made by managers or highlighted the contradictions of doctors' treatments.

Some conversations seemed to help members make sense of things, and sometimes even the ward manager was able to express herself. But the start of every session returned me to the powerful communication of the nurses' own experience of being disregarded and unvalued.

Some other important differences: the group will not necessarily be a small one but may feature median or even large group dynamics; and there is a hierarchy (formal power structure) as well as the usual variety of sources of power within the group.[4] The presence of individuals with greater formal power and status has been a source of discomfort for some group analysts, who have experienced it as being in conflict with the fundamentally egalitarian ethic of group analysis; in some settings this has been compounded by team members' resonating discomfort. Some common responses include excluding the managers (whether present or not, and they should be present); attacking them; recruiting the practitioner as an idealized substitute. This results from an unhelpful reification of the reality that all groups contain power dynamics.

The most useful approach is to encourage members to explore power dynamics and the associated fears and projections. An exploration of the dynamics of formal power can be liberating both for managed and manager.

Whereas in a therapeutic setting over time, patients learn a pretty sophisticated psychological language, the task of the organizational practitioner is to help team members work better and more comfortably, including a fuller range of emotional expression at an appropriate level. In a psychological treatment team this will likely also be quite sophisticated, but may be less so in a bank, waste disposal department, or retail organization. Learning the language of the team, and using it, is an essential first step: the practitioner must catch the tone of the team, and then express her/his ideas to them in terms with which they can connect.

The application of group analytic theory is therefore different in organizational work, and the group analyst must hold all these factors in mind, and practice in a more flexible and responsive way to work with what the group may throw at her/him. S/he must be fast on her/his feet and willing to adapt her praxis as well as her language to engage with the reality of the team in front of her/him.

Why is group analysis a valuable discipline in organizational work?

There are six factors: attention to the individual in the group, sophisticated grasp of the nuances of interpersonal communication, attention to context, tolerance and value of multiple perspectives, creative incorporation of difference, and a flexible developmental approach to managing anxiety and leadership projections.

The six factors are explored further in the light of praxis in chapter four, where they are used to analyze the case study in chapter three.

Attention to the individual in the group

We all start life in a group. A Portuguese group analyst, Rita Leal, wrote in 1982, 'the relationship precedes the individual'. The individual develops a sense of self through interaction with others, and all our learning, from the earliest moments of life, occurs in a relational context (Elias, 2000). Though our Western culture strongly emphasizes our need to be seen (mirrored) as unique individuals, individuals also need a group identification, that is, to feel part of something larger than themselves. We experience a lifelong tension between these competing needs; it cannot be fully resolved. The tension between individual identity and group identification is a fundamental issue for each individual in every group.

Group analysis is unusual among group methods in its stronger focus on the individual-in-the-group: 'analysis of the individual in the group, by the group, including the conductor'. This responsiveness to the individual-in-context may be central to its effectiveness: a capacity to soothe the anxiety of the individual about engulfment by the group. It can 'hold' this fundamental tension.

In working with organizational teams, awareness of individuals remains a part of praxis and seems to augment our capacity to hold them and so reduce anxiety. In an increasingly anxious world, this is important in organizational as well as clinical settings. The aim here is to improve group functioning, but paradoxically, appropriate attention to the individual seems in practice to enable freer, fuller contribution to team performance. Group analysts are trained to assume that individuals are important in themselves, as well as because each contributes something unique to the total picture.

Sophisticated grasp of the nuances of interpersonal communication

Group analysis is a science of interpersonal communication, not only verbal but with all the nuance of movement, tone, glance, display, energy, and so on (Foulkes and Anthony, 1957; Foulkes, 1990b; Thornton, 2004, 2016). In prehistoric times, our survival depended on our ability to work effectively together as a group – that is, to be an effective team. The clan, bound by kinship ties and the drive for survival, was the earliest form of group, probably predating the development of language (Osborne, 2015). Babies communicate emotionally before the development of words (Stern, 1985), and the non-verbal elements of communication are widely understood to outweigh by far the verbal. Some people in modern organizations spend more time with their colleagues than with their families (Hochschild, 2001). Group analysts have 70 years of literature exploring how communication works in groups. When I published a popular book articulating these processes, a high rate of plagiarism demonstrated that the value of a group analytic perspective is well understood by those outside the group analytic 'clan'.

Attention to context

We never work just with a team. Any team assignment is also an organizational intervention, so we always also work with its context. The practitioner must pay attention to every layer of the context, in the team, particularly when negotiating the beginning. The sociological strand in group analysis (Elias, 2000; Waldhoff, 2007a and b) directs our attention to the broader context of what we see and hear in a team. The concept of communication requires us to 'entertain the possibility that everything is relevant' (Marshall, 2001) – a glance, a tee-shirt slogan, the way someone sits down.

Our stranger status and our curiosity are priceless here. What questions strike us about this team? The reflection process (Searles, 1955b) is also useful (see also chapter six). Which aspects of its context are echoed in its dynamics, and of these, which patterns repeat most often? Attention to context links directly with systems and complexity thinking. The task for the consultant is not to avoid getting lost in complexity, but to use the experience of sometimes getting lost to build with others a richer picture of 'what is really going on'.

Group analysis arose from the same scientific paradigm as systems and complexity theories, and its emphasis on interconnectedness and multiple perspectives means it can readily and fluidly bring into focus issues arising in the broader system. The team, as an entry point, sits at a midpoint from which thinking can move out:

- What has happened recently in the service?
- What is happening in the broader organization?
- What in society has contributed to this?

Or move in:

- Why does Fred look upset?
- Is his upset shared by others?

And make links:

- How did it come about?
- How does it relate to other things in the system?
- Does it relate to a wider disturbance in the team or in the organization?

In group analytic terms, we focus first at the level of the dynamic matrix, but can easily move towards the broader context (foundation matrix) or the person (personal matrix), and make links between the three (Bhurruth, 2008). All three are always present, we can work with whichever seems most pertinent to the needs of the moment.

Tolerance and value of multiple perspectives

One of the strengths of group analysis as a foundation for organizational work is that our theory is fundamentally non-fundamentalist – non-dogmatic and based in pluralism. This results from what some see as a weakness: the skeleton nature of our theoretical base. Having, usually briefly, articulated key concepts and processes, Foulkes left us to do much of the work ourselves. But he founded a discipline which enables us to be comfortable with the tensions of holding several views of the same phenomenon simultaneously. This multiplicity of perspective has immense value in the complex milieu of the modern organization. A central part of the group analytic approach is bringing these together to co-create a fuller picture.

The emphasis on the value of differing perspectives positions group analysis as a uniquely well-placed framework to accommodate a range of ways of understanding modern organizational life, including, for example, several varieties of systemic thinking, complexity theory, business development, and organizational psychology. Group analysts struggle less with this than those trained within a more fully delineated theory. It means not only that the team can develop several parallel narratives as to 'what is really going on', but also that the practitioner can have in mind several ways of understanding what s/he observes in the group matrix: s/he is not restricted to any single theoretical viewpoint. This is more fully explored in chapters three and four.

Although power may not be equally distributed in an organization, if the right conditions can be negotiated (mainly if anxiety can be kept within reasonable bounds) the process of team communication facilitated by a group analyst will tend towards an equality of interaction. This is not only useful in understanding a situation in the round, but in allowing the managed to feel more valued, and the manager to be more comfortable with disagreement and diverse views (Kapur, 2009). Group analysis exploits the organizational value of difference.

Creative incorporation of difference

Exchange is a key mechanism of learning and change in groups (Thornton, 2004). Information is 'news of difference' and the encounter with new information/experience requires us to shift our world view (or, by contrast, shut the information out) (Bateson, 2000; Stern, 1985). This is how we learn. This learning through exposure to others' views may be largely unspoken and/or unconscious in a therapeutic group, but in a work group must also be in the realm of words. The group analyst (or coach, or consultant) role here is to normalize difference, and learning from difference, typically in a more active and 'everyday' manner than in a therapy group. We can promote the process by expressing interest in minority or left-field contributions or, where one view reigns, ask 'what isn't being said'? In a tolerant climate, a more diverse range of views can be considered, leading to better decisions and performance.

A flexible developmental approach to managing anxiety and leadership projections

Sixth and finally, group analysis has a flexible approach to managing leadership projections and the anxiety associated with them, this contrasting with some other approaches. The beginning of any group is anxious. In Waldhoff's (2007a and b) fascinating account of the 'C' group, much of the discussion focuses on managing anxiety in the first meeting of a group; Bion's style of disappointing members' expectations is criticized, and members describe how they handled the tensions of a first meeting. Here is Foulkes quoted by Waldhoff:

> I make it understood either by words or by conveying that it is welcome; that they can say anything they like at any time
>
> (Waldhoff, 2007, p. 493)

> I do not agree that it is the conductor's job to keep the tension at a maximum level and make the group bear as much as they can . . . . I do not even think it is the conductor's job to keep to an optimum degree of tension . . . he is out to diminish tensions and anxieties consistently in the first group as well as in all the others'
>
> (p. 498)

Group analysts at first accept some of the leadership projections team members make onto them, in order to relinquish them as anxiety reduces; the group analyst can become less active as the team takes a lead. This is also broadly the pattern in organizational stranger groups, such as action learning sets or leadership coaching groups. Here, as with teams, the consultant must look like a 'safe pair of hands', and convey something of what is expected of members, offering a 'steer' in how to react to this new situation.

The situation with a team is more complex than in an organizational stranger group because a team already has a leader, their formal manager (this is true even if they are not present, and they should be present). The potential here for rivalry, conscious or unconscious, is great, and even if the consultant is rigorous enough to avoid this trap, the team leader may feel rivalrous.

The team leader has a more complex role and relationship mix than others, more vulnerable to projection, as is the practitioner; the potential for splitting is significant. Against this background the practitioner must forge an alliance with the leader, while maintaining the confidence of other team members, or the value and longevity of his/her work is always in question. S/he must support the team's leader to be as effective as possible, while working to reduce anxiety about competition. For this reason, I always consult one-to-one with the team's leader *alongside* working with a team; the leader can be coached on 'how to be in the group' and gain understanding and experience of the group analytic approach to the complex leadership task. The practitioner must respond to the waxing and waning of the team's projections, weaning the team leader and the team from primitive ideas of leadership towards a more distributed concept, enabling the team leader to enable others to 'take a lead' as needed. Foulkes again:

> While it is easy to become a leader – in the popular misconception of the term – it is much more difficult to wean the group from having to be led
>
> (1964, p. 193)

This is a both a key element in group analysis and in an organizational context, a highly complex task requiring a different praxis.

Two key processes in exploring the organizational matrix: communication and translation

Two key Foulkesian concepts, *communication* and *translation*, underpin the discipline of group analysis in organizational practice, because:

- Everything may be a communication
- Every communication carries data
- Communications carry data about the group, the context, the difficulties . . .

> 'Everything under observation is taken as communication, whether verbal or non-verbal behaviours, and therefore in need of interpretation. This rests on the notion that everything can be taken as an associative response, a reaction against or an unconscious interpretation of what was happening. Everything is seen as meaningful in the light of the total context of the group. For this the concept of a group matrix, both pre-existing as well as dynamically evolving during the group's procedure, has proved to be very fruitful'
>
> (Foulkes, 1990b, p. 172)

Group analysts are trained to observe and *translate* communications, putting into words and linking communications made in different modalities (expression, movement, sound, gesture, pace), by different people at different times, into a coherent hypothesis which can then be shared, tested, and improved by the team or group assembled. In other words, group analysts enable a conversation about the data.

In an organization the purpose is to clarify the meaning of data, to contribute to an understanding of the total situation. This is also shared challenging work, both serious and fun. Fun, serious work creates bonds between people, improving the quality of relationships and so of future work: it creates a sense of being part of a 'good' group, and that sense binds people to the organizational task. That is what a 'high-performing team' is.

The capacity to link and analyze apparently unconnected data is of immense value to organizations in our interconnected world. It is a methodology for engaging with complexity without being overwhelmed, that allows shared creativity – a shared puzzling out of 'what is really going on'.

I close with a fragment of conversation between the book's contributors which illustrates this free-ranging process of group-analytic dialogue.

A fragment of conversation: communication, translation, meaning and identity

VINCE – *There is a constant constipation of the English – consistent rethinking about what you might mean. (Laughter)*

GERHARD – *When I coach in English – men – I coach by phone because it is easier for them to hear what they need to hear. (Laughter)*

CHRISTINE T – *Vince I am also thinking about – you have lived in lots of different cultures, but like me, you sound English but are Irish, so that . . . .*

DICK – *I remember a consultant telling story – a guy who says his boss said 'you may like to think about'. (Laughter) The consultant asks 'where is he looking when he says it? . . . if it was out of the window it's a suggestion, if straight at you it's an order'.*

VINCE – *Use of language is extraordinarily difficult, this indirectness of the English.*

FARIDEH – *I used to live in Berlin before moving to the UK. In my experience, German racism is very direct, here you do not know it, it is very subtle; the context is vital. And I was in America before, the same thing in different contexts.*

GERHARD – *Some of the best things that group analysts do is to take the work of translation seriously.*

VINCE – *The difference between interpretation and translation – working with the leader of the group and doing a lot of translation for them, as well as your own interpretation.*

ABDULLAH – *When Vince and I talk about interpretation we mean conveying the meaning, as opposed to. . . . Speaking two languages, sometimes when speaking in Gujerati I will say something using English syntax and grammar because it conveys the sense of what I'm thinking better.*

VINCE – *Even groups which seem mono-cultural also have lots of differences that go unrecognized.*

DICK – *When I teach culture and difference, I survey people at the beginning about their background; so many differences come to the surface, families who migrated a generation before. There is just so much difference even when everyone seems English.*

CLARE – *To use the term 'English' seems rather simplistic and I am concerned about this because it could be conceived as a racist stereotype. 49% of the working population of London is from overseas. England is multicultural.*

GERHARD – *But there is truth in it as well.*

ABDULLAH – *I think people narrow it down. Experience of racism in groups – I think people try to make sure everyone is the same, then we can work towards shared task or goal. If we talk about difference it brings about anxieties. We put otherness on the outside – there is a group out there that doesn't get it.*

GWEN – *We're talking about boundaries that create identities and also differences – we sometimes think boundaries are valuable, they help to define the task and define the identity, but at the same time create difference/otherness. And then what is a violation or a crossing of the boundary? Because sometime it's an enactment of anxiety or produces more anxiety. I'm thinking of an environment where a member of staff has a sexual relationship with a patient and what that does to the organization. What I have noticed is the silencing, something that becomes unspeakable around difference and similarities.*

ABDULLAH – *Undiscussable. You don't talk about difference. When I talk about difference and get people to talk about white British identities, what comes back is trauma, 'why are you attacking me?'*

GWEN – *There are a lot of similarities between us, a lot of differences between us, and how do we use that space creatively in a way that may also include significant conflict without damaging each other?*

CYNTHIA – *The importance of 'dissensus'. You are all different and that is what makes it creative. It introduces the idea that it is not a downside.*

ABDULLAH – *There is an evolution of knowledge – if group analysis is situational and context-specific then we must move with the context we find ourselves in, we are not isolated as a community, we are interconnected. It's not just British culture – there is something about not throwing the baby out with bathwater, not throwing away our heritage, Shakespeare, but we need to recenter ourselves in Group analysis.*

CHRISTINE T – *That just makes me think, whose Shakespeare? He is central to the English language, and yet understood and translated differently in every generation.*

ABDULLAH – *Macbeth translated into an Indian context feels very different from seeing more traditional Shakespeare.*

CHRISTINE T – *I bet. There is something about the universality of Shakespeare which is shared with group analytical thinking. A universality of concepts people can relate to.*

CLARE – *I find Foulkes' interpretation of the leader and criticisms of his work incredibly useful. The matrix for me, in the context of the NHS is the most useful concept. I live with it, see it on a daily basis and also how it contributes to doctors' well being and disturbance.*

MARLENE – *Isn't that the value of group analysis – you use it when you can see it? Certain concepts are very helpful.*

CLARE – *As a GP I used to talk of unconscious communications, now I talk about the matrix.*

GERHARD – *The most powerful way of connecting with the other in the organization – everything depends on working together as a group, but we are still measured individually. This is a huge source of tension.*

IAN – *Part of the problem is that we practise group analysis in a neo-liberal culture.*

CHRISTINE T – *More fundamental, I think, is the sense of myself as somehow individual <u>and</u> my sense of myself as part of something else. This is the most fundamental tension to all human endeavor. How do you translate this into organizations?*

EARL – *I think that we have tried to use the term person rather than individual.*

CHRISTINE T – *That's helpful.*

EARL – *A person is socialized individual organism. You have to have a concept of person who is saturated by language and socialization processes.*

CHRISTINE T – *Taking in the notion of identity as a process rather than fixed.*

Notes

1 A 'team' may also be called a 'ward', a 'service', a 'project group', or a 'reflective practice group'.
2 Waldhoff's (2007) pair of fascinating papers give an account of the 'C' group, a gathering of influential early practitioners of group analysis, including the sociologist Norbert Elias. They illuminate the early development of group analytic thinking.
3 Customers, service users, patients or clients.
4 Such as expertise, wisdom, experience, popularity, longevity or eloquence.

Chapter 3

Persecutor, victim, rescuer

Imperfect consulting in an imperfect world

Christine Thornton

Adapted from Thornton, C. Towards a group analytic praxis for working with teams in organizations II. Group Analysis 51(1), pp. 72–90. Copyright © 2018 by the Author. Reprinted by permission of SAGE Publications, Ltd.

I am approached[1] by the Human Resources Director (HRD) of a not-for-profit company providing services to victims of crime, to work with a team of service managers. The members of the group previously ran small independent agencies, now amalgamated, unwillingly, into one regional organization of which they are branch managers. They are locked in conflict with the new Regional Centre ('Area'): there is much hostility and little communication. The Chief Executive Officer (CEO), the driving force behind the change, wants a management development program (MDP) to improve standards of work and get the branches 'in line' with the new Centre. 'Area' is one of several geographical regions fully affiliated to a national organization; the HRD informs me that the standard of management in other areas is uneven, mostly provided by ex-police officers. She distinguishes her own 'area' – 'all used to managing, we just do' – both from these other, less competent areas, and from the members of the MDP group: 'this is all very very new to those (branch) managers'. Branch managers' hostility towards 'Area' mirrors 'Area's' hostility to the national organization, described as 'patronizing' and having 'de-skilled managers'.

The CEO wants the branch managers to participate in the MDP, and the branch managers do not necessarily want this at all. The CEO 'has an MBA and her own coach' and so will not be involved. The purpose is to develop role awareness and management skills; the HRD greatly hopes

This chapter contains	

that it will reduce the managers' hostility towards 'Area', consolidating the merger. The MDP, framed as 'training', focuses on the 'dysfunctional' performance of the branch managers rather than the relationship between the branches and 'Area'.

Group analysis attends to context, and so dysfunction in a team is always considered as expressing dysfunction in the team's broader organizational context. Accepting the label 'dysfunctional' is a risky business: the dysfunction may not (all) be in the part of the system where it is currently 'located'. Having only the HRD's perceptions, I frame a contract that sets out the difficulties, sets up a feedback relationship with her, and incorporates an agreement to work flexibly with the managers; I only agree to conduct an initial one-day session, after which the rest of the program, a series of two-day events, would be confirmed. This is to give me more information, and an opportunity to win the confidence of the branch managers. The HRD thinks that her presence, or that of the CEO, would be counter-productive, and on the face of it, I agree.

The beginning

The CEO opens the first day event, staying for about 20 minutes. I am then left with around 18 managers, who are vituperative at many aspects of the new arrangements. They feel inadequately supported, stuck in a 'culture of blame'; the CEO's communication style makes them 'feel devalued'. There is a language of confrontation: 'eyeball', 'High Noon'. My countertransference is of dismay then indignation, that these seem 'reasonable people describing difficult circumstances'. On this day, and in the first two-day block which follows shortly afterwards, they speak repeatedly of traumatic loss: rapes, murders, child abuse, child rape/murder; one member is absent at a funeral. Another attends only half the day because it is her daughter's birthday; her daughter would have been 20, but died six months previously in a road accident a few yards from home. At one level this is to be expected as what 'comes through the front door' (Thornton, 2018). There also are strong personal resonances: the trauma in the material highlights its ubiquity in the managers' day to day work, and also the way in which the merger has been experienced as traumatic. There is a useful discussion of the dynamics of traumatic failed dependency in Hopper's introduction to *Trauma and organisations* (2012a).

The managers are highly critical of the CEO as 'very controlling and ambitious'. They are cynical about the value of the proposed MDP. I ask them, what could they get out of it? Several people comment that it has been useful to talk to each other, and by the end of the opening day there is some enthusiasm for starting the program, particularly as they have few other opportunities to work together.

It was helpful to have strong emotions and realise that they're okay to have . . . so this session also helped me handle strong emotions more effectively and then I started to talk about things with other people more, outside.

A divergence of purpose has already emerged; the CEO wants to 'get the branches in line' whereas the managers are focused on resourcing and running their own projects. 'Area' is seen as failing to take care of the branches, resulting in overwork and under-resourcing. Fight/flight and dependency basic assumptions (Hopper, 1997, 2012a) are visible: the CEO is a conveniently absent enemy. However, there is a universal belief that had she been in the room, the conversation would not have been possible.

'Area' agrees to commission the rest of the work. Interestingly, though my notes show I considered it, at this point I do not seek to renegotiate the contract to include communication with the CEO and dialogue between 'Area' and the branches.

Every team assignment is an organizational intervention in a wider system. Some, perhaps most, interventions are commissioned by clients who at the beginning have only a limited understanding of what may be involved or achieved. An invitation to do 'in-house training' or an MDP is a particular kind of clue, often an attempt to address an unacknowledged organizational deficit or difficulty. The hope is for a solution through a short event or events not involving all the players, usually only the less senior ones: that the problem can be 'trained' away. In this case, the scale of the program commissioned suggests that the problem is perceived as a large one. For the unwary practitioner, this will oftentimes be an invitation to be the scapegoat onto whom staff can unload their frustration, and the organization, its responsibility for the problem. My work as a supervisor as well as my own experience demonstrate that this can leave the practitioner with something highly indigestible. By the time of this commission, I am far from unwary; I have evolved a way of responding to requests, using the invitation to open a dialogue. In a successful piece of work, the client's capacity to understand and make use of what is on offer grows as the project goes on[2]. I hope that this approach will see me through the challenges already evident.

Even at this early point, the power of the context can be seen. The organization exists to provide support and care for victims of crime, against a background of spending cuts and 'rationalization', leading to the hated 'merger'. Victims of crime experience the impact of overwork and under-resourcing in the court system, as do, in their advocacy role, the branch managers. The struggle over resources is mirrored in the organization and even in the physical environment of the work. The service covers two neighboring cities and surrounding rural and industrial towns. One city is prosperous, the other, one of the most deprived in the country. 'Area' is located in the former city, and apart from the opening event, my work with the managers in the latter; however, the HRD arranges for me to stay in a charming rural location between the two. The rigid and hierarchical culture of the justice system is replicated in the relationship between 'Area' and branches; I am positioned 'outside' (irrelevant?) and 'between' (a hoped-for bridge?), my needs attended to as those of the managers are not. The central Foulkesian concept communication (Foulkes and Anthony, 1957) allows me to think this is relevant.

The first two-day event is similarly experienced as useful but tensions begin to emerge. In creating a holding space for the group's conversation, I am positioned as an effective container, different from the CEO, the formal leader. The difficult relationship between the group and its leader is untouched. There is no direct feedback mechanism between me and the CEO, and I am beginning to doubt the efficacy of my link with the HRD. She listens sympathetically and appears supportive; however, I do not experience her as a true partner in the work.

Resistance

By the time of the second event, the disorder inherent in the organization's work has come to the fore. The HRD has given members an incorrect start time, so that when I arrive at the agreed time, I appear 'late'; there is news of a car crash which has prevented someone attending; the member who could only manage half of the first day repeats the pattern, leaving half way through each day. Two other members are missing. We discuss the apparently intractable problems they face, and all ideas are greeted with the classic 'yes but' response described so well by Berne (1964). Members express disappointments and depression, they no longer want to try to influence 'Area', and ask me for 'training', a more conventional experience. My countertransference is of uselessness, being 'no help', and 'I don't want to come back here'.

It is a difficult session, with unsettling dynamics, disrespectful behavior, and challenges to my authority, in other words, quite strong resistance. It is no accident that this session represents the midpoint in my work with them, the fourth and fifth of nine days.

I adopt a pragmatic 'training' approach, waiting for a challenge to allow the real conversation to emerge. I introduce the Drama Triangle, a concept from transactional analysis (Karpman, 1968),[3] as a way of thinking about the dynamics in the organization, with the roles of persecutor, victim and rescuer moving around between Centre, branches, me, the CEO, and HRD. The Drama Triangle articulates the complex and volatile dynamic of persecutor, victim, and rescuer.[4] At first it is only possible to consider 'victimhood' in their deputies, not to see it in themselves. By the end of the event there is greater insight and some ability to recoup power.

Nevertheless, I leave feeling disorganized, and lose my sunglasses at the airport; an undigested fragment has got into me.

The organization can be seen as an assistant 'rescuer' to the justice system which does not 'rescue' victims after a traumatizing crime, despite their hopes that it might. Experiences of persecution and victimization are ubiquitous, played out again and again. As workers, the branch managers are stuck in a 'victim', failed dependency (Hopper, 1997, 2012a) position from which the MDP seems to offer some hope of escape; yet the idea of escape is both the opportunity for and the threat to real movement. Perhaps in the fantasy of escape there is an unconscious link to prisoners' adjustment to life 'inside'.

In an organization focused on real victims, the Drama Triangle has particular power in connecting members with their context. Condenser phenomena operate in members' converging experiences of identification with their clients' experiences, as advocates in the justice system, a sense of victimization as workers, and as agents in a far more highly controlled new regime. Linking these experiences eventually leads to 'aha!' moments for some managers (Stern, 1985). 'Area' is experienced as the (criminal) persecutor and the failed rescuer,[5] mirroring the failures of the courts with which the managers work day to day; perhaps also as the persecuting 'gaoler' depriving the members of their previous freedom. Members also identify as 'failed rescuers' and their frustrations with the 'persecuting' justice system is mirrored in their frustrations with 'Area' and the CEO. The concept proves invaluable to some members in understanding powerful feelings about their situation, and in being able to move to a more professional relationship with 'Area' as well as each other.

Who or what am I invited to be[6]? At the initial event, I am invited to be the witness to the 'criminally' negligent and uncaring parent of the merged organization, and also to be in some sense an arbiter. I succeed in walking a narrow line, valuing the perspectives of the members, while keeping the inevitability of the merger present: a neutral outsider whom they are willing, for the moment, to trust. As time goes on it becomes clear that I am invited to be persecutor or rescuer by 'Area', and rescuer/advocate/champion by the managers.

The middle of the journey

My repeated countertransference is to feel 'torn', put on the spot, under time pressure to deliver something that feels undeliverable. What the managers need and what 'Area' wants seem irreconcilable. My conversations with the HRD do not help; it seems that either her understanding or her power is limited, so that I feel alone with the dilemma. The 'rushed' feeling is a strong projective process rather than a real dilemma, as there is a good amount of time, although the end is now in view. The sense of hurry is the managers' experience, and perhaps that in 'Area' too. I also feel a pressure to be 'cheerleader', a style of leadership aligned with the group's predominantly massified position (Hopper, 1997).

I continue to prioritize the managers' exploring together their real situations and dilemmas, as the best route to promoting greater maturity and autonomy in the tasks and challenges they face. My loneliness in the work mirrors the managers' isolation in their day-to-day work, with people traumatized by the experience of crime. By the third block, a month after the second, members are beginning to function more effectively together, developing a shared understanding of their situation, tackling their grievances with 'Area', and sharing intelligence about practice.

My identification with the managers and their view of the problem is steadily increasing, but I am torn here too, because as a group analyst I am reluctant to believe that the problem all lies with one individual. Despite mounting evidence, I want to believe that the CEO is capable of more than her managers believe. Here perhaps a group analytic awareness of location, and a strong professional commitment to challenging scapegoating, is not helpful. While groups can usually reduce polarization, that relies on the consent and presence of all parties; here the 'scapegoat', if such she was, was not in the room. Looking back from a distance of many years, it is clearer to me now that group analysis, whether clinical or organizational, cannot work with those who simply refuse to play.

Very different positions in the group now emerge. Some managers are genuinely engaged and keen to sort out the problems; the largest group are cautiously willing to try to make things work, testing progress step by step; a few are interested only in maintaining a sense of grievance. These seem to be wedded to a 'victim' position (intensified by their identification with their clients, actual victims of crime) and continue to see 'Area', and its CEO, as an uncaring authority, justifying their anger and envious destructiveness; here the Drama Triangle is aligned with basic assumption theory. For this minority, fight/flight and incohesion are active still (Bion, 1961; Karpman, 1968; Hopper, 1997, 2012a).

The failed dependency and feelings of helplessness at the root of incohesion (Hopper, 2012a) can be traced here. Expression helps some but not all the members to let in another perspective, moving to a more differentiated position. The pull to massification is strong. 'Area' sees the managers as a rebellious mass and wishes them to be a compliant mass. This consolidates the managers as an angry mass. A process of differentiation begins through the MDP but cannot spread to 'Area' because the MDP is limited to the branch managers.

Although the managers recognize their need to communicate with the CEO, they are reluctant because they do not believe she will be receptive. I have by now concluded that my link with the HRD is not enabling any shift in 'Area'; I decide to seek a direct conversation with the CEO. I wish to negotiate a conversation between her and the managers. I raise this with the managers. There is a sense of danger and concern; they fear I will no longer 'support' them – 'change sides'. I fear I will lose their confidence. I explain that I feel it is my responsibility to try; they agree, though without enthusiasm.

In this third block, there are signs of increased confidence: discussion is about the real work and the frustrations of the criminal justice system; the Drama Triangle is used in thinking; quieter members speak; disrespectful behavior is reduced and easier to quell so that I am able to hold my authority more lightly. They comment that open challenge is the way to break the hold of the Drama Triangle and that they have made a subtle shift from 'I'm sick of this, I will say what I think' to 'If I think something, I say it'. One particularly articulate member of the group is emerging as a thoughtful leader. Towards the end members are animated and engaged, and there is a chorus of thank yous as I leave. I feel that a corner has been turned.

The CEO

My meeting with the CEO is frustrating. I find her impermeable, unwilling or unable to hear. She will not meet the managers. She holds me at arms length, viewing her managers as a mass of troublesome children who need to be schooled, though by the end of the conversation this tone is more muted, or at least more covert. The CEO identifies with the rigid, hierarchical leadership common in her sectoral context (the justice system), and is either indifferent to, or actually glories in, her positioning as 'persecutor-in-chief', keeping at bay all vulnerability. Persecutor and victim positions are both a response to an experience of vulnerability, or in Hopper's terms, the experience of failed dependency and helplessness.

Chris Argyris has coined a useful language for focal unconscious organizational problems: 'undiscussables' (Argyris, 1980, 1990).[7] For the CEO, much is undiscussable; her rigid self-image as a 'strong leader' precludes her engagement with any view that might differ from her own. Particularly undiscussable is any possibility of failure or dysfunction on her part, or that of 'Area'; all dysfunction (here a pejorative term for being human) has to be projected into the branch managers. The possibility of learning anything is held at bay. At the outset the managers' 'undiscussables' are any positive outcomes from the merger or reasons to adapt. However unlike 'Area', the undiscussability is not undiscussable (Argyris, 1980) and so more permeable, open to change.

The CEO's former idealization of me has become denigration. Rather than a potentially useful ally, I am now positioned as 'merely' the provider of an MDP to be done to the 'others', the ones who are at fault. The

CEO's leadership style broadly aligns with the Aggregation pole of Incohesion (Hopper, 1997). The fashion, or mania, for seeking to measure/control/manualize all aspects of social intervention was at that time at its height; the CEO had a conceptual and political context which supported her approach. However, such leadership categories are inevitably more nuanced in reality. She also wished to be a heroic leader/warrior saving the organization, whom others would follow; the managers' group had denied her this. Her solution was to hire me in to 'fix' them – which in her terms, I was manifestly failing to do. I then needed to be positioned as 'just as useless' as the managers themselves.

It seems that the managers' assessment is correct: the CEO cannot, at present, engage in the kind of dialogue of which they have become capable. It is unlikely I can change this or enable real dialogue between 'Area' and branches. I can only assist the managers in finding a voice and joining together for greater strategic impact.

The ending

From the midpoint, in any time-limited intervention, the question of its ending must be emphasized. As organizational work is frequently time-limited, managing endings is a key task. The managers have experienced a containing space which has enabled expression and dialogue. How will they keep what they have gained when the program ends? I persistently raise this question. My role as container has unavoidably positioned me as rival leader, or rescuer. Now I am departing. What sense can the group make of my loss, consciously and unconsciously?

Again, the response is differentiated; some managers have regained authority and autonomy, together with a shared sense of the limits on efficacy in this organization; some descend to spiteful retaliation for their disappointment in me – 'it's very nice for you, you come in as a high-paid consultant and then you go away again'. The majority are pessimistic about the ability for things to change very much under the current regime – an assessment with which I silently concur – but are grateful that they are better equipped to deal with it together. They consistently thank me for my 'calm', and indeed the group is less gripped by fear and panic; there is a greater ability to think through their difficulties. They arrange ongoing meetings with each other, planning to continue to work at the boundaries of their relationship with 'Area'.

I am satisfied that the group overall has made good progress. Members have pooled resources and expertise and have developed a habit of thinking together about how to tackle problems. They think more strategically about their services and have also made some progress against the explicit MDP goals. The attitude of most of the group to 'Area' is now questioning, rather than irrationally hostile; 'Area' is no longer monolithic: they acknowledge the efforts of some 'Area' individuals and negotiate for what they need, feeling more in control of their work. There is more lightness and humor.

I do not meet the CEO again. In a final review meeting, the HRD seeks to position me as 'victim'. Though acknowledging the cessation of hostilities between branches and 'Area', previously her main goal, she focuses instead on 'unmet training goals', which turns out to mean that her entire shopping list of 'topics' for the MDP are not listed on the outline programs.

A more competent and assertive group of managers was not wanted; compliance was the goal. Or at least it was the CEO's goal – was the HRD's original acceptance of my proposal a covert or unconscious recognition that something different was needed? Mindful of the dynamics of blame and scapegoating in the organization, I am determined not simply to accept her view without challenge. I remind her of our contract, and that the outcomes are a better test of value than agendas. But it seems a 'view' has been taken, which the HRD is only empowered to deliver; we part 'agreeing to differ'.

There is further discussion of this vignette in chapters four, following the six aspects of group analysis discussed in chapter two, and 15, using the 'five questions' (Thornton, 2019).

Notes

1 The five questions which structure this vignette appear on pages 141–143, and are discussed more fully in Thornton 2019.
2 This is true even if they have a fairly good understanding in the first place.
3 The theoretical framework of group analysis, with its value for multiple levels and perspectives, readily enables the 'borrowing' of ideas from other traditions. We are not only not restricted to one view of 'what is really going on', we are actively encouraged to have several views in mind.
4 I have assumed that this concept is fairly widely known. If not, Karpman's original paper (see bibliography), and a plethora of other material about the Drama Triangle, are freely available on the internet. The Drama Triangle is also known as the Rescue Triangle.
5 A failed rescuer in the Drama Triangle rapidly becomes indistinguishable from a persecutor.
6 Or, what is my countertransference?
7 Argyris' work is richly represented on the internet.

Chapter 4

Group analytic praxis and 'persecutor, victim, rescuer'

Christine Thornton

There are many potentially valid perceptions of any piece of organizational work. Within the last chapter 'persecutor, victim, rescuer', the 'five questions' are used to analyze proceedings, a lens taken further by Margaret Smith on page 141. Here, I analyze the case study using the six core aspects of group analysis set out in chapter two.

Linking with the commissioning organizational leader

The leader-consultant partnership is the element missing in this consultation; the apparent commissioner is in fact a 'messenger' with severely limited authority. To achieve organizational changes with a good prospect of longevity, the group analyst must work effectively with the commissioning organizational leader, with a shared understanding of the aims, periodic reviews of progress, and cooperation in seeing it through. No such true partnership was possible here. Any improvement achieved was unstable, subject to systemic pressures including the CEO's unchanged modus operandi.

On pages 218–20 and 247–50 are vignettes giving an account of consultations where this partnership is central to success.

Clients vary. Some are able to give a meaningful response to a question about their real challenges and hopes, the desires underlying the commission. Some are not. In some cases, the expressed purpose may be very far from underlying wishes. In *Persecutor, victim, rescuer*, initial perceptions of obstacles to progress were confirmed as the work progressed. 'Area' engaged me to tackle a problem that was firmly split off, projected into the group of branch managers. Group analysis offers an excellent praxis for improving communication and collaboration, but only by consent and with those who are in the room.

Heard as individuals: better communication within the team

The managers' group was certainly not a team at the outset. Practically speaking, it had a shared purpose, but geographical distance and part-time working made coming together difficult. At a dynamic level, it was a relatively undifferentiated mass of opposition to 'Area'. The work enabled more individual voices, not removing opposition, but rendering the managers more effective because they were less in the grip of a traumatized and failed dependency; the work helped the majority to process trauma and recover a sense of autonomy and authority. Communicating honestly also confirmed their sense of the real difficulties of the situation.

Thinking together in groups helps us return to the ground of our own real experience, and understanding others' experience, so that we can find a way through together (Foulkes, 1990b). This is where group analysis scores highly. However, because the broader organization was not represented in the room, there was no possibility of narrowing the fundamental breach. There were two conflicting sub-cultures with different values and no frankness between the two; further, within 'Area' sub-culture, any dissent was undiscussable. Perhaps that lay beneath the HRD's conflicting messages about program objectives; something useful could *only* be done covertly: an unconscious invitation.

Attention to context

The vignette clarifies the importance of context, illustrating the greater pressures and constraints arising from the interplay of the task, the system, and the matrix.[1] We can only be the practitioner that the group, and the setting of which it is part, allows us to be; it behooves us to pay close attention to the context, because members' shared experience(s) will intensify its power through resonance and condenser phenomena.

In organizational work, the close relationship between systemic and group analytic praxis comes into focus, particularly attention to relationships between different parts of the system, and a focus on communication and feedback (Foulkes, 1948, 1990a and b; Foulkes and Anthony, 1957). Systems thinking aligns with the sociological element of group analysis, enriching our language for considering context (Oliver, 2008).

Not attending at the outset to the boundary/communication between 'Area' and the managers necessitated later re-negotiation, which failed.

When working organizationally, it is essential to engage with questions of power relations and formal hierarchy (Spero, 2003). How far was my intervention with the CEO a 'responsible' correction of an earlier oversight, and how far an unconscious response to the group's invitation to become rescuer, or even to 'pair' with the CEO to produce a savior who would remove all difficulties (Bion, 1961)? The heightened affect in the managers' group about this meeting can be read as evidence for this.

Creative incorporation of difference

Because of the different purpose and short timescales, the role of the group analyst in organizational work will often be more active: to intervene to improve communication, rather than let its development unfold at a therapeutic pace. This is linked to what I have called 'the creative incorporation of difference', for example, more active linking of members' contributions to encourage emotional expression, underscore common ground, or minimize destructive conflict. This is not dissimilar from large group practice, where members are unfamiliar with the method and the purpose is understood as dialogue (De Mare, Piper and Thompson, 1991; Thornton, 2017a; Rogers, 2017; Wilke, this volume).

Pace is an important question. We have to hold the balance between a sense of unhurried time for reflection and the reality of organizational deadlines and time pressures. We must be reasonably in step with the team we are working with, but (usually) encouraging them to slow down and think more. We do at times have the pleasure of working with teams capable of deep reflection; but the majority of organizations require help to sit and think at all.

An ethical question

Was it right to proceed with the program after the gap between the CEO's objectives and mine/the managers' became clear? Indeed, was my failure to renegotiate the contract after the initial diagnostic day a mistake, or a kind of wise foolishness? Had an unconscious recognition of the dynamics influenced that early decision? Had I renegotiated then, the commission might not have gone forward; the managers would have had either nothing or an MDP more closely aligned with the CEO's approach. I could also have refused the commission, with the same result. Instead the managers had an opportunity for limited, conditional change which left most of them more satisfied and better equipped in their roles.

My MDP did not set out to produce compliance, but competent thinking and feeling about roles, my objectives unmistakably nonaligned with the CEO's. I offered the managers a coherent alternative to their previous 'refusenik' position. Was this ethical?

I believe on balance that it was. I could not have worked in the way that the CEO wished without violating my own ethics (Simpson, 2017a). Having started, it was more responsible to complete the work I had begun with the managers than to abandon it, and them. Further, 'Area' wanted an MDP to 'train' the managers out of their recalcitrant attitudes; and recalcitrance *was* reduced.

Value of multiple perspectives, selection of best metaphor, and complexity

Group analysts are trained to hold several views of a situation in mind at once. If all theory is understood as metaphor which explains and (over-) simplifies experience, a shorthand for processes that are highly complex, the loose framework of group analytic theory allows us to accommodate a rich variety. I chose to articulate the one (the Drama Triangle) with the most resonant language for the people in the group. While not the only nor necessarily the most powerful lens I used in thinking about this work, the Drama Triangle was a metaphor with high valency in this situation. Team members 'got it' almost immediately.

Complexity thinking takes this further, with its emphases on conversation, 'tweaking' rather than orchestrating change, paradox, self-organizing emergence, the tension between stability and instability, and the limits on the predictability of any intervention (Stacey, 2001a and b, 2012).

My awareness of complexity thinking helped me make sense of this intervention. It clarified that the CEO's controlling stance was doomed to failure; the inherent instability of any system implied a potential for future change. The managers began to organize themselves to tackle the frustrations and uncertainties of their shared role, and to develop a habit of conversation; in the event of future regime change, these capacities would not be lost. Complexity thinking ultimately helped me make my peace with the limits of my capacity to influence the organization's culture and modus operandi, and to accept that I had done something useful at least.

Organizational work offers many opportunities to develop nimble feet and virtuosity, but few certainties and no purity. As we engage with the client matrix, we will always make 'mistakes'; it is the nature of our mistakes, and our enquiry into them, that are the most illuminating part of the work.

In more fully successful commissions, exploration with the client builds bridges and strengthens their capacity to think about their own 'mistakes'. Where a working partnership has been achieved, this shared process can reveal the 'mistakes', tensions or paradoxes, which lie at the heart of the organization's conflicts. That can be transforming for the organization.

Our chances of success are highest where conditions in the team and in the broader system support change (Kets de Vries, 2005), and where we can form a successful alliance with both organizational leader and team.

Conclusion

To live means to live with paradox: I could not make a link with the CEO, nor work with the organization's core difficulty. Instead I worked with those able to make use of what I could offer. Any lasting value could only reside in those people, their improved understanding and capacity and their new habit of working together. There was no guarantee that the gains could be sustained in what was fundamentally a hostile environment for mature working relationships; however, there are rarely guarantees in organizational life, or organizational consulting. In the end, it demands of us what we demand of our clients; that we thoughtfully and responsibly own and use our power.

Note

1 The complexities of the relationship between the system and the matrix is beyond the scope of this chapter. There is a full and valuable discussion of the relationship between (the system), the matrix and the social unconscious in Nitzgen and Hopper (2017).

Section II

The art of conversation

Complexity, the matrix, and 'parallel process'

Praxis based on complexity and chaos thinking is a thread running through the book, and the focus of section II.

In chapter five, Christopher Rance deconstructs communication and the art of conversation which is the core of group analytic praxis. Following the work of G.H. Mead, he explains how meaning is made between people through gesture and response, listening as well as speaking. He gives us the benefit of his mature thinking about many years of organizational practice in handling common difficulties.

'Parallel process' (see also the reflection process, isomorphism, equivalence and refracted counter-transference) is a concept much used but little examined. David Wood's erudite chapter six gives a scientific account of how it works. David traverses several fields, including physics, biology, evolutionary theory, genetics, cognitive science, and computational neuroscience. He links these processes to Foulkes' core concept, the group matrix, highlighting its far-sighted accuracy, and proposes a more accurate re-definition of 'parallel process'. Along the way he sheds light on the anatomy of learning.

Chapter 5

The art of conversation

Group analytic interventions in organizational life

Christopher Rance

Introduction

The relevance of group analysis, with its perspectives founded on psychoanalytic, sociological, and systems/complexity theories has been well demonstrated in its application to many types of work groups small, medium, and large. One of the founding fathers of group analysis, S.H. Foulkes, insisted from the start that it had applications in all contexts. Application to organizations takes various forms depending on the sector. It has been applied successfully to health, education, local government, civil service, banking, and commercial sectors among others.

What exactly does group analysis offer in the context of an institution and the organizing activities of its members?

I distinguish here between the many different institutions set in bricks and mortar with their various raisons d'etre and rules, and the universally present social dynamics, or organizing mental constructs, of the people engaged in undertaking the collaborative tasks of an 'institution'. An organization is not a concrete entity but a series of dynamic mental constructs that we may call organizing relationships. Although in some contexts group analysis is a therapy, in the context of the workplace we should consider its interventions, in as much as we can make the distinction, to be primarily education or training in the skills of relating, in the context of the collaborative tasks to hand.

Group work as a vehicle for organizational change has a long history. Forty years ago, Cary Cooper (1976),

This chapter contains

now Professor Sir Cary Cooper, was writing about developing social skills in managers via group training. We have come a long way since this top down, hierarchical approach. We now we realize that social skills are required by all in the workplace.

The group analytic concept of the integration of the individual and the group as interdependent realities lies at the heart of the idea of the promotion of the skills of conversation in the workplace. In my practice I initially tend to consider a group analytic intervention as helping to resolve dysfunctional organizational distress or conflict. There is a current trend in team building and training which focuses on task completion (bridge building and so on). I consider here the context, content, and process of relationships in the workplace but mainly the process. The primary group analytic task is to foster the art of creative conversation while taking the context and content seriously.

One aim of a creative conversation is to divert mental energies from the task of surviving dysfunctional organizational stresses into new possibilities of co-operative relationship. This is what group analysts would call ego training in action.

The two volume *Shorter Oxford English Dictionary* defines conversation as the act of 'living, or having ones being, in or among others'. This is a fundamental social characteristic of us humans; the social origins of our individual personalities. This conversation is not just speaking and waiting to speak again, presenting pre-thought thoughts, opinions, or 'truths', but more a process of listening, speaking, then hearing the response and moving on to a new, previously unthought thought, spoken out only if appropriate.

This key concept comes from the writing of the sociologist George Herbert Mead of the Chicago Pragmatists (1964). My contribution to the conversation, my gesture, spoken or otherwise, towards the other is only fully made sense of, to me, by my understanding of the response, spoken or otherwise, from the other. Gesture and response are the creative link between us. It helps create not only my own social personality in the group but those of all the other individuals who make up the group, and of the group as a whole.

The group analysts Pat de Maré, Piper and Thompson (1991) observed that conversation, which he called dialogue, is 'the hallmark of the human species and is an a priori form of currency: it is the skill that has to be learned and used if humans are to survive the onslaughts of human mismanagement let alone Nature. People speak to each other in a creative emerging manner. Mind does not emerge automatically: it is the outcome of a dynamic tension continuously in dialogue, a miracle of psychogenesis'.

This process of conversation is not one of transmission and reply but one of a mutually creative iterative process, sometimes an agreement, but often more creative if revealing difference. This forms the immediate local interaction in a complex network of gestures and responses that we call the mental construct of organizing – the organizing that exists only in the minds of the participants. There are as many organizings in the mind as there are participants. We have no control over the outcomes of these interactions, they are so many, varied, and complex that it would not be possible to control them all (like the mental constructs of, say, traffic or mind itself). We can influence by our participation and our skilled recognition of the emergent patterning of creative thought, but no one can control the result. Skilled recognition does not mean a psychoanalytical interpretation, but a recognition of the new meaning for me in the response for me in the other(s) gesture. We may be in charge, but we are not in control, even of our own thought processes, let alone anyone else's.

One way to plan a consultative role or intervention is to invite in the organizational expert who can quickly see what's wrong, tell everyone what to do next, and to act as an inspired leader; singlehandedly to pull the group out of the swamp that is impeding its effectiveness, and to contain the high levels of anxiety thus generated. This we call the politics of salvation (Lawrence, 2000). It never works.

Another way however is to facilitate the members of the institution to learn, from the conversational example of a group analytic conductor, how to find their own way out of the swamp. This we call the politics of revelation. This is what group analysis has uniquely on offer. As convener and conductor of the group, the analyst offers an experience of creative, revelatory group analytic conversation to the participants. The purpose is to attend to and attempt to understand any dysfunctionality they are experiencing by reframing the network or matrix of conversational relationships in the team. The group itself is not a problem solving one but an exercise in tentative exploration of relationship. The resolution of any actual problems, based on this experience, will by and large tend to happen outside the group sessions themselves in the day to day functioning of the institution.

The main problem we all face when working together is not usually technical expertise as such (which can be supplemented as a separate exercise if necessary) but the quality of the social interactions of the participants. Both sets of skills are learned skills, and this is often overlooked. It is assumed that the skills of the first, technical, set automatically lead to skills of the second. They do not. Participating in a genuine conversation is a hard-learned art, it does not come naturally. Many people are initially not only quite bad at it but find it very threatening. Avoidance of the challenge of a real conversation is one of the indications of an underlying dysfunction in the institution.

In selecting and promoting staff, the presence or absence of technical skills are easily verified, but those of social abilities, less so. Initially it is best to assume that no-one is inherently very good at relating to the other, only that they may or may not be just good enough. In my experience, organizational functioning is a very wide spectrum with exceptional technical and social skills often being found at opposite poles, the upside of each concealing its downside. The key skill in conversation is the ability to listen and process a new thought. The ability to do this diminishes under stress. Added to this we may well have to cope with living examples of the Peter Principle where people are promoted until they arrive at their level of incompetence, technical, social, or heaven forbid, both. The question is, how can we develop the social skills of the work group, or larger institutional grouping, to cope adequately and productively with all this?

In many cases we cannot directly address the problem of poor leadership, as often the one who invites us in will be part of that problem. Nor can we remove the wider structural stresses of sub-optimal social skills in the organization or in society as a whole, but we can work to enable the team to function optimally in the face of it all. Much has been written about military incompetence but less so about organizational incompetence. Professor Norman Dixon's (1976) famous analysis of military incompetence is worth reading as it is a brilliant commentary on incompetent leadership applicable to all situations. It is a standard text at the Royal Military Academy at Sandhurst. The common factor in failures of all types is that after the event it becomes apparent that many people foresaw them but could not prevent them because no one would listen.

In the civilian sphere a prime example was the sinking of the Titanic. Its cause, and its becoming a disaster, were direct results of not listening to telegraphic messages. Another case in point was the Challenger Space Shuttle explosion where management ignored the repeated warnings of the engineers. Yet another was at the Royal Bank of Scotland, where the Manager of Risk was ignored and fired by the CEO for pointing out the catastrophic danger ahead, just days before the crisis. The question is not the mind-boggling incompetence of the CEO in this case, but why all the other highly intelligent board members and executives let him get away with it. Just before the 2008 financial crash, Warren Buffet called Credit Default Swaps financial weapons of mass destruction. He was ridiculed. All this applies just as much to the many less seriously sub-optimally performing work groups, as it does to these disastrous ones.

Negotiating the entry to the organization is a separate subject, but once we are there, how do we conduct a group to promote the art of conversation? I convene the group, meeting weekly, in neutral ground and at a fixed time for ideally 90 minutes, seated in a circle facing each other. A model of interaction where the participants only see the backs of the heads of the others is perverse. Body language is as important as speech and should be easily visible. However, some find this very threatening. One contra indication of good leadership is hiding behind a large desk.

Ideally the size of the group should be no more than 8–10 with a maximum of, say, 12. This number eight is not 'magic' but has been accepted as an optimal unit of group coherence from the time of the Roman Legion's conturburnium of eight men to the current size of a British Army's section or squad of eight men, and also in group analysis. In current management thinking, if there are more than eight or so persons reporting to someone, that person may well be a supervisor rather than a manager. The exact composition or membership of the group, and any formal task to be agreed are again separate subjects in their own right. There should be no set agenda other than any subject/s adopted or raised willingly in the moment by the members present. These could address political (terrorist?) anxieties, organizational tensions, financial worries, personal problems such as the demands of parenting, or just the quality of the canteen food.

The contract is to discuss anything remotely relevant in a free floating, free associative way; to talk about but principally to listen constructively to anything whatsoever in an exploratory, courteous way in the spirit of provisional learning. In any group everyone spends – or should spend – the greater part of the time listening. The principal role of the conductor is to encourage the group members to relate meaningfully with each other. It is the quality of the process of relating rather than the content of the conversations that is of primary importance. The development of conversational skills is the primary task of the group. Although the improved quality of relating, if and when successfully achieved, may enable the participants to optimize both their technical and their social abilities, this ideal outcome can be moderated by the possibility that the interests of any particular individual, those of the group or the institution as a whole may be incompatible, and the satisfaction of everyone is impossible.

In group analytic groups everyone is equal irrespective of their rank or role outside the group. This includes the conductor who facilitates good conversation by example and not by ostentatiously demonstrating a specific expertise of leadership. If there are particular characteristics of such a conductor, they are a courteous curiosity to see what is 'at the other side of the hill', and a care for the well-being of all concerned. The conductor must assume that many if not most of the group initially do not want to be there, and that each member likes or dislikes their fellow group members in equal measure.

One model of conducting is that of a good chairman whose task is to facilitate the creative exchange of thoughts and only intervenes to help overcome obstacles preventing conversation, ensuring that everyone has their say. I personally promote the British Naval chaplains' tradition of adopting the rank of the person who spoke last.

A group analytic work group can also be regarded as Improvization Theater in that it forms the play, the players, and the audience all at once. It follows the four main rules of Improvization Theater: to make the other feel safe on the stage with you, trying not to be clever, trying not to control and dealing with one's own demons off stage. You don't need to train at RADA but it does need practice to participate comfortably and creatively. Like all good theater, a good conversation is a matter of cues and timing.

Although organizational and institutional failures of all kinds can be summed up as not so much failures to speak as failures to listen, overcoming this is never easy. This can be for many reasons, anxiety, ignorance, arrogance, laziness, fear of misunderstanding and then saying a wrong or foolish thing, or just not paying attention to the realities of others. In the group it can be manifest by the lack of confidence to be able converse easily – to chat – irrespective of rank or role. We have of course seen many examples of good practice but these generally go unremarked as no problems are experienced. There is no swamp. But the task at hand is for the team members to free themselves when they are trapped in this swamp of silent failure. No one can do it on their own but only together, within the development in the group of a network or matrix of supportive collaborative conversation. The slow emergence of trust can only be earned.

This however may not be immediately obvious to prospective clients: 'Is that what we can expect to pay for in both time and money?' At one level, 'yes we can', but at another, 'is it worth the risk?' As group analysts, when faced with the serious doubts of the clients, we have a duty to warn them that the outcome of a group analytically inspired experience of creative conversation may not be what was expected, or perhaps wanted. The outcome of an authentic conversation cannot be foreseen although it can usually be recognized as it emerges. The management of expectations is, of course, a fundamental skill of organizational life at all levels, but any attempt to control the outcome, even with the best of intentions, corrupts the quality of the conversation and makes it just another attempt to exercise inappropriate power, usually disguised as responsibility.

How can we dispel or mitigate this reasonable anxiety about failure? We have anecdotally many satisfied clients to date, but to demonstrate it experimentally would require long-term, stringent audit of the outcomes of our interventions in all contexts; this is not research in the sense of randomized controlled trials but qualitative outcome audit. Sociological interventions cannot be evaluated like pharmacological interventions, with their one variable and one constant (the drug), but rather more like major surgical interventions which have no constants and which, for ethical considerations alone, can never be evaluated by double blind trials but only by outcome audit. This may well be the challenge for the next generation of organizational group analysts.

Conclusion

The experience of promoting and enjoying a good and effective organizational conversation, made possible by an experienced group analytic conductor, is a powerful gift in its own right whatever the outcome. Immediate utility is dependent on many imponderable factors, not all relating to task, but invariably the participants benefit, one way or another, in terms of reduced long-term stress and improved psychological energy, which in turn benefits the institution in unforeseen ways.

Chapter 6

Complex reflections

Notes on 'parallel process' and the group matrix in group analytic organizational consultancy

David Wood

Introduction

The concept of 'Parallel Process' has taken root within group analytic discourse, particularly in relation to supervision, reflective practice, and organizational consultancy. It is often invoked to 'explain' phenomena in ways that suggest that, as a concept, it can be taken as given. But what is 'parallel' about the process and how does it work?

This chapter explores parallel process from a wider perspective. Links will be made to concepts from other disciplines: physics, biology, evolutionary theory, genetics, cognitive science, and computational neuroscience.

The concept of 'parallel process'

'Parallel Process' is ubiquitous. Therefore, although the focus here is on organizational consultancy, what follows takes in the entirety of group analytic praxis.

The term usually refers to an observation that a pattern of relationships, process, and communication in a particular system A is analogous to, congruent with, or similar to, a pattern of relationships, process, and communication in another system B.

For example, in a consultancy to a training institution, a teacher relates how a student had disturbed classmates by talking about her experience of being sexually abused as a child by her father. As the teacher describes this, other members of the consultation group report feeling disturbed that the teacher is over-identifying with the student. After reflecting on this, the teacher talks about her own discomfort at work because she experienced the Institution Head, a charismatic man, as being inappropriately sexually interested in her. Although he had done nothing overt, she felt that she was being 'groomed'. The Consultant becomes aware of feeling disturbed by finding himself more conscious of this teacher's attractiveness than he had previously been. He was curious because international news at the time was dominated by the disclosure that a well-known, powerful, charismatic man had been for many years abusing his power by demanding sexual favors from employees in return for preferment. There are striking 'parallels' in these patterns in feelings and relationships between a student and a member of her family, her teacher and the Head of the Training Institution, the Consultant and the members of the consultancy group, and what was current news in the wider social context.

But invoking 'parallel process' does not, of itself, explain the congruity between these patterns at different scales of system – how does the structure and process observed at one scale come to be reflected in another?

Origins in psychoanalysis

> The idea of parallel process . . . has its origin in the psychoanalytic concept of transference. Analysts involved in supervision observed that the transference of the therapist and the countertransference of the supervisor within the supervisory session appeared to parallel what was happening in the therapy session between client and therapist.
>
> (McNeill and Worthen, 1989, p. 329)

In the early decades, despite brief forays into group psychology, anthropology, and religion, psychoanalysis essentially remained a discourse concerned with a one-body psychology in which instincts or drives sought their satisfaction but were inhibited or blocked and the analyst strove to remain as detached as possible. Eventually Freud, and his successors, noticed that processes taking place within each individual patient became reflected in the relationship between patient and analyst (theorized as *transference and later, counter-transference*), and subsequently observed that these processes were also reflected in the relationship between analyst and supervisor. One of the first references to parallel processes was made by Searles (1955a, p. 135), who labelled it the reflection process, suggesting that

> processes at work currently in the relationship between patient and therapist are often reflected in the relationship between therapist and supervisor
>
> (McNeill and Worthen, 1989, p. 329)

Field theory

The concept of *field*[1] developed in physics to explain the phenomenon of 'action over distance' – *how* did the moon influence the tides, or a magnet influence a piece of iron, or the planets maintain their orbit without some sort of invisible attraction (McMullin, 2002)? In 1852 Faraday formally introduced the notion of a magnetic *field*, a field of force surrounding a magnet which was responsible for continuous action over distance on magnetic objects placed within it. Shortly after, Maxwell introduced his electromagnetic field equations which posited the existence of a field containing not matter but energy, followed by Einstein's General and Special Theories of Relativity, and the Einstein Gravitational Field Equations, which paved the way for wave-particle duality and Quantum Field Theory.

The general idea that the computational difficulties arising from considering the interaction of many different entities simultaneously could be alleviated by considering the entities as existing in and being acted on by a field spread to other disciplines that dealt with complex systems; Lewin (1939, 1947, 1951) in psychology, and, later, Bourdieu (1984, 1993) in sociology, developed explicit 'Field Theories', and in psychotherapy, Foulkes' introduced the 'cornerstone' of group analytic theory – his notion of the group matrix (Foulkes, 1983, 1984, 1990b; Foulkes and Anthony, 1957) – a *field theory* if ever there was one (see Tubert-Oklander, 2016).

Problems with the terminology

Geometrically the term *parallel* refers to two lines which, if extended to infinity, will never meet. Similarly, in cosmology, the notion of 'parallel universes' implies the existence of other universes which cannot interact with our own. This disconnection is certainly not what is meant when applying the term to the consultancy process.

Hopper (2007, p. 36), in a discussion of *group microcosms* as a kind of group transference, introduced the term 'equivalence', and importantly, remarked that these are *'not merely* (my italics) a matter of "parallel process"'. There are *causal connections* between the co-creation of microcosms and the experience of situations in the foundation matrix, 'based on . . . the inability to mourn authentically and completely' experiences associated with the profound anxieties of helplessness and powerlessness. The term 'equivalence' derives from a conjunction of 'equality' and 'valency'; that two (or more) entities share identical (or similar) structural properties, particularly in terms of their power relations. But the term does not sufficiently imply the causal connectedness between different orders of complexity that is needed.

'*Resonance*' (Foulkes and Anthony, 1957; Foulkes, 1990b), borrowed from acoustics, originally referred to the way in which sound waves from one source induce vibration in an object at its natural frequency. But acoustic resonance implies a transmission of energy from one entity to another. We are then pushed back into distinguishing one object as originator and another as recipient of a transmission, when what we need is a concept that better reflects the properties of a field.

If, as Dalal (1998) encourages, we take the group seriously, we need a term that better reflects the nature of groups as complex non-linear dynamical systems (comprising relational fields). A more useful and more accurate terminology describing the phenomena of 'parallel process' is, therefore, one derived from the study of complex non-linear dynamical systems – that of *fractal self-similarity* (Gleick, 1987; Stewart, 1989).

(Non-linear dynamical) systems theory

A system can be defined as: *a set of elements in mutual interaction*. The central tenets of systems theory (Bertalanffy, 1973) have been summarized (Commoner, 1971) as:

1   Everything is connected to everything else
2   Everything must go somewhere
3   Nature knows best
4   There is no such thing as a free lunch.[2]

To explore in greater depth how human organizations are constituted as dynamic systems it is necessary to consider the elements of the system (that is, human persons) and how their behavior is brought forth. Human persons are living organisms whose behavior is organized and coordinated by a 'nervous system'. About 3.5 billion years ago, single celled organisms (e.g. bacteria) evolved the capacity to move towards energy sources and away from harmful substances; random mutations increasing the efficiency of these capacities were preserved under the influence of natural selection. Bacteria sensed gradients in the concentration of nutrients or toxins in their environments through chemical receptors in their cell walls, triggering complex chemical reactions, eventually activating small whip-like appendages to move either towards or away from the stimulus.

> Thus, even in these most primitive organisms we find the three basic components for adaptive control of behavior, i.e., a sensorium, a motorium and in between information storage and processing
> (Roth and Dicke, 2013, p. 20)

The development of multicellular organization brought with it the problem of coordination of behavior: to behave in a coordinated way each cell needs to 'know' what the other cells are doing. Some way of communicating from one part of the organism to another is required. Natural selection favored the evolution of the nerve cell (neuron).

The essential feature of a neuron that specifies its function is its possession of a dynamically polarized membrane that allows the conduction of an impulse along its length.

Neurons connect to each other at 'synapses'; tiny gaps, into which are released 'neurotransmitters', which diffuse across the gap until they chance upon a suitable 'receptor', to which they 'bind', either triggering a further wave of depolarization in the downstream neuron (excitation), or alternatively, triggering *hyper*polarization, which inhibits an action potential (inhibition).

The binding of neurotransmitter to a receptor not only triggers or inhibits an action potential, but also triggers cascades of biochemical reactions within the cell, some of which reach the cell nucleus and, through epigenetic mechanisms, control the expression of genes that then produce more receptors, which become incorporated in the cell membrane. Thus, the amount of stimulation of receptors can under certain circumstances produce an *increase* in the density of receptors on the cell surface, increasing the probability of further triggering of an action potential.

Conversely, other biochemical cascades can stimulate the cell nucleus to express genes that produce enzymes that destroy receptors and hence decrease the density of those or other receptors.

Changes in the receptor density in the cell membrane alter the way that the neuron responds to future stimuli. Thus, activity at synapses not only determines whether or not an action potential is produced, but also determines changes in the neuron structure influencing subsequent behavior. This is the anatomical and physiological basis of *memory*, and a specific form of neuroplasticity. It is the central mechanism underlying the way that nervous systems become capable of *learning*. The probability of any specific *future behavior* is influenced by *past experience*.

About 500 million years ago, complex networks of neurons comprising 'nervous systems' emerged. Insects evolved brains capable of the sophisticated visual processing required for the control of rapid flight, and vertebrates began to develop a highly uniform brain structure, which continues as the basic brain 'plan' in all currently living vertebrates, including Homo Sapiens.

The human brain represents on average about 2% of body mass,[3] and is about 7–8 times larger than would be expected given human body size. It contains astonishing complexity, with about 10 billion neurons,[4] each with, on average, 1,000 connections to other neurons. Not for nothing has it been described as the most complex object for its size in the known universe.

Neural nets and cognition

Different arrangements of the excitatory and inhibitory receptors ascribe a 'weight' to the synapse; a value that corresponds to the readiness with which an action potential will fire in the downstream neuron.

The configuration of synaptic weights in the net determine which output neuron(s) will fire given any particular stimulus. Because of neuroplasticity, synaptic weights are altered by experience, and once the network has 'learned' to 'read' the input, each output neuron has become *coupled* to a particular 'input' state. The activity of the output layer comes to represent the state of the input layer and then can itself become an input layer for further processing.

If the output layer becomes recursively connected to itself, such that the output can be maintained in the absence of the original input, then an internal representation[5] of the original stimulus can be said to have formed.

By developing different arrangements of neural nets, a nervous system can develop the capacity to become coupled with its environment in specific ways which allow the nervous system to generate models of the environment, and to use these models in planning future activity in the absence of the original external situation. This has the following implications:

- Simple representations can be put together to form more complex ones
- Representations can be nested hierarchically
- Representations created through recursive networks can themselves become recursively elaborated, to form representations of representations
- Further recursive elaboration gives rise to the development of what Hofstadter (2008) has called 'strange loops' and the origin of self-awareness and consciousness.

The problem with classical cognitive science

Classical cognitive science was founded 'on the idea that mind is a digital computer and that thinking is computation' (Chemero, 2000, p. 1), and moreover, the 'mind' doing the computing resides within an individual brain.

This approach has come under scrutiny following growing dissatisfaction with the computational model of cognition, and with the idea that cognition is a property of *a central nervous system*, rather than something that takes place, not only within the organism *as a whole* (embodiment) but within the *coupled system of organism-environment* (radical embodiment or extended-phenomenological system (Silberstein and Chemero, 2012)).

From the perspective of computational cognitive science, bacteria can 'compute' the required direction of motion to enhance survival by comparing concentrations of particular molecules at one moment to those a moment later, inducing biochemical reactions which result in movement. However, from a different frame of reference, a bacterium does not actually 'compute' anything; what it does is become *coupled* with its environment so that *changes in the environment produce changes in the internal milieu of the organism* in reliable and predictable ways. Mechanisms that couple an organism with its environment in ways that enhance survival become conserved by natural selection.

This *coupling* is very significant, as it means that, although nervous systems are *thermodynamically* open, they are *dynamically* closed – what an observer might describe as input (receptor or sensory) or output (effector or motor) surfaces are *connected by the environment* (in which the observer stands), which effectively closes the system[6] (Maturana, 1978, p. 18). Thus any 'output' of the system will have some effect on the 'input' (however small) meaning that not only is input connected to output but output is connected to input, and the system becomes dynamically closed. 'Inside' and 'outside' the system 'exist only for the observer who beholds it, not for the system'.

Instead of seeing the individual organism as performing computations on representations of the environment 'in order to' determine an action, the radical embodied cognitive perspective considers how an organism becomes both phylogenetically and ontogenetically coupled to its environment through its structural relations, forming a single dynamical system. Such dynamical systems can have parameters both inside *and* outside the skin of an organism. As the organism becomes coupled to its environment, groups of variables that represent the state of the environment at any given time become part of the function specifying the state of the organism, and vice versa; they can be represented as a single system. See also 'autopoiesis' on pages 215–18.

Moreover, as Silberstein and Chemero (2012, p. 39) state:

> When the constituents of a system are highly coherent, integrated, and correlated such that their behavior is a non-linear function of one another, the system cannot be treated as a collection of uncoupled individual parts. Thus, if brain, body, and environment are non-linearly coupled, their activity cannot be ultimately explained by decomposing them into subsystems or into system and background. They are one extended system.

We now return to Foulkes' revolutionary idea, the group matrix: that the individual is 'a nodal point within a network of interactions'. This dictum is now supported by contemporary thinking in cognitive science: *'brain – body – world are dynamically coupled and thus mental states and cognitive functions might be viewed as extending spatiotemporally beyond the skin of the organism'* (Chemero and Silberstein, 2008, p. 1). Human agents as cognitive systems are *not* confined to existence within the human skull, but are *embodied* and *extended* (functionally coupled with their environment, which includes other human agents).

The behavior of dynamical systems

'Behavior' can be defined as *'change of state over time'*. When an observer tracks the behavior of a system over time, the observer is tracking the *trajectory* of the changes of state in the system.

As a dynamical system (in the physical world) evolves, it tends to settle into a regular pattern of behavior. The mathematical description of this pattern is known as the *attractor*[7] of the system – the behavioral trajectory of the system is metaphorically 'attracted' to it. In opposite ways, systems may have *'repellors'*.

As systems increase in complexity, so does the complexity of their attractors. Before the development of non-linear dynamical systems theory, it was difficult to understand how deterministic systems could behave in apparently random ways. In fact, these systems were *not* behaving in *random* ways, but were *unpredictable*; unpredictable because prediction is the activity of an observer, and any observer is limited in their capacity to calculate future trajectories with sufficient accuracy. Small errors in measurement lead to wide margins of error in prediction.

The attractors of complex non-linear systems were labeled *strange* attractors, a reflection of their strangeness or unpredictability. Properties of strange attractors include:

- The impossibility of predicting with certainty where on the attractor the state of the system will be at any specified time
- Two points that lie close to each other at any particular time may be arbitrarily far apart from each other at a subsequent time
- Trajectories never repeat exactly – they are non-periodic
- They demonstrate fractal self-similarity.

Psychoanalytical constructs, developed to explain patterns in behavior, such as the *Oedipus Complex* (Freud), *Unconscious Phantasy* (Klein), *Object Relations* (Winnicott etc.), *Internal Working Models* (Bowlby), or *RIGs* (Stern), can all be conceptualized as manifestations of *strange attractors*. These concepts refer to hypothetical structures that influence or determine behavior. A child who was sexually abused by her father is likely to develop an internal-working-model of 'abusive father'. The behavioral trajectories of neural networks that have developed in the context of such experience will carry an ontogenetically derived representation of an abusive-father that contributes to an attractor influencing responses to situations that are appraised as involving 'fathers' or 'father-like figures'. Such an attractor also has a phylogenetic component, reflecting the evolved behavior of dominant males in primate groups. Behavior in such situations is 'attracted' to certain patterns, deterministic but not fully predictable.

We know that it is impossible to predict *with certainty* how any of our clients (or indeed our friends or relatives) will behave in any given situation, although we can make quite reliable predictions, provided we acknowledge uncertainty. Further, how an individual behaves in relation to any other individual today might or might not be different to how they behave tomorrow. Patterns of behavior never repeat exactly, although they may be highly similar.

But what about fractal self-similarity?

The fractal properties of strange attractors

Mandelbrot (1977) introduced the term *fractal* as a contraction of the words *fractional dimension*, a mathematical concept involving sets of objects that exhibit repeating patterns at every scale ('self-similarity'), and whose dimensions are thus not integers.[8]

Fractal objects look roughly the same when viewed either close up or from far away. A common example is that of a coastline, which looks roughly similar when viewed from space, as it does when viewed from an airplane, from the top of a cliff, or from the beach (Mandelbrot, 1967).

An important aspect of this is that there is no idea that the structure of the system at one scale is determined by the structure at another scale; *the determinism is a property of the system as a whole.*

The behavioral trajectories of complex non-linear recursive systems have fractal properties which involve self-similarity; their structure will be similar when viewed at different scales or from different frames of reference. See also *Complexity theory and bounded instability* on page 69.

Human organizations as complex non-linear dynamical systems

As a consequence of developing coupled extended embodied neural networks, groups of persons acting within relational fields constitute complex recursive non-linear dynamical systems. Considered as such, their behavioral trajectories will demonstrate fractal properties, and particularly, fractal self-similarity; similarities of behavior at different scales of observation.

It is important to stress that self-similarity does not imply identity; the behavior at one scale is not identical to the behavior at another scale. It is *analogous* rather than *homologous*. But as the elements of a system become coupled and start to form more complex systems, the underlying attractors and repellors begin to influence the whole system, at all scales. So, the dynamics of the system at the scale of $depart\langle member\rangle ment$ show similarities with the dynamics of the system at the scale of $organ\langle depart\langle member\rangle ment\rangle isation$ and with the dynamics of the system at the scale of $consultant\langle organ\langle depart\langle member\rangle ment\rangle isation$ or even at the scale of $soc\langle consultant\langle organ\langle depart\langle member\rangle ment\rangle isation\rangle\rangle\rangle iety$ and so on. These dynamics are not running 'in parallel' but are properties of the system-as-a-whole, as a complex non-linear dynamical extended cognitive system.

Parallel process redefined

We can now redefine *parallel process* as the manifestation of fractal self-similarity within the complex non-linear dynamical systems (comprised of coupled extended embodied cognitive systems) that are human organizations.

Because human organizations are complex non-linear dynamical systems, the trajectories of their behavior may be considered, by definition, to be described by strange attractors. One of the properties of strange attractors is that of self-similarity at different scales; patterns of behavior at one scale of observation are similar (but not identical to) patterns of behavior at other scales. These similar patterns are *not* determined by behavior at any one scale of the system, but are a property of the system-as-a-whole.

Understanding 'parallel process' in this way helps us resolve the questions that result if we move from earlier concepts (such as projection and projective identification, transference and countertransference) to the logical consequences of Foulkes' insights: that *inner* and *outer*, *self* and *object*, *mind* and *body*, *individual* and *group* are abstractions, made by observers who themselves are part of the system they observe (see Dalal, 1998; Stacey, 2003). Self-similar patterns of behavior within complex organizations are not only commonplace, but are ubiquitous and inevitable.

Thus, the meaning of the events in the example above can now be reconceptualized. The similarities of pattern in the behavior described by the student in relation to her father, the teacher in relation to the Head of the organization, imagined in the mind of the Consultant, and press reports of the behavior of a powerful individual at the time, are all reflections of a feature of self-similarity in the strange attractor operating in the behavioral trajectory of the entire system. There are no mystical processes involved, neither is one scale of system responsible for another. It is no longer necessary to consider who is projecting what into whom and why; we can be content to reflect on the beautiful complexity of it all.

Notes

1 In Physics, a field is defined as a physical quantity that has a value for each point in space and time.
2 Strictly speaking, Commoner was referring to Ecology when he came up with this neat aphorism, but Ecology is nothing if it is not a Systems Theory and therefore I feel justified in using it here.
3 Brain size in vertebrates is principally determined by body size, although not proportionally; as body size increases, so does brain size but by a relatively smaller margin. Small mammals such as mice have brains that are about 10% of their body volume, whereas the brain of a blue whale, although comparatively enormous, represents only about 0.01% of its body volume. Primates, of all mammals have the highest ratio of brain size to body size (RBS).
4 To illustration the size of this number: 10 billion seconds is equivalent to approximately 317 years
5 From the perspective of computational cognitive science, the word 'representation' is used here in the Kantian sense of an internal state which 'stands in' for something in the 'outside world'.
6 It is not possible to construct a nervous system in which the output surfaces (as described by an observer) are not connected to the input surfaces by the medium in which such a system exists (and in which the observer also exists).
7 Attractors come in several types: they may be point attractors, such as those in a system which evolves into a resting state, such as a simple damped pendulum, or limit cycles, such as those in systems that reach a steady state of regularly repeating patterns, such as a pendulum in a clock which continues to swing for as long as energy is put into the system.
8 To understand this more easily, imagine measuring the length of a piece of string with a tape measure. To do so, one puts the tape against the string and reads the length off the marks on the measure. Any fold in the string must be matched by a fold in the tape measure. However, if the piece of string were fractal, one could never put the tape against the string completely because however much one folds the measure, more folding would be required because of the repeating patterns – the length would be infinite.

Section III

The wider organizational context

Section III consists of two passionate chapters on the place of group analysis in the wider world.

Dick Blackwell traces the global economic and societal context(s) within which organizations now function, highlighting the ubiquitous anxiety and reactive control which deaden so many workplaces in all sectors. Chapter seven is a plea to create work environments for creativity and job satisfaction, and an indispensable critique of the managerialism which stifle them.

Not all 'organizations' are formally constituted; organizations working for social change usually begin with the 'organizing' of activists. Christopher Scanlon develops his work on *disappointment* in a societal context, describing some 'organizings' which use group analytic principles in seeking to address global/local challenges. Chapter eight challenges us to 'get out more'.

Chapter 7

Stability or chaos, authoritarianism or dialogue

Towards a matrix of critical and creative thought at a time of uncertainty and threat

Dick Blackwell

Introduction

In times of anxiety and uncertainty a tension emerges between stability and chaos. A state of bounded instability can produce creativity. Much depends on the way that anxiety is managed. Group analysis suggests an approach for containing anxiety by facilitating communication and dialogue to overcome the regressive tendencies that lead to rigidity or chaos. This chapter is a development of two earlier papers. The first (1994), given at a conference on 'Thinking Under Fire', was entitled, *When everything needs to be thought about, more things become unthinkable'*. Based on my experiences, first as a staff member in a human rights organization working with victims of torture, and second consulting to a community mental health team struggling with constantly changing and increasingly unsympathetic organizational processes within the NHS, its title is perhaps even more apposite now than it was then.

The second paper, published in 1998, sought to develop Ralph Stacey's work on Complexity and Management (1996), particularly his idea of 'bounded instability' as a context for creativity. Since then the context of organizations has significantly changed. That applies not only to organizations in the UK, nor just in the Western world, but globally. So, it is worth beginning with a review of relevant global history.

In 1973, the coup d'état in Chile provided the opportunity to implement what had previously been regarded as an extreme and even unrealistic economic model: the neo-liberal model advanced first by Hayak and later by Milton Friedman at the economics department at the University of Chicago. The university's economists had already established a presence at the Catholic University of Santiago and within days of Pinochet's bloody coup Friedman flew down to Chile to help him re-organize the Chilean economy. There followed a decade of state terror across Latin America as all opposition to this model was eradicated so that when elections finally returned there was only an extremely limited opposition in most countries.

The model is now well known. It involves shrinking the 'state' and handing over its traditional functions to private enterprise. State budgets are drastically cut so that education, healthcare, roadbuilding, railways, all suffer except in so far as they can attract private investment whose primary goal is profit. Taxation is reduced to encourage 'enterprise', and this, it is argued, 'incentivizes' entrepreneurs to 'create wealth' which will then 'trickle down' to the rest of the population. The principal features and some of the contradictions of this model, including the increasingly globalized demonization of the poor are outlined elsewhere (Blackwell and Dizadji, 2014).

The model came to the UK courtesy of a highly orchestrated media campaign claiming an economic crisis in the late 1970s, which succeeded in bringing Margaret Thatcher to power. At the same time, Ronald Reagan became president of the US giving us twin versions of this neo-liberal model: 'Thatcherism' and 'Reaganomics'.

In the early 1980s the lending policies of the IMF and the World Bank imposed this model globally. The collapse of the Soviet bloc subsequently paved the way for its development in Eastern Europe in a new wave of economic colonization. The emergence of the so-called 'tiger economies' of South East Asia and the later development of China as a global economic power (implementing the neo-liberal model in what is still officially a communist state) has completed the global hegemony.

This hegemony has certain features. First, castrate trade unions so that there can be no serious opposition to managers running organizations solely in the interests of profit. In the UK a raft of anti-trade union legislation effectively curtailed what power the unions had prior to 1979, while in Colombia there was widespread assassination of trade unionists. Then an authoritarian style of management can not only be imposed but become unquestioningly accepted as 'normal'. Underlying and fueling the authoritarianism is a conscious and also unconscious level of sadism which finds its counterpart in the masochistic acceptance of a supposed necessity: 'We have to do this . . . We have no choice. ' It is an echo of Thatcher's statement for which she became known as Tina, (TINA – There Is No Alternative.)

The problem is, if there *is* no alternative, then there's no point trying to think about alternatives. Increasingly, there's no need to think at all. Just follow orders and pass them on, and unthinkingly follow policies and procedures. The echoes of fascism here should not be overlooked. One of Mrs Thatcher's first actions after coming to power, was to reject a delegation from the TUC, saying she had nothing to talk to the unions about. Thus, she established a principle of not talking to people representing alternative interests. This principle, in Northern Ireland, led to a further decade of violence, death, and political stalemate. The 9/11 attacks on the World Trade Centre and the subsequent 'war on terror' have served to advance a culture of authoritarianism, affirming the weakness or futility of dialogue and outlawing certain forms of thought.

There has also emerged a cult of the 'dynamic leader' who can guide the organization through uncertainty and change. This is a messianic rescue fantasy not so far removed from fascist ideology. This expectation/fantasy might be amusing were it not for its more serious consequences. One thinks inevitably of the Weimar Republic.

More recently it has been suggested that prior to the financial crisis of 2008, there were numerous executives in the sector who could see the contradictions developing but failed to point them out for fear of 'rocking the boat' and undermining the dynamic leader.

Binney, Wilke, and Williams (2009) have suggested that the kind of leadership needed is a more low-key approach that acknowledges the problems and seeks to draw on the expertise and experience of all staff to facilitate solutions.

Ballatt and Campling (2011) in their description of the current problems of the of the NHS have highlighted both vicious and benign cycles to be found within the formal and informal systems.

Simpson (2017b) describes a model of the collective containment and management of anxiety, along with a description of how that system was undermined and ultimately destroyed by an ideologically driven management system, rooted in the political economy of neo-liberal capitalism.

We see here the inherent violence of this model and its hegemony which persists in apparently 'civilized' systems managed by apparently 'civilized' people.

Complexity theory and bounded instability

Complexity theory presents hypotheses about the dynamics of networks of agents interacting with each other in a non-linear fashion. At low levels of information/energy flow, and/or sparse interconnections between agents, and/or little differentiation between agents, the system dynamic is that of stability – the network of interacting agents generates regular and therefore, predictable patterns of behaviors. When information/

energy flows are very high and/or agents are richly connected, and/or agents are extremely heterogeneous then the network produces completely random, patternless behaviors – chaos. However, at critical points, when information/energy flows are high but not too high, and/or agent connectedness is rich but not too rich, and/or agents are heterogeneous, but not too heterogeneous then the network system produces behaviors which are simultaneously stable and unstable. Such behaviors have recognizable patterns but over the long term the specific forms in the pattern are radically unpredictable. Such bounded instability is thus characterized by uncertainty.

It is only here, at the 'edge of chaos', in a state of 'bounded instability' that a non-linear network system is capable of endless variety. It is conjectured that living systems evolve to the 'edge of chaos' since it is only there that they are both fluid and stable enough to adapt creatively to changes in other living systems (Kauffman, 1995). It is further proposed that human systems are also non-linear networks of interactions and that these dynamics apply to them too. Human systems then will be creative when they operate towards the 'edge of chaos' in bounded instability.

I doubt that human organizations necessarily evolve towards the edge of chaos. Experience and observation suggest that many evolve towards stability, particularly under authoritarian leadership. Often the flow of energy, information and the richness of connectedness are actively restricted in order to retain such stability.

Complexity theory also introduces the idea of the 'shadow system'. This is the informal network of relationships and communication between members of a system, among themselves and with others outside. This network exists separately from the formal system and is not normally acknowledged. It has similarities with what Goffman has called the 'underlife' of an institution. 'Surfacing' the shadow system, that is, bringing it into play within the formal system, is a key to producing creative solutions to systemic problems.

Anxiety, thinking, and imagination

The psychoanalyst Wilfred Bion's (1962) theory of thinking was based on the mother's capacity to contain the overwhelming feelings of the infant as they are projected into her.

While the mother is present the infant can feel merged with her. But the mother's absence engenders frustration and fear in the infant leading to rage, panic, and persecutory anxiety. If the mother provides sufficient containment by not being absent for too long and by being able to take in and process the infant's feelings, then the infant will be able to 'think' about 'her', the object (the mother/breast) which is absent. When the object is present the infant need not think about it. When it is absent it can only exist for the infant as a thought.

Sartre (1991) notes that while 'what is' can be encountered and directly perceived, what is not can only be imagined. Thus, the absence of the breast or the mother becomes the basis of imagination and thought. The existence or representation of the mother as a thought is the product not the cause of the infant's thinking.

Crucial to the possibility of thinking is the need for the powerful feelings of the infant to be contained through its relationship with its mother. Otherwise the infant becomes overwhelmed by its feelings and is unable to think.

When, in an organization, anxiety is high, there is a tendency to seek psychological refuge to provide a sense of security. Marina Mojovic, following John Steiner's concept of the individual's 'psychic retreat' has suggested the 'psycho-social retreat' as a collective refuge. The retreat here is into the infantile state of merging with the mother as a single psychic entity. The organization symbolically becomes the mother's body.

Hopper (1997, 2012a) proposes a fourth basic assumption, incohesion: aggregation/massification. Massification involves a merging into a single mass where differentiation of individual experiences and viewpoints become submerged and disagreement becomes impossible. Aggregation is the opposite pole where the individuals withdraw from the group going their own separate ways. Incohesion is a non-dialectical oscillation between the two positions.

In times of uncertainty levels of anxiety tend to rise. States of bounded instability close to chaos and can only produce creativity if the level of anxiety is contained. If not managed it will escalate to a point where thought becomes increasingly difficult, if not impossible, and the system either tips over into chaos or rigidifies into authoritarianism.

Authoritarianism is necessary to police a collective state that is fragile and readily threatened, particularly by creative, independent, and critical thought. Regimes develop in which managers appear to be tough and resilient yet are extremely sensitive to criticism. Policies and approaches are developed in which criticism of any aspect of the organization, or any member's performance become officially prohibited.

Then the formal organization exhibits massification while the shadow system falls into aggregation, which substantially diminishes its potential as a source of creativity, since the dialogue which can generate creativity can only happen if individuals engage with each other rather than withdrawing into isolation. Furthermore, the time available for shadow system activity – informal conversation, socializing, and play – becomes more and more restricted for increasingly overworked and closely policed staff. And the massified formal system becomes largely impenetrable with regards to any new ideas from the shadow system.

Thinking, language, and imagination

For the French psychoanalyst Lacan, the 'word', language, is essential for thought (Lacan, 1966). The infant merges with the mother, becoming aware of its separateness only through recognition of a third person to whom it and the mother are related/connected. This is the symbolic father, not the actual father but the 'other' who is recognized to exist in the infant's and the mother's life. It is this recognition and location of the other, the father, that requires language. It is the intrusion of thought into the thoughtless state of being merged with the mother. The 'name of the father' demands the thought of mother as a separate being.

Thus, language becomes synonymous with the father's existence and the emergence of the infant's own separate identity. It is also the means of naming the absent, the imaginary.

Researchers in human and animal communication, Gregory Bateson and Jay Haley, in 'A Theory of Play and Fantasy' (1954), study the 'play' of baboons. 'Play', they argue, is the simulation of some other activity (fight) which it precisely resembles. How, they ask, do the baboons signal to each other that these actions, which would normally denote an attack, do not in this case denote what they would normally denote? This capacity to communicate about communicative behaviors (meta communication) is the birth of language. Thus language, play, and imagination are intimately connected.

Group analysis introduces the concept of 'matrix' (Foulkes, 1964, 1975). The matrix is a system or network of communication in which a language of communication, both verbal and non-verbal, develops between its members. Non-verbally there are numerous exchanges of looks, smiles, frowns, posture changes, voice tone and volume, speech rhythm, sequence of interaction, and so on. Intertwined with and overlaid on this is the verbal language seeking to articulate the thoughts, feelings and themes generated, and to meta-communicate about this network of communication.

Group analysts now speak of three matrices (Bhurruth, 2008), though here I am principally concerned with two: the foundation matrix is the network of communication shared by all members of a group prior to its formation. The dynamic matrix is the communication system developed within a specific group through the communication between the members. The foundation matrix gives them a common language through which to communicate. The dynamic matrix is the evolving product of that communication. It is within this dynamic matrix that thought, imagination, play, and creativity become possible, and within which the foundation matrix may itself be recognized, analyzed, and critiqued.

Managerial and organizational defenses

Philip Boxer (1996) has argued that a common response of professionals to anxiety and uncertainty is to engage vigorously and often inflexibly in those activities that characterize their profession. So, when flexibility and creativity are most needed, they affirm their professional identity by enacting professional activities regardless of their suitability to the actual situation. Such activity confirms personal identity through merging with others in the maternal entity 'the profession'.

In the psychotherapy world, national regulatory bodies, initially set up to standardize basic principles of ethics, have rapidly moved on to standardizing, not only psychotherapy training, but psychotherapy practice, too. Thus, whenever faced with uncertainty, psychotherapists are now able to seek security by acts of conformity that define them as psychotherapists. Individual intuition and critical thought, once the sine qua non of analytic psychotherapy, become deviant if not subversive.

Much contemporary managerial language developed over the last two decades indicates this sort of merging. The terminology of 'excellence', 'quality', 'audit', 'performance', 'evaluation', 'targets', 'competency', 'good practice', 'best practice', 'monitoring', 'lead bodies', 'evidence based', and so on, all has a sort of edge to it; an echo of potency, power, control, assertiveness, and indeed, mastery through conformity.

Yet serious questioning of these terms suggests that they serve mainly to obfuscate rather than illuminate. Behind the facade lies uncertainty and vulnerability which cannot be acknowledged. Thus, we have a 'management-speak' that is not a language in the sense that it facilitates thought, but is instead an Orwellian NewSpeak. We move increasingly towards a style of management in which real anxiety, uncertainty, and other human emotions and frailties (anger, frustration, vulnerability, and sexuality to name a few) have to be denied in favor of assertive posturing. Managers can increasingly speak the language of management without being able to manage.

In organizations where resources are insufficient to meet the demands (the UK National Health Service for example) and the 'job' is essentially impossible, there has emerged a notable woolliness making it difficult if not impossible to identify what is really happening or what is being attempted, and what the boundaries and limits actually are. Awesome collections of policies and procedures create the appearance of order and control but obfuscate a state of chaos that cannot be named or thought about. We might characterize this state as bound, as in constipated, or bondaged, rather than boundaried or bounded instability.

We also see those members of an organization with certain management roles become grouped together under the title of 'management'. This impersonal term, often used by both the members of 'management' and those managed by 'it', becomes a convenient screen for all sorts of projections and avoidance of individual responsibility. It is another version of the 'fudge'.

Additionally, there has developed what I have called the organizational buffer. This is the level in the organizational hierarchy where the nature of the work and its most problematic and painful aspects gets fudged if not denied, to be replaced by a more sanitized version which is passed up the line to the top where strategies and policies are formulated. Thus, in a charity dealing with the homeless, the senior management and trustees can discuss the provision of accommodation with its rules and regulations, along with educational programs to help the homeless to learn how to manage a household budget, while the reality of work at the 'coal face' involves drugs and knives and guns coming off the street.

Along with this is a repertoire of what I call, 'appearances and masquerades'. The latter involves performances that give the appearance of addressing problems without really engaging with the problem at all. The repetitions affirm a conformity in thought and action providing a collective defense against anxiety and critical thought.

In all these scenarios the defensive merging is maintained at the expense of thought. Critical thought would symbolize the introduction of the 'father' and the end of the merger. Real thought involves differentiation, difference, disagreement, and dialectic. It requires that anxieties be named and discussed and that various alternative courses of action be considered. It makes it no longer acceptable to engage in unthinking action, or the unthinking use of language merely to signify membership of a club.

Containment, the matrix, and the shadow system

The alternative to this merging identification is containment and management of the anxiety. This means the anxiety has to be experienced and recognized, named and discussed rather than repressed or projected.

Twenty-five years ago, I saw it as the task of senior management to 'contain' the anxiety of the staff and to provide 'good enough mothering'. However, I now believe this to be an error inviting senior managers to infantilize their staff, making them dependent on a symbolic parent figure. This was perhaps, my own version of the messianic leader.

The alternative is that the group provides the containment. That is to say, it is the pattern of relationships and communication between the members of the organization – its matrix – that is the container, as at the start of the vignette on pages 242–43. The task then is to facilitate the evolution of that containing matrix – a system or network of reflective and reflexive communication through which changing circumstances and the anxieties they provoke can be recognized and discussed; thus, creative solutions can emerge. The shadow system is then understood as part of the matrix to be surfaced and engaged within the formal system. In the vignette, the containing matrix develops but ultimately fails, in large part because of the unaddressed and uncontained anxieties of the organization's board.

Crucial for creative thought, and usually found more readily in the shadow system than the formal system, is a capacity for play and humor, along with an awareness of sexuality, aggression, and destructiveness, and the part they all play in creativity; plus a recognition of how anxieties and defenses inhibit thought.

Group analysis is the analysis of the group, by the group, including the conductor. This is an essentially democratic process, necessarily in conflict with authoritarian and hierarchical models of communication. Group-analytic dialogue is particularly concerned to develop the reflexive dimension of the matrix – to recognize and bring to the surface the unspoken, the non-verbal, the invisible and the unconscious dimensions of communication including all levels of the organization. Creative thought may readily be experienced as subversive: different points of view, disagreement, argument, and challenges to established modes of thought and received wisdom must flourish. Creative shadow systems can only develop where staff engage with each other outside the formal system without too much fear for the consequences.

Chapter 8

'Practising disappointment'

From reflection to action in organizations and communities

Christopher Scanlon

Introduction

> 'Never doubt that a small group of thoughtful citizens can change the world. Indeed, it is the only thing that ever has'
> Margaret Mead, Anthropologist and Scholar, 1901–1978.[1]

To struggle with *disappointment* in our interpersonal, organizational and social settings is an inherent part of being human. It is an aspect of what Foulkes (1975) described as being permeated to the core by social processes: a narcissistic injury arising from the inevitability of our and others' death, and the necessary *compromise* that is demanded from being alive. Disappointment is also about needing to, and failing to, recognize our frailty and vulnerability in social matrices within which disappointment, like all other social and material resources, is not equally distributed (Craib, 1994; Butler, 2004; Honneth, 1995; Benjamin, 2018). Gilligan (1996) suggests, in the vernacular, that to be 'dissed' (e.g. disrespected, disappointed, disillusioned, and so forth) is to be humiliated, and that this shaming is at the core of much of the traumatizing interpersonal and structural violence that blights modern society. Indeed, accumulated empirical evidence demonstrates that the *differential* extent of these shameful disappointments; the difference between those who are extremely *disappointed* and those others who are extremely *disappointing* which gives rise to the widespread ill-health and social insecurity of our fundamentally unequal modern world (Dorling, 2010; Wilkinson and Pickett, 2009,

2017; Cooper and Whyte, 2017). In this sense to take *disappointment* seriously is to understand it as a profoundly unsettling experience that permeates to the core of all of our family, friendship, neighborhood, and community matrices, disturbing both our relatedness and relationships, and so shaping all our (failing?) efforts 'to love and to work'.

Elsewhere I have discussed the mechanisms through which Reflective Practice Team Development (RPTD) might be deployed inside social public organizations and workplaces (Scanlon, 2012, 2017). Here I explore how disappointment, as a synonym for 'psychosocial trauma' can rather be addressed in less formal organizing within neighborhoods and communities. My challenge is to ask how we might we extend our group-analytic attitude to become more politically, socially, and civically engaged, making psychosocial links between the inner reality of 'the organization-in-the-mind', and the outer organization-of-the-social (Armstrong, 2005; Gould, Lucey and Stapley, 2011; Kraemer and Roberts, 1996). In other words, I would like to begin with a challenge and suggest that we psycho-socially informed analysts, researchers, and consultants might want to consider how to 'get out more'.

Practising disappointment: practising equality?

In earlier work John Adlam and I made use of the life and times of the ancient itinerant Cynic philosopher Diogenes of Sinope, who lived in a barrel in the Agora in ancient Greece, from where he made trenchant commentary about the inequality and unfairness he perceived in the world surrounding him. We suggested that his life stood as a metaphor for the psychosocial challenges facing both the dis-enfranchised and those seeking to engage them (Adlam and Scanlon, 2005, 2011; Scanlon and Adlam, 2008, 2011a and b, 2018). We re-tell the story about how on one occasion Diogenes was seen begging from a statue of a goddess in the Agora and when asked what he was doing replied that he was 'practising disappointment' – perhaps a useful skill for us all to acquire and cultivate.

In discussing *disappointment* from a group-analytic point of view Craib (1994) suggests that disappointment, as an inherent aspect of our social condition, demands that we be in a complex and ambivalent relationship with something *that doesn't happen*. He suggests that the more we deny the extent of our individual and collective disappointment, the more we break the links and connections between people, and within ourselves. These sentiments chime well with Bion's (1967a and c) discussion of importance of the linking-up up of concepts in order to be able to think and act. In these ways disappointment can be understood as a reciprocal interplay between intense longing, and profound unrequited sadness:

a push-me-pull-you bipolar encounter with regressive-and-progressive forces that demand a relinquishing of something in order to make a space and a place for something else – in the mind and in the social world.

Whyte (2015), a poet and social commentator, however, suggested that disappointment might also be thought of as a *'hidden, underground, engine'* and a potential source of trust and generosity to provide an opportunity for transformation. He describes the experience of disappointment as a 'merciful heartbreak' which we might compare with Shakespeare's thoughts on *mercy* proclaimed by Portia:

> The quality of mercy is not strained.
> It droppeth as the gentle rain from heaven
> Upon the place beneath. It is twice blest:
> It blesseth him that gives and him that takes
> > William Shakespeare, *The Merchant of Venice*; Act IV, Scene 1.

I find the idea of 'twice blest' mercy helpful in imagining *disappointment* as also 'twice blest'; it too affects those who are disappointed and those who disappoint. Honig's (1996) more philosophical perspective argues that much 'social work', often associated with 'mercy', takes place in *dilemmatic spaces*, which she describes as opening up when conversations about things that do not fit together *must* take place, and when actions are demanded that will inevitably *disappoint* someone. In the reciprocal impossibility of *dilemmatic space, therefore,* there are always those who are *disappointed* and those who are *disappointing*. Lawrence (2000) in contrasting the *politics of revelation*, with the *politics of salvation* suggested that the real dilemma at the heart of these necessary conversations is how to engage with them in such a way as to allow *disappointment* to be revealed and talked about, without expecting that something or somebody can be saved from the *heartbreak*.

Freud (1937) suggested that psychoanalysis, along with education and governance were three impossible professions (although if he had known more about 'social work' he might have added a fourth); yet even as this recognition dawns we find ourselves further confounded, because we must then face the more complex double-edged, inside-out/and outside-in, psychosocial reality that, more often than not, we are both disappointed **and** disappointing. We are disappointed in ourselves because we are so disappointing and we are disappointed in others because we feel so disappointed. The 'twice blest' nature of disappointment then also could be understood as an aspect of double-suffering (Frost and Hoggett, 2008), *ressentiment* (Hoggett, 2009; Hoggett, Wilkinson and Beedell, 2013), or the *reflexive violence* (Scanlon and Adlam, 2013) that arises when *insult is added to injury* (Adlam and Scanlon, 2018) in ways which eat away at our body and soul, and interfere with our capacity to engage with, much less love, our neighbors (cf. Žižek, 2001, 2008).

In these muddling inside out/outside in/ s(S)tates mixed-feelings run high, but are difficult to *articulate*, links are not made, needful compromises are not made, and the open public sharing of failure and disappointment is problematic. The desire and longing, and the grief and mourning, that is at the heart of our ordinary human vulnerability is denied or disavowed, and anger and resentment prevail in ways that are not only distressing for individuals but are also corrosive of the structures and the cultures of the very social institutions that we depend upon for our sense of social security (Butler, 2004; Hoggett, 2009; Hopper, 2003, 2012; Volkan, 2004). To paraphrase (Roberts, 1994a) this deep sense of disappointment brings with it the existential realization that there is nowhere to run and nowhere to hide from the *self-and-other disappointed/disappointing impossible task.*

On Agora-phobia: a realistic fear of the marketplace

Zeldin (1998) charted the changing nature of *conversation* from the Agora and the Forum of ancient times through to the *Salons* and *Cafés Scientifiques* of French High Society, and on to 'public conversations' that gave rise to peoples' revolutions, workers' rights, women's suffrage, civil rights, and universal [sic] human rights. He maps the changing nature of the conversation and argues that the right type of conversation in the right place at the right time has the power not only to change minds, but also to transform the social world. For Benjamin (2018) the aim of creating places in which these conversations can happen requires what she describes as a *moral third space* in which members as citizens can listen to each other's stories, see ourselves reflected in others' pain and so, in coming to recognize our own frail and interdependent vulnerability, to bear witness to others' traumas and disappointments: literally and metaphorically, to *re-member* [sic] ourselves and each other.

Discussing 'disappointment' from an organizational and management learning perspective Clancy, Vince and Gabriel (2012) similarly discuss how organizations frequently become arenas of disappointment where emotions, such as shame, guilt, and anxiety prevail, and a sense of failure is followed by defensive blame and recrimination. They argue that a judicious appreciation of the affective and dynamic implications of disappointment and failure can offer a way of moving beyond these dynamics, turning it into the basis for social and organizational learning.[2] Likewise, arguing from a *Complexity Theory* perspective, other group and organizational theorists (Mowles, 2015, 2017; Stacey, Giffin and Shaw, 2002, 2003) argue that creating optimal conditions for *conversation* is *necessary and sufficient* to enable change for the better in all organizational and social situations – 'one conversation at a time' (see also Rance in chapter five of this volume).

Whilst in agreement about the potentially transformative power of conversations, Arendt (1958) and Sennett (1974), nonetheless describe the ways in which the modern Western world has *spectacularly* failed to maintain effective participation in democratic processes and how our social, communal, and civic lives have become impoverished. Bauman (2000, 2002), in defining *liquid modernity*, described by how the conceptual 'Agora' and other modern public spaces have been emptied out, such that the philosopher, the poet, the seer, along with *the interested citizen* have all retreated to 'private places', leaving the 'marketplace' in the hands of powerful neo-liberal, highly monetized private/public institutions who deploy secretive agencies to promote 'fake news' in order to propagandize and manipulate the public. Social discourse about inequality, vulnerability, and lack have diminished, and the currency of social exchange is increasingly dominated by preoccupations about the rights of the 'deserving' and the 'hard-working', who are set against those who are represented as undeserving, feckless, lazy, or otherwise *worth-less* (Scanlon and Adlam, 2010; Scanlon, 2015).

In the context of this institutionalized dysfunction, subgroups have become places of refuge and psychosocial retreat from the normative hateful experiences social-exclusivity (Mojović, 2011, 2016, 2017; Scanlon and Adlam, 2008, 2011b, 2013). Young people who feel that they have no stake in the social world express their homicidal rage towards each other in criminally organized gang and ethnic violence, others become *radicalized* and turn their homicidal and suicidal rage against the unresponsive establishment through hateful terror-filled acts of violence. The failure to provide spaces and places for more engaged reflective conversations in the current socio-political climate becomes a double disappointment, so that rather than 'coexist in difference' (Arendt, 1958) we are sleep-walking into a post-truth, disinterested-future in which the relentless advance of 'market forces' privatizes profits and puts loss and failure into the public arena through blaming the victim. To be *agora-phobic* in this modern liquidity is less an indicator of neurotic anxiety than a sign of a realistic fear of the marketplace (Adlam and Scanlon, 2013).

One example of this anti-democratic tendency in the clinical domain, is the thoughtless destruction of the residential *Democratic Therapeutic Communities* movement in the UK. These places provided innovative, safe, and containing spaces for traumatized people to live and learn together to discuss their experience in the private/public world of the community setting (Rapoport, 1960; Jones, 1968; Whiteley, 1986; Norton, 1992a and b). See further pages 153 and 161. But they were closed down as 'no longer fit for purpose' and/or 'too expensive'.

'Repopulating the agora': dialogue in our neighborhoods, communities, and workplaces

On the world stage in recent times we have also seen the potential of 'reflective conversations' to bring peace to conflict zones. Restorative Justice methodologies (Zehr, 1990; Hoggett, 2009; Erlich, Erlich-Ginor and Beland, 2013; Ofer, 2017; and other contributions from Group Analytic colleagues e.g. *International Dialogue Initiative[3] and the Oxford Research Group[4]*) have enabled reflective conversations that *evidentially* allow different *parties* to share their profound sense of disappointment through truth telling, reconciliation, understanding, and perhaps even forgiveness. This type of organized *reflective-practice*, has brought peace, or at least a cessation of violence and exploitation, in South Africa and Northern Ireland, and has allowed the truth to be told about historical institutional abuse in Ireland (and elsewhere). If these more active types of conversations, drawing upon key group-analytic concepts of exchange, negotiation, arbitration, and compromise, can also be brought to bear within organizations, they may go far to address the profound splitting and fragmentation that characterize the challenges of *working with difficult people in difficult places* (Scanlon, 2012, 2017; Adlam, Lee and Kluttig, 2018; Simpson, 2010, 2016).

In their experiential working conferences exploring German-Jewish group-relations in post-holocaust context, Erlich, Erlich-Ginor and Beland (2013) suggests a metaphorical, development *'from blood, through tears, to words'*. Similarly, De Maré, Piper and Thompson (1991) in their groundbreaking book propose a movement 'from hate, through dialogue to culture' in which they make use of the concept of *Koinonia*, (κοινωνία), from the Greek, meaning something like, the gift of active participation in the community. Lawrence (1998) suggested that one way of allowing something to emerge, or be *revealed*, in *the Matrix* is through 'Social Dreaming' a methodology which is now widely deployed in the field. The social and organizational impact of a shared dream was perhaps never more clearly illustrated at a social level than by Dr King Jr's who dreamed a social dream *'that my four little children will one day live in a nation where they will not be judged by the color of their skin but by the content of their character'* – a dream which sadly is not (yet) realized – perhaps because we have been unable get beyond the *blood* or the *hatred*.

A number of practitioners have taken up the challenge of how we might re-populate the agora to enable people better to take up their membership of neighborhoods and communities through the notion of the 'Reflective Citizen' (Mojović, 2011, 2016, 2017; Gould, Lucey and Stapley, 2011). Dubouloy suggests that to be a reflective citizen requires individuals, families, and neighborhoods, as sub-systems, of wider communities, to ask the questions that will allow them to find their place and to take up their membership of that place, whilst allowing and enabling others to do the same (Dubouloy, 2011, p. 134). However, Krantz (2011, p. 96) suggests that whilst it is necessary to be *reflective*, it is not in itself *sufficient* to bring about change and so proposed a further movement from reflective citizen to 'deliberative citizen' within which we must first think-and-feel, after which we must find our voice(s) and then act accordingly. To offer an integrative statement of this development, paraphrasing De Maré, Piper and Thompson (1991), Lawrence (1998, 2000) and Erlich, Erlich-Ginor and Beland (2013), I propose a movement from *'hate-and-blood, through tears to words-and-dialogue, and by way of shared social-dreams to building a culture of collaboration-in-action'*.

To this end I have recently been 'getting out more' and have taken up ongoing staff roles in two inter-related collaborative projects which I would like to present as illustrations: the first is the Reflective Citizens (RC) project led by Dr Marina Mojović, a Serbian Psychiatrist and Group Analyst. This multi-site project aims to re-build traumatized communities in the post-war Balkans countries (particularly Serbia, Bosnia and Herzegovina, Slovenia, and the contested province/country of Kosovo), (Mojović, 2011, 2016, 2017), using a methodology integrating Group-Relations, Group Analysis, Social Dreaming and Therapeutic Community. The second project, founded and led by Mónica Valarde Lazarte is the *Asociación Civil Esperanza de la Amazonía* (Hope of the Amazon)[5] which aims to address issues of marginalization and social inclusion in former (and current) conflict zones in Peruvian Amazonian regions, using similar methods to develop deliberative citizenship and leadership.[6]

Conclusion

What these projects have in common is a democratizing aim to work with and to train networks of local people, using these complementary psychosocial approaches to explore the historical and contemporary disappointments of communities torn asunder by past and present conquest, occupation and/or colonization; painful inter-generational differences are played out between the un-mourned disappointment of the previous generation(s) and the disappointed hopes of the young(er) generation(s). I hope to return to these projects in future writing to show the ways in which they serve as exemplars for how to work together within social-networks of 'interested citizens' drawing upon and applying reflective-and-deliberative-practice-in-action in our neighborhoods and communities, as well as in our social institutions and places of work. All these have similar trans-generational ambitions, to find better ways to love our neighbors and live together so as to leave *the place in a better s(S)tate than we found it*. I hope that these reflections may make some contribution to these conversations.

Notes

1 Used with permission of the Institute of Intercultural studies www.inter culturalstudies.org/

2 One example, of this type of intervention at a socio-political level perhaps is in Finland, where there is an annual *National Day of Failure* which promotes a collective pause-for-thought and a coming face-to-face with these darkly permeating inner and outer failures and disappointments.

3 www.internationaldialogueinitiative.com

4 www.oxfordresearchgroup.org.uk

5 www.hopeoftheamazon.org/

6 Inherent in the *Hope of Amazon project* there is, of course, a central concern about the ways in which we *thoughtlessly* pollute, contaminate, and poison the land, rivers, forests, and jungles upon which we all depend. Clearly, this subject is beyond the scope of this chapter, however, I would not want to pass by without commending those who work tirelessly to promote reflective conversations and deliberative action that enable us 'to think globally and act locally' about this potentially cataclysmic shared problem (e.g. Weintrobe, 2012).

Section IV

Leadership, authority, and power

Leadership can *only* arise in a group. Leadership is most usefully under-stood as a *function* of the group, rather than a characteristic located in one person: a leader is someone whom the group is willing to trust with leadership; effective leaders share their real perceptions, seek help, and enable others in their groups to 'take a lead' when needed. In section IV, three leaders describe how group analytic thinking helped them manage in highly pressurized situations, and a fourth comments.

In chapter nine, Clare Gerada gives a moving account of being a lead-ing doctor who became nationally prominent for her courageous oppo-sition to the Lansley NHS changes, which passed into law in 2012. She describes the leader's internal process and the sense she made of it through experiences in group analytic groups. Clare, always a leader who acts on her convictions, has now incorporated groups into caring for mentally ill doctors.

For 18 years Raman Kapur has led a residential and support ser-vice for mainly psychotic people in Northern Ireland, a context where madness is intensified by 'the Troubles'. In chapter 10 he takes us through an incident highlighting how psychoanalytic and group ana-lytic thinking contain him, describing his use of intense experiences of projective identification as a daily tool in understanding and fulfilling his role as CEO, holding and containing the inevitable mess in this important, difficult work.

In chapter 11, Morris Nitsun comments on Raman's chapter, linking it with his own experience leading NHS mental health services. He raises an important topic: the appropriate style of group leadership, on a spectrum from active/authoritative to understated/enabling – a debate he has done much to stimulate.

Farideh Dizadji focuses on the leader's role in containing chaos to create a situation for creative therapeutic work in chapter 12. She draws on her experience as clinical director at Kids Company's main

Centre and at two other community agencies. In services where members bring chaos, holding boundaries is a creative and flexible process (Thornton and Corbett, 2014) simultaneously allowing members to flex those boundaries, which is crucial in their development of increased agency and control.

Chapter 9

Using groups in leadership

Bringing practice into theory

Clare Gerada

Introduction

In April 2012, the National Health Service (NHS) suffered a near-fatal blow. After a two-year gestation, the Health and Social Care Act (HSCA) finally passed into English law. This deeply unpopular piece of legislation – branded 'Lansley's Monster' by the British Medical Journal (BMJ), named after the Secretary of State for Health – wrought changes on the health and social care system so large that the then Chief Executive of the NHS said it could be seen from outer space.

As the head of my professional body, the Royal College of General Practitioners (RCGP), from 2010 to 2013, I argued against these 'reforms' as an unnecessary and wasteful distraction for the NHS. I was the first leader of an established medical body to say so, despite the mountains of supporting evidence. During my chairmanship I encountered denial, dissociation, and fragmentation amongst organizations drawn from medical and other professional groups, think-tanks, trade unions, and Parliamentarians. As part of my post, I became a member of dozens of different work groups of varying sizes, configurations, and make-up. These groups both sustained and wounded me, almost in equal measure.

To understand the destructive forces I was experiencing I worked with a clinical psychologist, who introduced me to the ideas behind group analysis, encouraging me to train with the Institute of Group Analysis (IGA). I began this training as the Bill made its final passage through the House of Lords. On the training, I became a member of different groups and in them, I was able to see parallels with the experiences of my working life. I began to make sense of what was going on below the surface. I learnt about my strengths, but more importantly my weaknesses as a leader. I also learnt about fear and how it stops good people doing good things and about the power of groups and how only by forming/joining them can one be sustained as a leader through difficult times.

In the beginning

In 2009, David Cameron, then leader of the British Conservative Party in opposition, gave a speech to the Royal College of Nursing. He promised 'no more pointless top down reorganization of the NHS'. The American health policy leader Don Berwick (2010) commented 'In good faith and with sound logic, the leaders of the NHS and government have sorted and resorted local, regional, and national structures into a continual parade of new aggregates and agencies. Each change made sense, but the parade doesn't.' Mr. Cameron seemed to understand that the cycle had to stop. In May 2010 however, he became Prime Minister and formed a coalition government, which six weeks later published the blueprint for the largest re-organization in the history of the NHS. In order to justify the proposed changes, the Government had to attack and undermine the NHS, its achievements, and by implication the 1.2 million people who worked in it. I became Chair elect of the RCGP in April 2010, taking over the reins of leadership in November 2010.

My groups

I want to look at three of the groups in which I have belonged and explore how these impacted me as a leader.

The first group to which I belonged was the NHS, in which I have worked for more than 40 years. The NHS is the largest single employer in the UK and the third largest in the world. British people hold the NHS in higher esteem that the Queen (Mori, 2012). Established in the dying embers of the Second World War, it has been described by the conservative politician Nigel Lawson as a national religion, and forms part of the collective unconscious of over 60 million people. Progressively funded through national taxation, the NHS transcends racial, ethnic, gender, party-political, and socio-economic boundaries. The letters N.H.S were beamed out to 2 billion people during the opening ceremony of the 2012 Olympics.

The NHS has been described as one of the most outstanding human endeavors of modern time and as the embodiment of kinship and one of our last expressions of community togetherness, of being part of a group (Ballatt and Campling, 2011). This 'chosen glory' of the British is shared via experiences built up over generations (Volkan, 2009).

Given its size, the NHS functions not as a single group but as a web of interdependent systems connected by a meta-matrix of connections formed through historical and cultural links – groups within groups. Constant reorganizations, which successive governments have engaged in, fracture relationships and the fragile ecosystem which keeps very large systems functioning. They are corrosive, creating institutional trauma, each attempt to fashion a new order creating a new state of disorder. Morris Nitsun describes the all-too-familiar pattern over decades of restructuring and its effect of reducing institutional and individual resilience (2015, p. 39). Constant change also reduces the authority and power of doctors, perhaps explaining why so many feel unable to speak out.

My second group is the Royal College of General Practitioners (RCGP), the largest of the medical Royal Colleges, with a membership of over 50,000 doctors. On 15 November 2010, I become its head, only the second women in its history to hold this position. My council, a group of 60 or so general practitioners supported me, challenged me, and were loyal and loving. Jean Claude Rouchy talks of 'belonging-groups' and the fundamental human need to be part of a group (1995). Due to the long and grueling training, medicine is the group of belonging for many doctors, encapsulating a sense of self (Gerada, 2016). Whilst my primary group of belonging is my family, the intensity of the work and contact with the College groups made them my secondary group of belonging, an attachment which became crucial for my mental health.

On the surface, my decision to stand as head of my profession was a natural progression from holding most of the senior officer posts. On reflection, it became apparent that the reasons went deeper. The desire to redress my sense of not belonging, of being a perpetual outsider, was part of my personal matrix. My default is to be 'the stranger', both 'near and far at the same time', outwardly a member of the group but remaining distant from it (Simmel, 1950, pp. 1–3). In my training group, this was easily demonstrated by me moving my chair back to break the circle, so remaining in and out at the same time. These experiences were built from my own past. My father was a single-handed general practitioner. He arrived in Britain in the 1960s, accompanied by my mother and four (soon five) young children, looking for work. As a fluent Italian speaker, he eventually got a job caring for a large Italian community in the East of England. My father taught me a love of medicine, but more importantly a love of general practice. He also opened my eyes to a darker side of the profession. When taking on a new partner he rapidly sifted the applications – and there were a lot – into two piles. I asked him what the two piles were. He said the one on the left was for those with the (not yet compulsory) examination from the RCGP, and those on the right who had not got it. He only short-listed from the right pile. Like many foreign doctors, my father did not feel welcomed into the growing movement of the Royal College, which he saw as belonging only to the white, male, South of England elite – and not to foreigners like him. Whilst he worked for decades in the same city, building his practice into one of the largest in the area, he never felt part of this group. He remained an outsider.

This feeling of alienation was passed like a baton to me and played out in my dealings with different groups during my Chairmanship. It was most starkly evident in my third group, made up of all the senior medical leaders from across the NHS. As had my father, I felt a stranger to this group, an outsider on the periphery of their circle. For the most part, certainly in the early days, I experienced the group as isolating and destructive.

Becoming a leader

My first RCGP Council was held in a magnificent room in the Worshipful Company of Skinners. Surrounded by ancient tapestries I took the chain of office. That morning I was the main item on BBC news and front-page story in the Guardian newspaper (Campbell, 2010a) and other media. This was because I had given an interview challenging the Government's proposed health service reforms. I stated that they would create a fragmented health system, were an unnecessary distraction, would lead to worse care for patients; would cause irreparable damage to patient care and jeopardize the NHS. As I walked in to chair this meeting – seeing my fellow council members clutching their own copies of the newspaper – I wondered how many would sanction me for being so overtly critical of the government. This was after all a Royal College, a charitable body that had to stay clear of party politics. That day, the first of my tenure, I feared for my survival, doubting that I would last even 24 hours. This fear never left me, and in varying degrees of intensity was a constant companion. That day I had crossed the boundary into the lonely space of leadership.

The confusion

I lived through that day, making the decision not to retract my criticism (as some outsiders suggested I should) but to continue raising concerns on behalf of my constituency, and through them for the patients we served. In doing so, and as time passed, I was subjected by the media, politicians, individuals and others to tremendous forces of personal attack, envy, and ridicule. I was exposed (if that is the right word) in the newspapers for having 'socialist views' and underlying motives for my dissent were questioned. I was name-called even on the floor of the House of Commons. To balance this, I received unquestionable support from my College; and many other health professionals and strangers would write, tweet, and email me to thank me. Others, including senior government and medical officials would seek me out to tell me privately that they agreed with me but were too fearful to speak out. I received accolades, including one for bravery from the *British Medical Journal*. I became City Woman of the Year and voted one of the most powerful women in the UK. I kept a personal diary, though a public account of this period is also written in the book, *NHS SOS* (Davis and Tallis, 2013).

This part of my leadership (balancing the needs of my College with not being overly critical of the Government) took a personal toll on my psychological health. Outwardly I was the strong, determined, powerful leader. Inwardly I lived in a state of anxiety; I lost weight, could not sleep, and was concerned that I was being watched (this turned out to be true but not to the extent I believed). At the same time, I continued with my clinical work, caring for doctors with mental illness, the archetypal wounded healers. Doctors have high rates of mental illness (depression, anxiety, and post-traumatic stress disorder) but are low users of services – reluctant for many reasons to seek the help they so readily prescribe for their patients. My symptoms matched theirs, and it was important to address them for my own psychological survival. Through individual reflective practice, and in the safety of the consulting room, I was able to contain the madness I was experiencing. More importantly I began to understand that what I was experiencing in one group was being mirrored in another, that I was the recipient of painful envious projections and as I will discuss later, others' fear of annihilation.

The flu

The week the NHS Bill passed through the House of Lords, meaning an unimpeded passage to becoming law, I attended the introductory course at the Institute of Group Analysis and began my journey through group analytic training. Suffering from influenza and distressed by what had happened I played out my grief in the group. I blamed other group members for not doing enough to stop the Bill – in fact I even accused them of complicity. This was nonsense, since they were drawn predominantly from the public sector – as committed to public services and to the NHS as I was. That weekend, I learnt about projective identification and malignant mirroring. As time went on, I encountered some of the same conflicts in the training groups as I did in my work groups, the outside being reflected inside and through the individual work, I delved deeper into this phenomenon to make sense of it. Being a national leader on the one hand and an 'ordinary' group member on the other created tensions in me and the other group members. Rather than a wounded healer I was a 'wounded leader', needing to show vulnerability in one setting in order to be able to function in another. The group was unable to tolerate this fall from grace, and either ignored my vulnerability or fought to exclude me.

Lessons learnt

Fight – flight

In retrospect, what I was experiencing was the inevitable splitting that happens in groups at times of stress. In the NHS, these splits tend to occur between clinician and manager, or nurse and doctor. Paradoxically and difficult to understand at the time, the group of senior medical leaders were angry with me. They saw me as the representative of GPs, theoretically the beneficiaries of the reforms and so the profession that had brought this chaos to them (the rhetoric behind the reforms was to bring about a 'GP-led NHS'). The group task was overwhelmed by strong emotions of anxiety, fear, and guilt, all played out in the group meetings where the future of the NHS was being discussed. I believe these groups lost their core purpose of protecting the values of their members and therefore of patients. Bion's fight-flight was played out in fleeing not from the danger of the Bill, but from me and other voices of dissent.

Leadership

Even before becoming Chair of the RCGP I had held a number of leadership positions and had been a senior clinician for over two decades. Nothing had prepared me, however, for that first day, when I experienced for the first time the deep loneliness of leadership. For Foulkes, the aim of a group conductor is to contain the anxiety of the group to enable it to work. Foulkes teaches that the conductor 'does not lead' in the traditional 'heroic' sense, rather creates a climate of acceptance of all communications. In the book Living Leadership the point is made that effective leaders need not be 'heroic', akin to a military officer, leading from the front, marching to war (Binney, Wilke and Williams, 2005). However, the public demands that leaders demonstrate invincibility, though of course leaders are human, not demigods. During my leadership, I learnt that a leader must recognize the disparity between the expectations they experience (strong, secure, invincible) and the hidden reality (fearful, lonely, fallible). This is the true burden of the leader – living out two lives, one hidden from the other. To survive being a leader, as I did, it is important to find a safe outlet where this disparity can be safely and honestly explored and understood.

I was not a traditional 'heroic leader', but as with the conductor of a group, ultimately the leader has to move to the front, be visible and rise or fall by their decisions. Nitsun (1996)argues that the conductor does exercise control. The same process had parallels with my leadership of the Royal College. Leadership can never be fully given away, only shared or lent for periods of time to the wider group.

Effective leaders have to rely on their groups – no one can have all the knowledge, all of the time. On pages 200–01 is a description of a group analytic consultation which supported my work with GPs. I have written elsewhere about dispersive leadership (C. Gerada, 2014), using the analogy of a peloton (the pack in a cycle race). The peloton protects the leader until they move up front and win the race. Sharing the burden of leadership – both in my functional work groups (namely the College) and my training groups – and individual reflective practice allowed me to survive longer than if I had been alone. Whilst I drew on the advice of the different groups to which I belonged, in the end, authority lay with me and the position I held.

Fear

I lived with the sense of fear throughout my tenure. Fear is now sadly ubiquitous in the NHS and an emotional driver at all organizational levels: individually in the consulting room and collectively in those who deliver care to patients (Miller and Gerada, 2017). Obholzer and Roberts (1994) writes that the NHS is a container for all our fears of death. During my leadership, I experienced different groups acting as an echo chamber for this shared fear. Instead of group members finding solutions and acting together, they became dysfunctional and split, with me embodying this fear on behalf of the groups and the public. The psychoanalyst Isabel Menzies-Lyth, in her classic studies, described similar processes and behaviors in nurses – driven by fear and paranoid anxieties within organizations (1959).

Group norms

In time, I began to understand the motivations of the various work groups of which I was a part. Like many organizations, the group members embraced a set of shared beliefs which defined their behavior and status. For many, the group norms seemed to aim to continue the status quo and to remain influential. Paradoxically, with each period of silence, they became more disempowered.

Challenging the status quo

Trying to make sense of why so many people were failed by so few took time. One aspect was a deep-rooted sense of being right based on a position in society (medical leader, politician, policy maker) superimposed on ideological beliefs. I was considered a threat because I challenged these beliefs and, in time, other groups (virtual and real, professionally or publicly led) did the same. Most of the organizations purporting to represent doctors and other health professionals did too little, too late. Davis and Tallis in *NHS SOS* (2013) write that the NHS was betrayed through the 'active collusion, passive acquiescence or incompetence of . . . politicians, journalists, unions and leaders of the medical profession'. Without these players, it would not have been possible for Andrew Lansley's 'nightmare vision for the NHS' to be enshrined in law [2–3].

Scapegoating

My training groups helped contain my anxiety and process displaced feelings of hate, disappointment, and despair. But I also became a scapegoat – disturbance was located in me on behalf of the group. This echoed the position in which I was put in my professional life – I was identified as the 'spoiler', the individual set to defy the government and impede the passage of their legislation. Identifying and working through this allowed me (and other group members) to understand that the disturbance lay not in me, but in what I was bringing in, the madness of what I was dealing with in the outside-group world. This allowed me some psychic relief, and absolution of the self-blame for being unable to stop the passage of the Bill. As leader of the RCGP I might also have been carrying the desperate need of many people to save the NHS – an enormous pressure for a single individual. I was simultaneously scapegoat and idealized savior to different people. Scapegoats often have real (or imagined) differences from the group in which they belong. These differences threaten the fantasized integrity of the group. Conformity provides safety and because I did not conform, the groups unconsciously required me to be expelled. The enactments in the work groups were processed in my training group, where they could be thought about and the differences viewed in a positive light.

Restoring normality

Time passes and I have returned to clinical practice – caring for doctors with mental health problems and my patients in mainstream general practice, as well as to other leadership positions. I have learnt so much. Fundamentally, I have learnt not to blame. Especially leaders. Everyone has their point of fear, beyond which they become paralyzed and cannot move on. For many of the senior doctors it was about moving into a space which felt overtly (party) political. For others their fear was existential – what I was saying, that the NHS was at grave risk, was too much to comprehend fully, and therefore had to be denied, and I, the speaker of such foreboding, expelled. I was fortunate. I found myself a matrix of care – both individual and group. This allowed me to test, observe, feel and resolve many of my fears. It is clichéd to say there is a crisis of leadership – but like most clichés there is truth in the statement. Many leaders remove themselves and surround themselves with non-dissenters, with those who say what the leader wants to hear. I had no choice. My leadership was played out in groups where I was either savior or scapegoat, idealized and denigrated by different audiences. Without the space to reflect, these projections could have become internalized. Instead in my spaces of reflection, they were understood.

Chapter 10

Another fine mess you've gotten me into

Effective leadership in a difficult place

Raman Kapur

Introduction

I have written before (Kapur, 2009, 2016, 2017) of the pressures as a leader/CEO of a voluntary mental health organization offering a specialist therapeutic service to people with severe mental illness. In this role I try to integrate my clinical expertise with the reality of leading and managing. So much gets activated, consciously and unconsciously, when people come together to carry out the primary task of any organization. Often the personality and task of the organization group will dictate the content of emotional processes, but the actual mechanisms remain the same. In this chapter I describe a particular incident and use group analytic and psychoanalytic theory to understand the mechanisms at play, navigating through the emotional and management issues. Our agency is one of five main voluntary organizations in Northern Ireland providing services for severely mentally ill (usually psychotic) patients coming mainly from psychiatric hospitals. We have 94 residents 'beds' (spread over six residential units) along with a 'floating support' service for 30–35 people, which provides support to people suffering from mental ill-health to enable them to stay in their own homes, a turnover of £2 million and around 65–70 staff on our payroll. We are a provider, being commissioned by local Government Housing and Health Trusts to offer accommodation and support services to patients in the mental health system.

A new unit had been commissioned at a cost of £2 million pounds, with the 'decant' property previously used as temporary accommodation being returned to the Housing Association. A 'new baby' representing the good work and growth of the agency was born. This good moment was quickly attacked.

In the temporary accommodation, vivid pictures of sinks filled with dirt and overflowing, empty Chinese food cartons and bottles strewn across bedroom floors, dirty bathrooms, un-flushed and dirty toilets, un-emptied over-flowing bins. The vacated house looked totally chaotic and trashed. Photographs were sent to head office complaining about the trail of disaster that had been left. A 'messy' butterfly effect unfolded with senior management and staff embarking on a clean-up operation. Blame was everywhere, pride in our services was lost and fantasies of being inspected, closed down, and humiliated were in the atmosphere.

I will now analyze the reverberation of this incident throughout the whole organization.

Transference

As CEO, who am I to staff and Board members? For me this has been the central question since I took over this role 18 years ago. Am I an ordinary mental health professional who has specialized in offering therapeutic atmospheres to people with psychosis (Kapur, 2016), or am I a mad, destructive narcissist only interested in sadistically projecting my messy mind into others, to fuel a damaged ego that gains pleasure from dominance, power, and greed?

'In' the transference with disturbed parts of patients is a difficult place to be (Kapur, 2018) but being 'in' the transference managerially, with all its legal and financial responsibilities is a terrifying place to be. So 'in' the transference, or in working directly with managers to resolve this situation, how could I have been seen?

Perhaps

- Blaming and shaming staff involved
- Sadistically gain pleasure from their failure

- Projecting my 'messy parts' into them to collude with an ego-ideal view of my leadership
- Thinking 'you should be grateful for what I've provided for you'.

I want to emphasize that in every leader, in all of us, there is always a capacity for the 'destructive narcissist' to be activated. Here is Rosenfeld's (1987) definition of this state of mind:

> Putting forward a theory of destructive narcissism, I suggested that in some cases . . . there was an enormous idealization of the destructive parts of the self which were felt to be attractive because they made the patient feel omnipotent. When destructive narcissism of this kind is a feature of the patient's character structure, individual object relationships and any wish on the part of the self to experience the need for the object and to depend on it are devalued, attacked and destroyed with pleasure . . . . Secrecy is part of feeling omnipotent destructive superiority
>
> (Rosenfeld, 1987, p. 22)

In most organizations the CEO is seen in this way, and unfortunately in many instances it reflects reality (see also chapters three and 19). Often those in leadership seek a 'superior position', wait for weakness and vulnerability and sadistically attack at the first opportunity. I have certainly been on the receiving end of this from Board members and Commissioners. So, it is crucial for the leader to recognize the emotional and organizational catastrophe that ensues if reality meets this fantasy. If we, as leaders, are operating out of a 'secret sadism' of perverse abusive authority, then the organization and ultimately the patient will suffer the consequences.

To resolve this issue I not only had to recognize how this messy part of my mind could be (and momentarily was) activated, but also had to ensure the structure of communications or the group/organizational matrix remain intact for the 'mess' to be worked through and contained (Zinkin, 1989; Knauss, 1999). In other words, maintaining the regularity and consistency of 1:1 supervision with senior staff, senior management meetings (fortnightly) and the monthly middle management meetings (see also chapters 22 and 23). These meetings had to be conducted with an openness to discuss 'messy' issues where appropriate, and I needed to 'hold and contain' the messy part that could have become a contagion in the organization. However, it is very important not to become a toilet for the mess of others, and it is crucial to help others retrieve parts that belong to them, if possible. That is wholly dependent on the quality of their internal worlds. Here I reference psychoanalyst Eric Brenman's work, substituting the word 'manager' for 'analyst':

> The "manager" needs to provide the strength to withstand the omnipotent contempt and resist the power of the repetition compulsion, where the "manager" is "blue printed" to act out sadistic moralizing, or the masochistic pseudo-tolerance or to supply an ideal provision to obviate problems
>
> (2006, p. 33)

So rather than acting out these negative reactions, I have to do what I do with my patients, contain and alpha process these primitive beta-elements, and put words to the prevailing atmosphere, which I did (and repeated):

> I suppose we have to be careful that the mess in our minds doesn't get put into the project and make things worse.

Gradually, after considerable working through over the subsequent days and weeks, the staff involved became seen as 'whole' rather than 'part-objects', who recognized that they found themselves spoiling (Meltzer, 1986) or sabotaging the 'new baby' while, as CEO and senior managers, we recognized the huge pressures of 'moving house' with 14 patients with severe mental illness. Understanding, coupled with firm boundaries that this 'shouldn't have happened' led to a realization of all of our capacities to create a mess when a 'new baby' arrives. Greater attention to this has left us wiser to attending to the complexities of something 'new' replacing something 'old', which inevitably stirs up deeper anxieties that Wilke (2014) succinctly comments upon:

> As group analytic consultants, we would do well to refrain from pathologizing oedipal conflict and outbreaks of sibling rivalry in organizations and treat these instead as the symptoms of severe distress connected with the transition from the old to the new
>
> (p. 57)

It was crucial that I did not become the 'big destructive moralizing Daddy' but rather contained and held the mess that meant we could learn from experience and thus be creative rather than destructive (Nitsun, 1996; Knauss, 1999; Mojovic, 2007).

Countertransference

For CEOs of any organization, large or small, public, private, or as in my case, the voluntary sector, there is an automatic pull towards destructive narcissism both from the reality of the power and authority in the role and the inevitable projections of power and authority. To remain sane, human, and in the depressive position is central and also one of the most difficult jobs in management (see also chapter nine). The contrast to running psychotherapy groups couldn't be starker as freedom to speak and free association is replaced by an omnipresent legal backdrop with an adversarial discourse that by its very nature destroys open discussion.

Thus, managing the countertransference well is crucial for the effective functioning of the organization. In my first several years as CEO I did not do this at all, as I assumed staff would relate to me, as I did to them, as a clinician who wanted to protect the work of the agency (Kapur, 2017) in a hostile public sector world (Wilke, 2014). A near-fatal mistake. Only after considerable retrieval and amalgamation of my clinical insights with organizational work (Kapur, 2009) did I begin to use my own reactions to understand the internal world of staff and my Management Board. With this in mind, how did I manage the vignette incident?

I have described my negative reactions to the incident: blaming, potential sadism, projection, and persecution. So, via projective identification how could I better understand the internal worlds being projected into me and offer a strengthening introject (Brenman, 2006), something that strengthens rather than weakens the workforce?

First, the newness of the project made it likely that there would be a destructive and envious attack, either from inside or outside the project. The goodness of the new building was simply going to be too much, with a 'high risk' of a spoiling attack. Although 'named' and spoken about, it still occurred, with a messy fall out. As CEO, I had completed all my financial and strategic management tasks and felt pleased the project was 'safe and secure'. This was particularly pleasing because 10 years previously I made the decision to close a Personality Disorder Project, to protect our work with psychotic patients as we had taken on too much. So, I was quietly pleased with past and current decisions. However, while I kept my feelings of quiet satisfaction private, I believe the tangible existence of this 'new baby' was overwhelming for staff and patients and had to be attacked.

Second, the incident was a reminder that everyday work as a CEO is about dealing with the messy minds of staff, Board members, stakeholders, patients, and oneself. What a reminder! As with clinical work, I believe it is imperative not to underestimate destructive potentials (see below 'Attacks on Linking'). Potentially, this 'mess' could have destroyed our relationship with our Commissioners (threatening the existence of the service) and the local regulatory body (Regulation and Quality Improvement Agency, similar to the Care Quality Commission in England). I had to let the 'shit hit the fan' with the Senior Management team (three people) and allow them to react within the container of our regular fortnightly meetings (maintaining the group matrix), putting words to the atmosphere created:

> So what do we do with the mess in our minds, you always worry it will be my messy mind that mucks things up, but maybe we all can do this. Look at . . . referring to other conflicts.

The re-iteration of this in other settings led to less acting out and blaming, and more thinking about a way forward. Staff were made aware in a matter of fact way of the seriousness of the mess and helped to emotionally 'clear up the shit'. The goodness of the service was recovered.

We know from our clinical work that the movement between paranoid-schizoid and depressive position (or in Nitsun's model, anti and pro group) is a two-way arrow. As CEO I have to do my best to start the day in the depressive position and allow myself to be affected by the complexities of the internal world of everyone connected to our service. Recognizing projective identification is my tool, and my reactions have to be recognized and processed. A final point: several months prior to this, this Project had failed an inspection. As the Registered Provider, I had to appear before the regulation authority. I had ignored acting out by other managers and was now placed in a 'guillotine' situation where I could get my 'head chopped off'. This time I couldn't ignore the impulse to oedipal attack (Wilke, 2014) nor the associated murderous impulse against the hated and envied father. So, I had to put words to this in our 'open discussion' (held every three months with Project Managers) to recognize that primitive forces are always operating against the leader, but as CEO I will, can, and do openly declare 'I have no wish to harm anyone in this organization. Quid pro quo please'!

Connecting and fragmenting

The internal worlds of all of us will 'fragment and connect' according to the stability of our own internal objects and the external projections we are exposed to. A patient once described this to me as being in free-fall:

'Part of this world
Acknowledged
Accepted

Undeserving but nevertheless
Existing
But in the space of a second
Obliterated
A nothing
Falling
Again
That downward spiral
Ever downwards
Where will it ever end'

This 'dread of annihilation' (Meltzer, 1968) captures the subjective experience of 'falling to pieces' which this and other patients have described as 'falling into a black hole'. This is a feature of the paranoid-schizoid position so if we assume that it potentially exists in us all, then in a group the effect would indeed be catastrophic and the cause of huge distress.

I believe in the workplace this catastrophic butterfly effect (Thornton, 2016; Kapur, 2017) is omnipresent in day-to-day organizational life, with deep hidden reactions potentially triggered by this kind of incident. The potential for a descent into chaos is huge, for these incidents can connect people so quickly with a 'sinking despair' or hostile, persecutory paranoid responses. I have seen moments like this escalate into full scale industrial tribunals where the internal world of the persecutor and victim are acted out in the most damaging and destructive ways.

Hopper (2003, 2009, 2012a) describes this experience in his fourth basic assumption, incohesion: aggregation/massification or (ba)I: A/M. He is referring to psychotic anxieties like those described above when he writes (2003):

> In a sense each of the three basic assumptions conceptualized in Bion is a source of in-cohesion in groups and group-like systems. However, this fourth basic assumption pertains specifically to the dynamics of incohesion, the bi-polar forms of which are aggregation and massification. The terms "aggregate" and "mass" are taken from early sociology and anthropology. The underlying basic assumption is that the group is not really a group but is either an aggregate or a mass. Although a mass seems to be more cohesive than an aggregate, in fact these two bi-polar forms of incohesion are equally incohesive. They are transitory and incapable of sustaining co-operative work.
>
> (p. 220)

Importantly, for our understanding of the vignette and of organizational life, Hopper identifies the etiological role of the 'fear of annihilation' in producing this incohesive state:

> Trauma provokes and activates the fear of annihilation. The phenomenology of the fear of annihilation involves psychic paralysis and the death of psychic vitality, characterized by fission and fragmentation, and the fusion and confusion of what is left of the self with what can be found in the object. Fusion and confusion are a defense against fission and vice versa. For example, the fear of falling apart and of petrification is associated with fission and fragmentation; the fear of suffocation and of being swallowed up is associated with fusion and confusion; but the former infers protection again the latter and vice versa.
>
> (p. 223)

Finally, Hopper (2009) describes the people who take up particular 'leadership' roles when psychotic anxieties dominate a group:

> For example, the "lone wolf" role is typical of aggregation, and the "cheer leader" role of massification. As Foulkes would have put it, traumatized people with crustacean character structures are likely to "personify" aggregation processes and those with amoeboid character structures, massification processes. In other words, people with crustacean defenses are likely to become lone wolves and those with amoeboid defenses are likely to become cheer leaders.
>
> (p. 224)

So how do anti-cohesive basic assumptions, particularly (ba)I: A/M become repaired? In the incident described, the crucial task for me as CEO was to facilitate some linking between fragmented, psychotic particles to 'hold and contain' the situation. Hopper's analysis helped me recognize the potential fall-out from the trauma and guided me towards 'prophylactic interventions' (naming negative events) to lessen incohesion.

Binney, Wilke, and Williams (2012) suggest it is helpful to ask for support and guidance from colleagues to begin a connecting reparation of a messy situation. However, after many experiences of asking for help from the wrong people (Kapur, 2017), I have an important caveat on the existence of 'destructive narcissism (Rosenfeld, 1971, 1987; Steiner, 1993). For proper re-connection and linkage to occur, there has to be a 'linking object' (Volkan, 2004), firmly based in the depressive position. Seeking help from a 'false self' helper who pretends to offer support, care, and concern is a tragic and terrible mistake for a leader in need. However, differentiating between a true and false helper is not easy, particularly if they have the sophisticated defenses of a personality suffused with narcissism (Britton, 2008). In particular what Rosenfeld (1998) describes as the 'libidinal narcissist'.

> In considering the libidinal aspect of narcissism one can see that the over-valuation of the self plays a central role, based mainly on the idealization of the self. Self-idealization is maintained by omnipotent introjective and projective identifications with ideal objects and their qualities. In this way, the narcissist feels that everything that is valuable relating to external objects and the outside world is part of him or omnipotently controlled by him.
>
> (p. 105)

When good linking/recovery occurred, staff saw me and senior managers as human beings (Thornton, 2017a) who had a serious responsibility to keep the organization safe rather than dehumanized, sadistic objects. This is an important observation in external interventions where there is often an over-identification with staff. Thornton (2017b) comments on this:

> The presence of individuals with greater formal power and status has been a source of discomfort for many group analysts, who have experienced it as being in conflict with the fundamentally egalitarian ethic of group analysis, in some settings this has been compounded to by team members' resonating discomfort. Failed strategies for dealing with this include excluding managers (whether present or not, and they should if possible be present), attacking them and recruiting the practitioner as an idealized substitute.

Attacks on linking (coming alive)

In his seminal papers on 'Psychotic and Non-psychotic Personalities' (1967) and 'Attacks on Linking' (1959), Bion emphasizes the effects of the 'destructive attacks which the patient makes on anything which is felt to have the function of linking one object to another' (p. 32). I will 'link' this phenomenon to the vignette and to the idea of an 'alive' organization (Binney, Wilke and Williams, 2012):

- Well connected
- Able to think clearly
- Tolerates complexity and uncertainty
- Tolerates reality as it is
- Able to use the whole self, feeling as well as thinking
- Able to ask for and receive help
- A short- and long-term focus.

These are contrasted with 'surviving' (less alive and focusing on survival) and 'coping' (managing to exist with some connections). In Kleinian terminology, an alive organization would be in the depressive position and the latter two in the paranoid-schizoid position.

This is a common emotional event in organizational life and I have found, as in clinical work, offering a 'considered amount of goodness' is essential to minimize triggering these attacks (Kapur, 2009). An early mistake I made as CEO of a voluntary agency was to adopt a charismatic and enthusiastic style – so characteristic of this sector. Often this kind of individual commitment is needed to generate the energy to secure income streams and recruit staff to deliver public services: unlike the statutory sector, there is no automatic government funding. However, the negative effects of this style are twofold. First, it can quickly lead to burn out with so much energy put into seeking funds, often from skeptical Commissioners (even more so if your services are psychoanalytic). Second, you can elicit attacks from staff and colleagues who simply can't bear your enthusiasm, which they often see as you following your own narcissistic ambitions (which you may be).

So, I have found, after much 'trial and error' that maintaining a quiet emotional attitude of recognizing your own good work, and that of others, is most effective. Not unlike having a good session with a patient on the couch, I don't smile gleefully at him or her when I open the door at the end of the session. Rather, I quietly digest the good moment and hope that both the patient and I have been satisfied by the good work undertaken by both of us.

Conclusion

For me, the hard work of 'holding and containing' everyday organizational human relations, internal and external to the agency minimizes the chance of a 'mess' becoming an exploding 'bomb'. Not unlike working with the psychotic parts of our patients (Kapur, 2018), so much ordinary work is required to manage the patient/staff members view of me (transference), detoxify my own human reactions to this (counter-transference), pick up and connect things together, and manage attacks on the goodness of our professional work.

Over my 18 years as CEO I have moved where possible (and within what organizational reality permits me to do) from the normal 'disciplinary and grievance procedures' to working with the limitations of my and others' internal worlds, to create an 'alive' working atmosphere, where people can do their work as well as possible. This inevitably means putting clear boundaries on (and at times humanely excluding) people who, in Rosenfeld's terminology, have a 'secret libidinal self' aimed at destroying good work, addicted to a 'mess becoming a bomb', and the over-excitement (often sexualized) that comes with this. However, I have realized that this alternative approach aims, as best as I can, to protect the primary task of the agency from psychotic processes. This painstaking work has lessened the persecutory or annihilatory anxiety (Hopper, 2009) in the organization so that people have the best chance to work from a 'good object' knowing that I am trying to do the same. This is an endless, iterative task to maximize an 'alive' depressive position atmosphere and so lessen organizational trauma while looking after people with severe mental illness.

Chapter 11

Leadership and 'another fine mess' by Raman Kapur

Morris Nitsun

Raman Kapur's chapter underlines the unswerving importance of leadership in organizations. It is an intense and searching exploration of the burden of responsibility he carries in a leadership position, the terrors and traps of the role but also the potential to influence a stressed, dysfunctional system for the good. Group analysis tends to emphasize the group as a whole, systems within and without the organization, and the social processes informing these, and needs to be balanced by attention to the very real challenges of leadership and authority, and the way different incumbents in that role mediate their influence in the organization. The wider environment, including culture and current political and economic pressures, deeply influences the organization, but so much also depends on how the leader or leaders (there may be more than one) manage the interfaces.

In the decades in which I was an NHS manager, with wide responsibilities for a large psychological service, I was at times exercised to the limit by the challenges and difficulties of the role, despite recognition as a competent and creative manager.[1] I found the job rewarding in various ways, but an almost constant struggle. In those days (roughly the 1980s and 1990s), I felt a distinct absence of interest within the group analytic milieu for these leadership difficulties. But today, against a background of more fully articulated group analytic organizational thinking, Raman and others in this book do appreciate and attend to the leader's dilemmas.

How does this compare with running an analytic psychotherapy group? Raman contrasts the demands of organizational leadership with those of running a group, strongly emphasizing how much more difficult the organizational role is than the psychotherapeutic. I agree, but only to an extent. Organizational leadership carries more crucial responsibility and accountability, but the anxiety produced in the conduct of an analytic group is often underestimated and constrained by the strand of group analysis that emphasizes passive leadership.

Raman quotes Christine Thornton (2010, 2016) who writes about this strand as an avoidance or denial of the real significance of power and authority given the democratic stance imbued in group analysis. Keen as I am on democracy, I have no doubt that leadership is an important and facilitating component, not an impediment. This was the basis of my Foulkes Lecture in 2009, titled 'Authority and Revolt: The Challenges of Group Leadership' (Nitsun, 2009). In this, I questioned the validity of what I believe is an idealized view of the democratic process in groups, and Foulkes' insistence on 'leading from behind'. His was a conscious reaction to the authoritarian leadership that played such a destructive role in World War II, and of course authoritarianism remains a problem in the world, recently resurgent. Foulkes famously rejected the term *leader* in favor of *conductor*. But the leadership issues we are dealing with as clinicians or consultants are not of the same import, even if they mirror some of the processes of larger-scale and more traumatized groups. I am all for group empowerment, be it organizational or therapeutic; but I see the leader as integral.

We could think in terms of a developmental process in which the group first needs to trust the authority of the leader, his/her capacity to hold the boundaries, to be fair but firm when necessary, and to be sufficiently comfortable with his/her own authority to take on the responsibility of a group or organization (the essence of what Foulkes referred to as 'dynamic administration'). See also pages 153–55, 192, 194–204. With this reasonably assured, the group can find its own ground and the leader can afford to step back and let the group get on with the job. However, even when a group finds its strength, there may be periods of impasse, disruption, or threat that require the exercise of authority. Further, since there is potential in most groups for conflict, including disappointment and anger with the leader, it is necessary for the group to feel that there is something or someone they can kick against. My own training group analysis, while beneficial in general, was at the same time problematic because of what I felt was the passivity of the conductor. I found this frustrating and at times disempowering rather than empowering in my struggle to find my own authority. Ultimately, I did find my authority, but it was not because I had helpful role models.

In my writing on the anti-group (Nitsun, 1996, 2015), I have drawn attention to the conductor's responsibility when the group plunges into particularly difficult waters, when there is uncontainable conflict, group demoralization and fall-out. In my experience as a supervisor, this happens more commonly than is generally recognized, leaving conductors feeling very anxious and uncertain of how to manage the group. There are no easy answers, but the impasse is reinforced by a lack of robust vision of the group analyst's authority, denying the need to take an active stance when required. Anti-group developments are often a reflection or consequence of inadequate or unconfident leadership, and in turn an inadequate leadership model tends to exacerbate the difficulty. I believe this is as true of organizations as it is of the psychotherapy group.

Another aspect of the leader's authority illustrated in Raman's chapter is the capacity to deal constructively with communication difficulties in the organization. In my writing on the organizational mirror (Nitsun, 1998a, 1998b), one of the most notable features of dysfunctional organizations is the poor, confusing, and contradictory information that is passed down the line. I describe how this *dysfunctional mirroring* reflects organizational stress and anxiety, often setting in motion a process of destructive organizational mirroring. Being able to recognize and understand this process, and potentially intercept or correct it, is in my view an important requirement of a leader, be it a manager or a clinician.

In Raman's chapter, part of his struggle and his achievement is the ability to communicate effectively with his team. As leaders, we are not just receptive containers. We have responsibility for communicating clearly with others and offsetting the organizational drift to dysfunctional mirroring. This is easier said than done, and leadership requires training and support, protecting the leader from vulnerability to enmeshment in the organizational maelstrom. I am aware that these views portray the leader as to some extent separate from the rest. There is a credible argument that this is false separation, that the leader is as much part of the organization as the others. But there are times when s/he is required to take a bold, authoritative step and perhaps this is the real challenge of leadership – to be both a part of and to be separate and to know how to steer one's way through the ambiguities of the role. In my own long experience as an NHS manager, much of my attention was directed to this process. I think I was able to steer my way most effectively when I could understand the complexity of this process, differentiate myself and others, and identify organizational mirroring in ways that could restore thinking and coherence. Raman's chapter gives us a real sense of how this feels, and how we can make a difference, in action.

Note

1 Morris Nitsun received the President of the Royal College of Psychiatrists' Award in 2015 for contributions to mental health services.

Chapter 12

Creative chaos

Containing transforming space in Kids Company and other stories

Farideh Dizadji

Introduction

In 2010, I wrote *Organization on the Edge: Chaos and Creativity*, reflecting on working at Kids Company Children's Centre in London. I used group analytic thinking to understand the organization's unique, complex structure and dynamics, particularly focusing on the keyworking model. Perhaps more than any other aspect of the Centre's work, the relationally based keyworking model exemplified how the Centre worked creatively at the edge of chaos, creating space for members to develop emotional attachments (Lemma, 2010).

Camila Batmanghelidjh details the traumatic shutting down of Kids Company in *Kids: Child Protection in Britain: The Truth* (2017). Working since in similar settings, and reflecting further on the organizational dynamics, I have come to appreciate the importance of group analytic thinking in understanding organizational chaos and how one can work creatively within such contexts. I have also become more aware of the limitations of such understanding: is creative thinking and understanding of chaotic situations sufficient to hold, contain, and facilitate changes in such settings in the long term? I am wondering about the impact of power and authority, both internal and external to these settings.

Thus, here I revisit my earlier work to explore how 'therapeutic chaos' has a transformational potential for change. Reflecting on the complex external political forces with power to interrupt these transformational processes is beyond the scope of this chapter. However, one of the architects of The Big Society, Steve Hilton, in *The Sunday Times Magazine* on the 18th of September, 2017, commented that Camila Batmanghelidjh was put forward as a 'poster child' for The Big Society, and as a result, became a victim of attacks on it from among parts of the establishment that were threatened.

I will also touch on more recent experiences of 'chaotic' settings to see whether there are correspondences between them.

I have come to realize that the common factor among all these organizations, all charities, is that they have become economical substitutes for statutory institutions as the result of government's neo-liberalist policies; 'economical' in the narrow sense that they are without the resources, capabilities, and power of the statutory sector. This has fundamental and decisive impact on leadership, function, and ultimately survival.

> If we sanction a health care system based on a business model where profit is the motive for efficiency or the rationale for decisions about resources, we get one where the desire to reduce financial cost pressures triumphs over ethical, professional and clinical judgement. If we sanction a health care system where financial incentives are the priority we get a system which is likely to become less concerned about staff and patient needs and more like to cut corners to maximize profit.
>
> (Simpson, 2017a)

Let me then start by reflecting on my experiences working at Kids Company, an organization dedicated to providing practical and emotional support to vulnerable inner-city children, young people, and their families. I was the Clinical Director of its main street level center (the Centre) for over six years before its forced closure in 2015. Over those years I witnessed its growth from a developmentally 'adolescent' center, to 'adulthood'. I aim to explore how the chaotic nature of the Centre led to positive therapeutic outcomes. I draw upon a range of group analytic and psychoanalytic literature. In particular, I suggest that the Centre was analogous to a therapeutic community in the group analytic sense, in a state of bounded instability, at the edge of chaos, where creativity became possible. I locate my own role at the Centre as one of providing a 'therapeutic presence', (Solomon and Nashat, 2010; MacDonald, 2002), enabling and extending the Centre's functioning. This was about building a therapeutic relationship in flexible ways with different boundaries than usual therapeutic work, less obvious but nevertheless strong and containing. Is this 'real group analysis'? I think Foulkes would recognize it as such, because of the crucial role of thinking in terms of the group, the matrix, and relationships.

> interlocking systems ranging from an individual mind nested in group, in an organization . . . and a society . . . The interaction between these nested systems is always circular . . . with one level affecting and being affected by the levels above and below.
>
> (Stacey, 1996, p. 190)

The organization

Kids Company was set up to help deprived inner-city communities operating from various settings. At the heart of the Centre was its main hall, with a dozen round tables, a kitchen in one corner, and a library and a few couches to one side, representing a big 'home' for its community; colorfully painted walls were covered with pictures of kids: some dead, victims of gang crime. Everything happened in this space: eating, meeting, interacting, or simply belonging. Young people, families, and staff mixed there, in constant interaction with each other. The Centre's visitors ranged from members of local communities to royalty, celebrities, students, professionals, politicians. It was open six days a week offering various activities: a day school for a group of 11–16-year-olds excluded from mainstream education; daily afternoon school and Saturdays clubs; 3 nights a week it opened for youngsters aged 16–25, as an alternative to involvement in gang culture. 'Therapy House', within walking distance of the Centre, provided psychotherapy and complementary therapies for the members and staff alike. The workforce combined professionals with various qualifications with people with relevant skills and experience, but no formal qualifications, including some former service users. Daily operational issues were decided collectively by 'keyworkers' and Centre managers working that day.

The Centre as a therapeutic community

The Centre's history is fascinating. It became an 'unintentional therapeutic community' similar to the 'Peckham Experiment' in the 1930s (Bridger, 1985). It started as an afternoon school for local children, it soon took on a 'life of its own' as a crisis center for troubled young people who had nowhere else to turn. Leaders embarked on a risky process of inception, development, and growth through many chaotic and interdependent phases.

As word spread, the number of people who came for help increased rapidly. From the simple slogan 'no child will be rejected', it grew, becoming a space expected to fulfill everyone's needs: not just children's, but their communities'. By this stage it was a chaotic space, and managing it became extremely difficult. At its inception the Director had contained staff's anxieties, so they could function. But this virtually single-handed role could not be maintained after the rapid growth. To cope with the influx of users, many more staff, 'keyworkers', were employed. But more staff led to a more chaotic atmosphere; newly thrown into 'the thick of it', they brought their own anxieties.

As clinical director of The Centre, I too was thrown in at the proverbial 'deep end'. I was struck by the level of chaos and fascinated by the lively dynamic of creative interactions and communications between staff and service users, the members. In conversation with a senior clinician, I wondered about this: 'The chaos is an integral part of it', he replied: 'without the chaos it would not function'.

The Centre's state of chaos and creativity

The Centre functioned as a large and complicated matrix with very complex unconscious communication, wherein 'shadow systems' were created and dissolved constantly, a multifaceted conveyor belt of social interactions including unconscious mental processing, naming, 'dialogue', and other therapeutic engagements. One could never expect linear progress with the Centre's members; rather they needed to be seen, heard, and understood in a variety of ways before change could begin.

Group psychotherapy was not available, while other types of therapies were, and I wondered why? Perhaps the Centre itself acted as a container, forming a therapeutic space, a group analytical situation, facilitating all the other therapeutic interventions at play. It seems there were some similarities between this experience and the Northfield Experiments, where democratic and psychoanalytic principles were introduced. 'Neither the commanding officer nor his staff was able to tolerate the early weeks of chaos' (Kennard, 1983). Indeed, during the second Northfield experiment, the therapeutic community was developed slowly by Foulkes, Rickman, and Main in such a way that it facilitated other therapies at Northfield (Foulkes, 1990b; Kennard, 1983).

I conceptualize this notion of 'therapeutic chaos' by looking at the context, content, and processes and dynamic of the Centre.

Stacey (1992, 1996) moves away from traditional organizational and psychoanalytic theory, and links group analytic, management, chaos, and complexity theories, along with Bollas' 'Unthought Known' (Bollas, 1987), for a novel view of human relations in groups, organizations, and societies. His complexity perspective of mutually constructed individuals and groups focuses on transitional and transformational phenomena. Drawing from Chaos Theory, he developed the notion of Creative Chaos to study human organizations. Chaos is an 'intricate mixture of order and disorder in which behavior patterns are irregular but recognizable' (Parker and Stacey, 1994, p. 11). An organization's future cannot be planned, and its direction will emerge from the spontaneous, self-organizing interaction between people in the condition he calls bounded instability (Stacey, 1992). Hence, constant innovation, which happens at the edge of chaos, is the key to success.

Stacey locates the space of novelty in the human mind, in the human group, and at the level of organizations. This space is located at the edge of chaos: in the world of transitional objects and the depressive position. It lies between the stability of concrete reality and the instability of disintegrative psychotic fantasies. Within this space, the mind can reflect upon itself; can play to manipulate the symbols and rearrange them; and can achieve double-loop learning (Argyris, 2009), with its potential for creativity. With a good enough holding environment which strengthens the ego, individuals can manage their anxieties. The space of creativity needs to be understood within a collective space, where group members, while bearing anxieties, can jointly reflect on the paradoxes of their interactions. Stacey associates all learning and creativity with the ability to play – individual, group, and organization.

Blackwell's (1998) contribution is particularly relevant. Drawing on complexity theory and identifying different systems' parameters and their dynamics, Blackwell suggests that the network system achieves a state of bounded instability when the flow of information is high enough, the interconnections are intense enough, and the agents are heterogeneous enough. Then it produces simultaneously, recognizable stable and non-stable patterns of behavior. At this 'edge of chaos', a human system is capable of creativity. See chapter seven for the further development of his thinking.

He draws attention to two parameters of human dynamics, introduced by Stacey (1996): the need to contain the anxiety and the creation of shadow systems as a result of the impact of the power on human dynamics. He, like Stacey, suggests that by bringing the shadow systems into play alongside formal systems, creative solutions to systemic problems can be achieved. Blackwell suggests group analysis offers a model that endorses dialogue, through which anxiety is turned into a source for creativity. 'Shadow systems' are informal networks of communication, developed in parallel to formal systems in any organization, for example in the forms of personal friendships. Through creative dialogue, organizations can be prevented from tipping into chaos. This is different from Stacy's view of shadow systems, created as the result of uncontained anxiety caused by the impact of power on human dynamics, formal systems, and hierarchies. Blackwell suggests that the formal matrix produces predictability, while an informal matrix is a source of creativity.

Reflecting on the Centre's history and my own experience, I can see that both Blackwell's and Stacey's ideas are salient. The Centre was functioning between 'instability' and 'stability', at the edge of chaos. Here behavior is stable enough for the system not to fall apart, and unstable enough not be stuck in one pattern. Creativity is possible, a state of paradoxes, of excitement and tension, the state of 'unknowability', similar to Foulkes' 'unknowing state of mind': 'I feel like a conductor, but I don't know in the least what music is to be played' (Foulkes, 1975).

Management structure

As the Organization grew and needed a 'Head Office', a new hierarchical management structure was formed in contrast to the flat management structure of the Centre. These differences of management styles caused miscommunications and conflicts between the two. Consequently, anxieties and frustrations reached a high level regarding prospective changes; social defenses were deployed, the simultaneous idealization and denigration of the Centre.

On reflection, it seemed that the split which gradually occurred between Head Office and the Centre kept anxieties at bay. Indeed, whilst the Centre staff reacted negatively at first to the arrangements imposed by Head Office, they served to bring some structure to the Centre and thereby 'bounded' and stabilized it. More generally, by describing the matrix of the organization and showing its interconnectedness, better communications were facilitated; a space for dialogue was created.

Creative models of therapeutic interventions were practised at the Centre. 'Keyworking', modeled on attachment theory, was offered by keyworkers who worked with young people and their families. A 'therapeutic presence', was offered by Clinical Director and therapeutic staff, the case managers. Case managers held and contained individuals (staff or client), group (staff support group), and The Centre as a whole (through, daily briefing/debriefing and Quality Yard meetings), providing a safe place so a therapeutic community space could develop. In the next sections I illustrate these different creative aspects of the Centre's functioning.

Therapeutic presence

I thought of my role at the Centre as being like a room around its contents. I defined the boundaries – as a room provides a frame – a space where keyworkers and young people felt safe enough to develop their own relationships, to 'decorate and furnish'. The room space – space – was created through holding and containing the Centre's keyworkers and case managers, providing consistent support, helping them to recognize, understand, and work through organizational conflicts. Drawn from the concept of 'therapeutic presence', this is different from a conventional management role.

'Therapeutic presence' is a conceptual framework – 'a way of working' in the broadest sense which has been used in nursing (MacDonald, 2002) and in educational settings (Solomon and Nashat, 2010). It offers a framework for thinking about change using key psychoanalytic concepts, such as Bion's Theory of Thinking and Containment, and Winnicott's Holding.

I came across this concept while trying to describe my role as the Centre's clinical director. The concept could be extended beyond its literal meaning within a structured organizational system, to a setting functioning at the edge of chaos. My role had been essentially to contain the Centre's anxieties as a whole, and those of its membership. This later helped me suggest a 'management structure' for the Centre.

As the Centre mainly functioned at the edge of chaos, clinicians often offered 'therapeutic presence' informally and spontaneously, such as opportunities to reflect on specific interactions and promoting 'reflection in action' (Schon, 1983). Via 'therapeutic presence' the Centre's emotional experience was used as 'intelligence' (Armstrong, 2004, in Solomon and Nashat, 2010, p. 291) to have a better understanding of its dynamic interconnectedness.

One of the main functions of 'therapeutic presence' is containment as described by Bion, based on the relationship of the mother and infant. When I joined the organization, the Director said to me: 'I am giving my baby to you to look after . . . there are similarities in our approach . . . so I feel I can trust you. If you look after it, I can concentrate on getting funding for it'.

I took to the role instinctively and intuitively, like a 'mother', without knowing its full complexity. I soon realized that I was 'mothering' not an infant but an angry adolescent center, one with a 'know it all' attitude. Gradually, I realized the sense of loss and abandonment by the original 'mother', the Director, led to unwillingness to trust or accept easily the new 'mother', or better to say, the 'step-mother'. These feelings were shared by existing clients and staff, perhaps reflecting too some of their own earlier personal experiences.

My attempts to encourage staff to use supervision to reflect on those feelings were not initially successful. On one occasion, I offered an experienced youth worker some space for thinking and reflection, as his behavior had become impetuous and colleagues were finding him difficult to work with. He had been with the organization from the start and adamantly insisted that he did not need help: 'therapists want to get into my head . . . and I have no time for that'. Accepting his anger and projections, acknowledging his concerns, we had our first session 'on the move', walking up and down the street outside the Centre. It became apparent that he was vulnerable and fearful despite his tough front. At the end he agreed to a weekly session for the following next six months. My informal 'therapeutic presence' helped me understand his anxieties, which in turn helped our therapeutic relationship to develop.

Important in 'therapeutic presence' is Winnicott's concept of 'holding' a 'transitional space' which seems similar in function to Bion's 'containment'. Winnicott suggested (1958, 1971, in Solomon and Nashat, 2010), that with a good enough environment as a transitional space, a capacity for symbolization and creativity will develop. A 'therapeutic presence' fulfills a similar function where participants use the space to play with their thoughts and test reality, leading to new and creative ways of thinking about dilemmas and challenges.

The containment given through 'therapeutic presence' allows staff's emotional experiences to be felt, processed, and fed back in a modified form which can be internalized. Rather than a fixed role, offering 'therapeutic presence' in the Centre was a developmental process in which therapeutic professionals – the case managers – helped keyworkers make sense of some of the inevitable challenges in the work. As a consequence, they were able to tolerate anxiety and become freer to explore, experience and contemplate new ideas and ways of working.

> Creativity is then possible when one can manage frustration and anxiety. A restored thinking capacity encourages individuals to become more curious about themselves and others and not fear to take risks and try out new ideas
>
> (Solomon and Nashat, 2010, p. 302)

It was a joy to be part of the growing up of the Centre, from an adolescent to a young adult.

Over the last 3 years I have been working at two small community psychotherapy centers. Despite their good reputations and the great demand for their services, often very complex and complicated cases, both organizations have been struggling to survive during the period of austerity policies (Dalal, 2017). Key factors were complex referrals, funding challenges, and the lack of creative vision or robust leadership. Drawing on the ideas above, in one case the organization was not at the 'edge of chaos', because 'the flow of information' within the Centre was too low, 'the interconnections' were too moderate or even minimal, and its staff, 'agents', were too heterogeneous. The level of organizational uncertainty and chaos, the complexities of its client groups, the lack of adequate funding, the increasing demands for evidencing and paper work, all resulted in high level of anxiety among non-clinical and clinical staff alike, including myself. The setting was operating only on Bion and Hopper's basic assumptions; no creativity was possible (Bion, 1961; Hopper, 2002).

The experience of the third organization was different in thought-provoking ways. There were, to be sure, similar challenges. However, I found the Centre potentially more creative. On reflection, that seemed to arise from its community-based context and culture. Its staff group and its clients were heterogenous and interconnected enough to acknowledge and accept differences so that similarities could become profuse and creative and exciting new ideas could be generated.

Conclusion

Success in the first and third examples was based upon a set of 'holding' principles formed by a thoughtful, analytic, and holistic understanding, with reflective spaces for staff to facilitate thinking and working through of difficulties and most importantly, the maintenance of the safe enough/good enough context as a container to 'hold' staff and patients (Simpson, 2017b).

'Therapeutic presence', holding and containing in ways responsive and apposite to the particular organization, was the foundation for creative solutions to dilemmas and challenges.

Section V

Inside the practitioner's mind

How we frame praxis

In section V, we gain insight into the mind of the practitioner as s/he works.

Chris Powell engages us with a witty and self-deprecating 'real-life' account of the lived experience of consulting in chapter 13, using the experience of the Self to help teams make sense of things. His 'three questions' encapsulate some of the most commonly encountered organizational dynamics.

In chapter 14, Christine Oliver treats us to another thoughtful dissection of a consultancy intervention, focusing on the *communications* within the process, both within the community and within the consultants. *Communication* is a core group analytic idea, meaning any event which may communicate a meaning. Like Chris Powell, she gives us a clear sense of how she uses her Self in making sense of communications made simultaneously at many levels, and how she makes praxis decisions.

Frankly bringing to bear her own experience of consulting in equivocal circumstances, in chapter 15 Margaret Smith gives us a commentary on the work described in *Persecutor, victim, rescuer* (chapter three). She draws in further useful perspectives such as systemic family therapy, exploring more fully the 'five questions' which structure the vignette in chapter three. This chapter was also originally published in *Group Analysis vol 51(1)* and the reprinted material is by permission of SAGE Publications, Ltd.

Chapter 13

Inside out

Chris Powell

Introduction: three questions

I spend much of my working week sitting with groups of people, trying to talk and think with them about their work. While sat there, I repeatedly find myself wondering about one of three questions: whose side am I on? Am I being sufficiently group analytic? Am I doing any good? Occasionally I wonder about all three at once. I doubt this is what the people paying me expect me to do with my time and attention. In general, they hope I will help them solve some sort of problem, change what they are doing, or help them sustain something successful. So, presumably, they would like me to pay attention to what this group is saying. Then, it seems, they would like me to say or do something that will help, change, or sustain. I do try to do that. However, I find my attention wandering, and I have learnt to make use of that as a way of understanding what is going on. This is 'free floating attention' (Lorentzen, 2014; Foulkes and Anthony, 1957) and it is central to the way group analysts work. More of that later, but for the moment I want to underline that my mind wanders to these three questions probably more than anything else, while I work as an organizational consultant.

I shall explain what I mean by these three questions, why I think they recur so frequently, and also why I think they generally hold a clue, if not the entire answer, to what is happening in the organization I am working for at the time. To put it another way, I shall try and explain why a temporary neurotic fascination with myself and my feelings, opens a door into what is being experienced by other people in the group I am working with, even though the content of their words may be about something else altogether.

Question 1 – whose side am I on?

The first question – whose side am I on? – occurs whether working as an external consultant to an organization, or internally to an organization of which I am an employee, or an integrated part of its structure. Am I on the side of the people in front of me? Or of the senior person who commissioned me to do this work? Or should I represent the interests of the wider organization? Or am I fundamentally here to support the needs of the organization's customers or service users?

There is often a conflict between the interests of the people in the group and the demands on them from their organization and the recipients of their services, expressed with irritable frustration, or else hopeless helplessness. I start to wonder whether their complaint is fair, or whether management might actually have a point. I wonder whether the people they serve are unrealistically demanding, or whether group members should be grateful for having a job and get on with it. Sometimes, someone in the group asks me if I think their situation is fair. I am being asked to pick a side. The impulse to choose can be strong, partly because I, like most people, am predisposed to need to belong to something. However, taking a side affects the direction in which thought or action is encouraged: to take a stand or comply, stick to protocols and boundaries, or be flexible in responding to needs. I believe I might have influence in these decisions, so want to use it correctly.

So it is a tricky, curious question, particularly when I have already entered into a contractual relationship defining for whom I am working and what they want me to achieve. However, it seems, in that moment, to make sense to choose a side, because where I stand clearly influences what I do and how I am regarded in this group. I am there to help the group, so surely I would be on their side. Anyway, the issues being presented usually demand that any right-thinking person would take a particular position. They are rarely presented as a finely balanced dilemma with arguments on either side.

Question 2 – am I being group analytic?

This second is more troublesome because I trained and qualified as a group analyst some time ago and now hold positions of seniority as a group analyst. Surely I need not worry about this? Even if I am in the middle of making a mistake in a group, noticing and addressing mistakes is part of being a good group analyst. Moreover, I am working in a role which is a modification of group analysis. My therapy groups need me to be group analytic, but as an organizational consultant I just need to do whatever is effective in achieving the desired outcome. This question is also foolish since group analysis is not a manualized discipline; there is a wide disparity in practice, with an inability to agree definitively on basic questions such as whether to have a chair for absent group members. There is no rule book and no direct scrutiny. We submit ourselves to reflection on our work in supervision, continuing training and in peer reflection and appraisal, but no one reviews video of our work and marks us on content, process, and presentation ('Your interpretations are passingly insightful, but the use of what you regard as humour is both psychologically defensive and not funny. Must try harder, C minus').

Nonetheless I find myself worrying what other group analysts might think if they could see what I was doing, and generally imagine it would be unfavorable. At these moments, I am sure that if only I was a better group analyst, I would be able to help this group and solve this problem. This is unduly neurotic. Even for me.

Question 3 – am I doing any good?

The third question is more reasonable, and perhaps necessary, as I accept payment to achieve something. However, it does not feel compatible with the inquisitive curiosity of balanced evaluation. Rather it has a dead weight, bringing a feeling that not only am I not doing any good (and they would do better without me) but that there probably is no point to any of it; not just this consultation or support group, but whatever the work of the particular organization is too. What is more, it seems difficult to construct an answer based on anything more than the perceived responses of people who think you do a good job because they like you, or a bad job because they don't.

This question is not as neurotic as the second: this is how I earn my living. I need to be good enough for people to keep hiring me. Also, consultation and reflection groups are often marginal to organizational priorities. Although some organizations and professions have culturally embedded them, for the rest these groups tend to come about because there is a problem to fix or because they have a particular champion. Their existence is often questioned on grounds of cost and effectiveness. So, there is often a threat of the work ending, and with it that part of my income. I ignore money at my peril as it otherwise has powerful unconscious impacts, so it must be acknowledged and worked with. This third question is an existential one: I need work in order to eat; organizations must spend their resources of time and money effectively to survive. My work must have meaning.

What these questions mean to me

The question of whose side I am on translates as 'who is my client?' (see also chapters four, 15, and 17). This is critical in any form of service provision, and long experience as an organizational consultant tells me that the books are right – without a strong contract and clear understanding of who the client is and what they expect, the work will inevitably and invariably fail (Block, 2011). Except when it doesn't, because there is an exception to every rule; but the work will at least be complicated and troublesome without this clarity. However, clarity often seems impossible to acquire. In which case, my task is to be clear about what I am not clear about. Psychoanalytic thinking holds a high regard for the notion that to name something (such as in making an interpretation) is to begin to understand it, and to understand something is to begin to change it (Freud, 1923). In mythology, to know someone's name is to hold a power over them and so reveal their true nature (as in the biblical story of Jacob wrestling an angel), or to be able to supplant them (as in Isis overthrowing Ra by discovering his name and putting her son Horus on the throne). Working out the name of the client gives me a position from which to work with authority. Otherwise, naming the lack of clarity or complications of this, gives me a position from which to work provisionally. It allows the group to share my dilemma and think with me. If I do not do this, I am thrown between competing needs and concerns and quickly lose sight of what I am meant to be doing.

'Am I being group analytic?' means I am wondering 'am I getting this right?'. There are two closely connected fantasies that underpin this. First, the wish to get it right expresses a deep desire for the approval of others. I accept the analytic notion this may well have roots in the longing for parental approval. This is all the more compelling because, in an averagely happy and helpful developmental journey, parents inevitably frustrate, let down, and separate from their children. This leaves an imprint of wishing to return to an earlier blissful state where, as a baby, we had our parents' undivided attention and devotion and believed them omnipotent and infallible. Now, other childhoods are available, as are other reactions to this one. Nonetheless, although our mature thinking minds understand the need to discover what is right for ourselves, a less conscious bit lurks, that somehow believes we lost parental affection and attention through some failing on our part. So the fantasy goes: if only I could get things right, I would be returned to my rightful place in others' affections. (Ideally as King or Queen of all I survey!)

Second, this connects to another sort of fantastical thinking: that there is a magical formula, a silver bullet, a philosophers' stone, something that will put everything right. Or, more likely, not a thing but a person, the kind of person a mother might seem to a young baby, capable of meeting every need, protecting from all harm, and proffering unconditional love. The wish for a savior, whether religious, political, or romantic, is powerful the world over. So it is that in the crucible of workplace pressure and distress, the wish for a formula or person to solve it all reveals itself.

However, group analysis is neither a sacred method to be applied devotedly, nor a standard for compliance. Rather, my training has allowed me to offer a distinctive perspective and set of skills from which to explore an organization. A conceptual framework is helpful in trying to understand a problem or develop a solution. Nonetheless, it offers neither a magic wand nor a guaranteed outcome; just a way of trying to construct some meaning, some insight, some change, some acceptance.

The third question, of whether I am doing any good, translates as 'how can we (I, the group, and the organization) evaluate our work together?'. This is preoccupying because evaluation and outcome measurement is complex and contentious in the study of human activity. For example, in mental health the intended outcome, such as relieving stress and anxiety, is not always easily observable, and so many factors are involved it is impossible to say with great confidence that one thing, not another, is responsible for a change. Research in psychology is a highly developed, scientific field, but it is also one in which much is contested, accepted views change rapidly, and there is often discrepancy between professionals and people receiving treatment. To extend this a little further, medical science works hard to be rigorous and verifiably scientific. However, I notice that aeronautical engineers do not factor in a placebo effect in building a new jet engine. Anything focusing on people and their work has to examine and understand something – human nature – that is highly complex, and apparently mystifying. Anytime you need a good laugh, just ask a neuroscientist what consciousness is, or where the mind is located.

So, it is hardly surprising it is difficult to find a reliable way of evaluating the impact of a reflective group in an organization. Even asking the people involved if it is doing any good is complicated, because if we are inviting people to look at difficult thoughts, feelings, and behaviors, that might be uncomfortable or even emotionally painful. A group might be discomforted by what I ask them to think about (such as how they might be contributing to making a manager behave in an apparently punitive way). Accordingly, they might express discontent with me and my method, whilst also deriving a great deal of benefit, and even, on a good day, going on and changing how they deal with that situation. Equally, a group might feel very comfortable with conversations I initiate about what they struggle with and what they have in common (which may well turn quickly to how useless senior managers are). As a result, they may feel validated by me and my approach, but without learning anything useful or achieving any meaningful change.

For my livelihood and self-respect, I need to believe I make a positive contribution to the people and organizations I work with. For my continuing livelihood, I need them to believe that too. Trying to prove that can feel like a fool's errand.

Effing the ineffable – where these questions really come from

The ineffable are things and ideas that cannot be expressed by mere mortals. This might be because they are too complicated or taboo. The philosopher Roger Scruton writes a blog entitled *Effing the ineffable*, and Douglas Adams' holistic detective, Dirk Gently, proposes 'Let's think the unthinkable, let's do the undoable. Let's prepare to grapple with the ineffable itself, and see if we may not "eff it" after all' (Adams, 1987). In a group, my three questions seem unanswerable, and perhaps ineffable.

If the difficulties facing the people in a workplace group were easy, they would have solved them for themselves. It is both foolish and grandiose to think I can solve things for them, particularly through the quaint process of sitting quietly in a circle and waiting for someone to say something. The problems seem not just impossible, but even ineffable, beyond understanding or constructive discussion.

When I read a joint degree in Philosophy and Psychology, back in what now feels like the Middle Ages, I thought Psychology would be occupationally useful, while Philosophy was for my own entertainment. Certainly, in a career in organizational development and psychotherapy, a degree in Psychology is useful on my CV. However, day to day, I often get as much value from Philosophy, in particular from studying the work of Karl Popper. I can condense three years study into five words: everything I know is wrong. His contention is that since every great scientific theory has been proven subsequently to be wrong, we should not imagine we have achieved inviolate truth in whatever our latest idea or theory is. Rather we must put things to the test, find out what is wrong with them, and then improve them.

As I sit in my group, wondering about my three questions and their ineffability I realize they are not my questions at all. I usually do know who I am working for, how to work in a way that tends to work, and most people in most groups I run will find them helpful, one way or another.

The clue to the ineffable I have to 'eff' lies in the group analytic concept of countertransference. This is a development of the traditional psychoanalytic concept. In psychoanalysis, transference describes the ways a person projects their experiences and feelings of others, usually authority figures, onto a therapist, and so imagine him or her be like a character from their past. Countertransference describes the feelings evoked in the therapist by the person he or she is working with. In group analysis, however, with lots of people together in the same room, countertransference can be understood as any feelings that arise in the therapist, and are understood to be connected, one way or another, to what is going on in the group at that time (Prodgers, 1991).

Back in the context of organizational groups, this means that what I find myself thinking and feeling whilst working with a group could be about me, but is equally likely to be an expression of what is going on in the group – at least if I am self-aware enough to separate out my own tendencies and preoccupations.

This means I find myself thinking about these three questions because these are very often what people in my groups are thinking or feeling, but can't find a way to put into words to each other, or even to themselves. I end up thinking about these questions because the group members, individually or as a whole, are anxious or troubled about them.

Nietzsche asserted that 'thoughts are the shadows of our feelings – always darker, emptier and simpler' (Nietzsche, 2001, p. 137). My three questions emerge in my thoughts, because they arise from the complex feelings I pick up from the group about the struggles going on within and between people.

What the questions are in the mind of the group

Question 1 – whose side am I on? – is an expression of people in the group wondering 'where do my (i.e. their) loyalties lie?' Contemporary work practices with heightened efficiencies, internal markets, and global competition produce tensions between people in organizations, and between their work and the rest of their lives. So does a worker owe loyalty to their colleagues in challenging unreasonable demands from managers? Or to their line manager in achieving success for their department? Or to the organization as a whole, which is pressing for changes the immediate manager is resisting? Or to provide the best deal or service to their customers or service users? Or do their loyalties lie with themselves, their families, their lives outside work, and perhaps even their faith or culture? How can an individual caught in competing demands decide which come first? Your children might need you to make their tea and put them to bed, but what if you are told to finish your work before leaving and leaving becomes later and later, night after night?

Question 2 – am I being group analytic? – arises when people in the group are worried 'am I doing my job right?'. This is the problem of feeling unduly controlled, scrutinized, and at risk of punishment. The predominance of 'managerialism' (Enteman, 1993) in many organizations puts the focus on how things are done, rather than what is done, with disapproval and sanction being applied to failures of compliance. This leads to a preoccupation with doing the thing right, rather than doing the right thing. Gary Hamel identifies it in *Leading the Revolution* (2000) as causing loss of innovation, development, and ultimately profitability and market share. Nonetheless, as organizations face increasing competition and reduced funding, the demand for efficiency and compliance increases, leaving employees feeling insecure and impotent. To question this, though, is to challenge the organization's orthodoxy and often an exercise in futility.

Question 3 – am I doing any good? – equals a questioning in the group of 'what is the point of this?' People find themselves meeting impossible demands, insatiable needs, or producing meaningless goods or services, without even the gratification of appreciation from employers or managers. So they question whether they would be better off taking an easier job for less money. Or perhaps they would be better off taking an easier job for more money, and without the heartache of trying to make a positive contribution to the world?

Making use of the data

I often encounter an assumption that someone trained as a psychotherapist will be a good listener. This might extend to other professionals with backgrounds in human resources, organizational development, or certain types of management. This expectation is particularly high on a psychoanalyst or group analyst, with popular culture depicting analysts waiting patiently through long silences until the patient finally speaks. They are then expected magically to understand the true meaning of what is said and put someone on the path to recovery, insight, and – presumably – health, wealth, and happiness, through an incisive interpretation.

However, there are rarely instant fixes in either the psyche or organizations. Perhaps we shouldn't be listening all that well to the people in our groups. Rather, we should be listening to ourselves as much as to the people we are working with. Foulkes promoted the idea of free-floating discussion as the way the group begins to find a way to talk about what it really needs to talk about. Similarly, he proposed the group conductor listens using free-floating attention, as a way of hearing what may not be said (Foulkes and Anthony, 1957). So, we allow our attention and minds to wander, and notice where they go, and what thoughts and feelings are evoked. We attend not just to what the group is saying verbally, but also what is being said through feelings and non-verbal microcommunications, in subconscious and unconscious ways.

When I sit in a group, present and part of it, I become connected to the members of a group, and can begin to pick up the preoccupations they can't put into words for themselves. I am then left with the real three questions for myself:

> What's really being said (or unsaid)?
> How can I usefully bring this to the group's attention?
> When shall I do that?

By the time I've considered these, sometimes the group has moved on to something else, so I have to decide whether to bring them back. Sometimes the group has resolved the issue for itself, which is the better, empowering way, but does make it look like I'm earning money for doing nothing. That said, it turns out these things often aren't resolved if I'm not there, thinking hard, even if saying little. So perhaps just holding the group and thinking hard is a useful contribution.

Then sometimes, the group is still just going around in circles, repeating itself, worrying away at a moan, or despairing of a solution, and so I find a way to say aloud something about what I've noticed. Occasionally, I miss the mark, people are confused and I have to think again. Sometimes though, it turns out that what I've been worrying about is what they've been worrying about too without realizing it, and the opportunity is taken to say what had not been said, to look at what the real problem might be, and explore the real question at hand.

Chapter 14

Context and the interpretive act

Developing the language of the matrix for working in and with organizations

Christine Oliver

'The monastic life is something quite mysterious – it gives things to the church, often despite the people who are living it'

(from a text of the community's history)

Introduction

This chapter, taking the Batesonian notion that there is no meaning without context, offers a contextual framework for group analytic practice in organizations, developing the notion of communication as a contextualized unit of meaning (Thornton, 2010, p. 49). I define interacting units of meaning as *interpretive acts*, emphasizing the unique interpretation individuals make in any given communicative moment, relating to group-as-a-whole themes, shaped consciously and unconsciously by histories, the social unconscious, and by the cultural, relationship, and identity narratives and patterns alive in the interacting dynamic matrix of which, as a consultant, one is always part.

The chapter describes a consultancy process with a community of Anglican monks, with whom I have worked for eighteen years, now preparing for an important decision. I share how we consultants made key decisions and explore contexts and consequences of those decisions, developing the language of the matrix through linking particular *interpretive acts* to the contexts that shape them.

The community

The monastery began its community life in the late 19th century with commitments to engage in theological and political innovation, social justice, serving the Church, and sharing the fruits of that engagement with the world. Daily life was characterized by the monastic tradition – mass, prayer life, and other routines. There were several houses in England and abroad; and a theological college offered a unique experience of monastic life to those in training. However, over the years fewer novices have arrived and work abroad diminished. Houses and works closed down until only the mother house remained; they became smaller and more 'family like'. A narrative is that God was calling them to find new ways to live community life. They developed partnerships, sharing their site with other organizations; and they developed their hospitality to guests and visitors. They are now assisted by a general manager, catering manager, and many other staff. They are about 15 in number.

I meet with the community with a colleague, for a few days, twice a year, and our agreed role as consultants is to facilitate dialogue in relation to the many themes and decisions of their daily life, for instance – whether they should build a new monastery; the implications for them of the ordination of women; the relationship between college and community. Our original engagement related to an entrenched conflict causing high levels of distress and polarization. Now the task was to help them to prepare, through dialogue, for election of a Superior (leader of community).

Not a typical 'organization', the community's communicative matrix is rich. Although there are comings and goings, many of the monks have been living and working together for forty years. They have well established narratives and patterns of interaction.

Context, the interpretive act, and the matrix

The relationship between context and meaning is central for group analysts with their core interest in the 'nuances of interpersonal communication' (Thornton, 2017b). It is the labeling or framing of a context that helps us give meaning to a communication exchange; and developing awareness about our framing of contexts provides us with opportunity for reflection on our communication choices (Oliver, 2005).

Bateson (1972) highlights the distinction between the digital and analogic as two separate but connected levels of context: digital – the content of a message – and analogic – its relational meaning. However, in a communication exchange, there are multiple contexts shaping how a communication is experienced and interpreted, not just the content and relational meaning of a message (Pearce, 2007; Cronen, Johnson and Lannamann, 1982). Dalal (1998) proposes that we not objectify context in considering how our experience influences our interpretations within our social worlds. Here, inspired by Bateson (1972), Dalal (1998), Cronen, Johnson, and Lannamann (1982), and Pearce (2007), I am treating context in narrative terms, as a frame for giving meaning to experience. Our frames are storylines which can be enriched or stifled within the communication dynamic of which we are a part; we can feel weighed down with layers of constraint, our reactions inevitable, rather than reflected-upon responses that reach toward conscious, contextual purposes.

Building on Bateson's original formulation, Pearce (2007) and others (Cronen, Johnson and Lannamann, 1982; Oliver, 2005), have developed a framework they call Coordinated Management of Meaning, for making sense of communication and for orientation to action, connecting macro and micro contexts in a communication exchange. Taking this further, I have developed the notion of the *interpretive act*, referring to the *emotional response* to a communication, the *meaning* given and the consequent *act* of communication. The *interpretive act* represents a reflexive opportunity for exploring links between emotion, meaning, and action and higher-level contexts that shape them (Frosh and Barraitser, 2008). This exploration can take many forms in organizational consultancy: a focus for curious inquiry; a frame for sense making and a tool for intervention.

To illustrate: the consultants were told that recently, in a group discussion about a shift in management arrangements for looking after guests, one monk stamped on his hearing aid. If we think of that as an *interpretive act*, we might hypothesize: an emotional response of *anxiety* about loss of agency (previously the monks themselves had been responsible for guests); an unconscious meaning of '*I don't want to hear this*', with the consequent action of *stamping on the hearing aid*.

If we imagine some contextual storylines shaping this response:

> *Culture:* monks finding it difficult that HR decisions about staff involve confidentiality; many feel excluded from power and this creates anxiety and feelings of loss.
>
> *Relational:* discomfort and confusion for some in being both 'host to' and 'guest of' a staff member. This change in relational dynamic symbolizes deterioration in ability and power.
>
> *Personally:* as the community ages there is, for many, personal fear of dependence and loss of control. . . 'the old are getting markedly old: two are confined to their room through illness; one keeps falling over; one has gone deaf as a post and does funny things; one can hardly walk; one rambles on about being near to death but carries on and runs the book shop marvelously' (Superior).

These contextual storylines are imbued with socially unconscious fears and defenses in relation to death and survival providing a context for enactments at organizational/community level.

These inevitably partial observations illustrate the framework, connecting small *interpretive acts* and the contexts that shape them, through sense making. The framework will be elaborated on further in the narrative of the consultancy process below.

First, I propose that our *interpretive acts*, over time, often become *patterns of figuration* sustaining or challenging storylines of organizational culture, relationship, and identity (Elias, 1994). Elsewhere I have offered a framework for hypothesizing about *patterns of figuration* and how they link to organizational contexts and have proposed that this can give meaning to the dynamic matrix (Nitzgen and Hopper, 2017; Oliver, 2016, 2019).

> *Reactive patterns* are repeated linkages between *feeling, thinking and action* characterized by unconscious defense, mistrust, paranoia, hate . . . polarization, and poor reflective capacity. A *culture* of dysfunctional mirroring contextualizes competitive/defensive *relationships* where the position of the other is delegitimized, further contextualizing *self* narratives of exclusive legitimation, difficulty in tolerating difference, uncertainty, ambivalence and poor discernment for decision and action.
>
> *Paradoxical patterns* are in a form, inspired by Hopper's 'non-dialectical oscillation' (1991) and the notion of strange loops (Cronen, Johnson and Lannamann, 1982), of a figure of eight, where patterns of *feeling, thinking, and action* stimulate the opposite meaning at each level, contextualized by processes of splitting and fragmentation so that when an individual or group are connected to one experience of *feeling, thinking and action*, they become disconnected from awareness of its opposite. *Cultural, relational* and *self* narratives are contradictory, ambivalent or polarized.
>
> *Reflexive patterns* are those characterized by the relational qualities described by Schlapobersky and Pines (2009) – mutuality, fairness, understanding, and reciprocity, but also by reflexive abilities whereby individuals and groups show preparedness to reflect on and evaluate the ways their own *narratives* and *feeling, thinking and action patterns*, contribute to the organization. A *culture* of functional mirroring and reflective learning contextualizes *relationships* of self/other legitimation and empathy, linked to *self* narratives of partial legitimation, i.e. the person takes a position of humility in relation to their own views and experiences and is curious about those of the other. Tolerance of difference, ambivalence and uncertainty becomes possible at cultural, relational and personal levels.
>
> (Oliver, 2019)

The linkage of emotion, meaning, and action responses can represent a typical *reactive pattern of figuration* for this community whereby storylines of survival, loss, and increasing dependence are denied, and acted out through projection of responsibility and control onto staff, and complaints that community leaders are initiating unnecessary changes, polarizing community members into those doing things to others and those that are 'done to'.

I will now describe the consultancy process, sharing the consultants' formulations and decisions about dialogue processes in relation to observations and sense making about *interpretive acts* and their contexts.

Consultancy narrative

The Superior (leader) and Prior (deputy), informed us that before the election for Superior (every five years) the community had agreed to focus on the following 'constitutions':

- The community's vocation in relation to church and society
- The particular needs of the community in terms of development, critical appraisal, or revision
- The gifts, qualities, and abilities perceived to be desirable in a Superior at that time.

Plenary 1

We invited the community, in a free-floating discussion, to think with us what would be most important to address over the three days in the context of the constitutions.

The first to speak was an elderly monk saying there was an 'elephant in the room . . . we have a tremendous problem with guests'. He spoke of the volume of guests, the busyness of the site, and the exhaustion of many; visitors were hungry and thirsty for what they found in the monastery but the community was *burdened by its own success*. Another agreed, adding that the Superior is supposed to be a pastor but seems now to be an administrator.

We noted the articulation of a binary here – pastor or administrator.

Another monk wondered how each might take up their mutual responsibility for living together in community, suggesting that this might mean not saying 'somebody else must do something about the guests'.

This seemed to be an attempt to take responsibility for integration of new ways of functioning with guests, rather than seeing guests as taking away from their calling.

Another added 'when we are busy looking outwards, the ability to get together is undermined'.

Our observation was that it was not easy for the community to 'get together' even when they were not overwhelmed by guests – the problem of 'getting together' projected onto guests.

Consultants' discernment

From these contributions and others, we perceived different storylines about changes facing the monastery in relation to staff, visitors, partners, and guests. Some felt 'done to'; others were encouraging a narrative of agency. This ambivalence no doubt included us consultants in its scope, one of the monks saying 'you always make us talk'. The election for Superior could become a potential container for the storyline about those in authority making people do things against their will, a storyline undermining and negating one's own and others' authority.

We formulated a paradoxical pattern linked to the interpretive act: 'we are burdened by our own success' with its associated feelings of ambivalence, anxiety, and frustration. In the context of fear about survival, the community developed its ability to welcome guests, for instance by providing a new church, B&B, a venue for weddings, retreats, and so on. Thus, the community became even more attractive to 'outsiders' and this encouraged a hope in the survival of community. However, before long, there was a felt experience of being flooded by guests which undermined the experience of community, the very thing that people were attracted to, which led to fear about its survival, and so on.

Plenary 2

We communicated in plenary that we hypothesized a dilemma which could become a paradoxical, stuck pattern at its worst but did not need to -, if it could be thought about together. We presented it in the following way:

'Burdened by our own success'

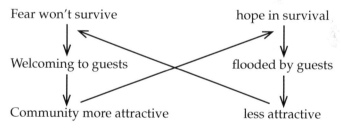

We made it clear that we were hypothesizing, not diagnosing their dilemma, i.e. that meaning was emergent not fixed and this could be one vehicle to explore the constitutions. We proposed that in so far as this pattern characterized their experience, it might be held in place by certain storylines. For instance:

A *cultural* dynamic of natives and immigrants, insiders and outsiders, included and excluded – a prevalent conscious and unconscious dynamic in society at large.

A *relational* dynamic which privileged the internal relationships amongst themselves – guests and so forth on the outside, rather than living alongside, as part of their vocation.

A *personal* dynamic characterized by fear of loss of the essential nature of community (vocation) – a diluting of power and energy, laid at the feet of guests, but an inevitable consequence of changes in the life of religious orders, individual ageing, and the demands of contemporary living.

The task we gave the community was to explore in groups of four:

First, what do you recognize of this pattern and how might you adapt it so that it fits more with your experience?

Second, to transcend the pattern and its thinking, what is required of you as community members and what is required of the Superior? How do you need to think differently and how do you need to act?

We invited them to report back to plenary after an hour working on this in small groups and said that later, building on this exercise, we would work more directly on the election of Superior.

Response from group 1

The core question for them was not about survival but about how to continue to respond to God's call in the new circumstances. They questioned whether they were actually burdened or whether they just thought they were and then questioned the assumption that being burdened was problematic. They suggested that 'running the show' was a modern form of burden that could get in the way of the spiritual burden which they wanted to have. They proposed that authority needs to be shared so that the Superior can be supported.

Response from group 2

They recognized words like fear and survival, welcoming and flooding, but overall saw their busyness with guests as productive and as a 'ministry of hospitality' and a welcome source of income. They recognized that operations had got bigger while their numbers got smaller and that people in their eighties cannot be so involved with guests and can then feel excluded. They emphasized the spiritual dimension of hospitality – that for St Benedict, guests *are* Christ. They acknowledged that negative perceptions could rob them of the spiritual dimension. They suggested it is important to find a middle ground that enables all to feel included without feeling burdened, and felt that the burden of authority was not sufficiently shared.

Response from group 3

They did not necessarily feel that the volume of guests was a burden. Someone said it was their vocation to look tired and that the aggravation they did feel said more about them and what they felt about 'the life'. They needed a balanced life and needed to learn better how to organize their time e.g. in their own rooms – reading, study, prayer. It was felt that if they did that better they might be less likely to think of guests as intrusive. At the moment there was more of a sense of recharging in rooms and then going into battle.

Consultant observations

We observed the ability in these responses to interrogate assumptions implied in the language of 'burden' and 'survival'; less projection of responsibility onto Superior in the language of 'shared burden of authority' and in owning their own difficulties in managing time and space for themselves; and potentially a move towards integrating the sacred and profane split of pastoral care and administration.

We decided to focus more directly on the constitutions, building on the dialogue experienced so far.

Process: in the same small groups for 30 minutes then moving into plenary with goldfish bowl structure.

Task: Building on the work from the morning, how has that dialogue stimulated and developed your thinking about the constitutions?

The dialogue included:

MONK 1 – I was reminded of X Superior who used to push letters down the side of the sofa and would 'just sit' when he didn't know what to do. My tip for the next Superior is to sit and think.

MONK 2 – is it just the responsibility of the Superior to be pastoral or is it everyone's responsibility? As brothers we need to take ownership of that.

MONK 3 – I was mildly disturbed yesterday as many brothers seemed to be worried about the future – I don't share that worry. We have issues and questions but I am confident that the Lord will provide and be faithful.

MONK 2 – I value the way you have put it – the fear was quickly attached to the busyness of having guests but this is God's place and we can work with it. The foundation of the community is to live together – this is a gift. It is not perfect but there can be a lurking fantasy that if we elect the right person all the problems will go away.

MONK 4 – on reality – it is going to be one of our number; none of us are geniuses or supermen; it will be a human being.

MONK 5 – generosity both ways is important. I should not be ready to say 'not him again and not that again'.

MONK 6 – one of my worries about busyness is our ability to hang on to our music tradition. The history of this needs to be more shared – and the responsibility for it.

MONK 7 (current Superior) – when I was elected I felt I was a coat that everybody climbed into. I'm aware of many things that I don't do well or I don't do. All you can do is be yourself warts and all. Though there is a desire to learn and grow, there are limits.

MONK 8 – we have to keep working at relating so that we can be warts and all. If I'm going to live authentically, there will be bits I dislike in myself and others as well.

Consultant observations

We had observed an underlying force in the group for splitting the sacred and profane – pastoral/administrative; a pure life/life contaminated by having to earn money – but there seemed here a stronger force for withdrawal of projection and integration. We took the view that the next part of the work could be more self reflective, focused on their own transference and tendency for projection. We called the next exercise: 'me and my inner Superior'.

Process: In 3s, in turn, A interviews B and C keeps the process on track, offering reflections and keeping to time.

Stance invited: be curious, exploratory, inquire into detail.

The questions to explore:

How have you related to present and past Superiors and what does that say about you and your history?

What did you perceive you needed from them? And how did you deal with these needs being/not being met?

What do you need to be conscious of in yourself in relation to your interaction with Superior and community?

What do you wish for the role of Superior having reflected in this way and how would you like to evolve in your relationship to Superior?

Some reflections following their interviews:

MONK 1 – there needs to be care for the Superior when he finishes. The ending has been disastrous in the past for recent Superiors. They have felt wounded and have needed a year to get the poison out of their system!

Concern/reparation for Superior.

MONK 2 – it could be helpful if the Superior goes away for a year!

MONK 3 – what struck me last time was – there is no moment of renewal, no thanksgiving or celebration. There needs to be a sacramental moment of letting go.

Gratitude for work of Superior; concern about new Superior.

MONK 4 – it is important that we accept the gift of what is offered now – it may not be the gift that I prayed for but it is the gift that I have been given, whether it is a new Superior or a re-election.

Lack of idealization; withdrawal of projection.

MONK 1 – the Superior carried the community story because we were not sharing authority enough.

MONK 2 – owning one's own wounds requires a Superior who is pastoral and notices sadness and has his door open.

CONSULTANT – it may be useful to interrogate the notion of the pastoral.

MONK 5 – I'm so glad you said that. I'm tired of this idea of a nanny Superior. He is a shepherd who leads his sheep to new pastures.

MONK 6 – the pastor knows the sheep are on the mountainside but from time to time he needs to help a sheep who has got stuck and it is very difficult to get to him.

MONK 8 – the Superior can only be the Superior of the community now. We are more fragile than we were – that shapes the task.

MONK 9 – in what ways are we fragile?

MONK 8 – age, energy. I've been accused of impatience but I'm 32 and some people can barely walk. The big dog gets tired and lays his paw on the puppy.

MONK 7 (current Superior) – should I leave the room at this point so that brethren can say things they may be inhibited from with me here?

CONSULTANT – I was actually thinking it would be helpful to hear from you at this stage rather than you leaving the room.

MONK 7 – ok – I can't imagine being wounded or poisoned and can't imagine going away for a year – this is my family. It exercises me, the gap between how the role of Superior is seen on the outside, the patterns that are seen and the actual experience of it which is messy.

Conclusion

This chapter demonstrates the value of taking notice of acts of interpretation and highlighting them in organizational consultancy, for making sense and for design and facilitation. In this particular consultancy process, *interpretive acts* have been taken to represent themes for the group-as-a-whole (while acknowledging that there are counter themes) which can be cultivated in consultancy exercises designed to develop *patterns of figuration*, all dimensions of the emergent dynamic matrix. A focus on the *interpretive act* can enable increased collective and individual consciousness of *patterns of figuration* including dynamics of splitting, transference, and projection. Consultancy processes can be designed to enable meta-communication in dialogue, rendering reflexive *patterns of figuration* more likely with withdrawal of projections, integrating of splits, developments in humility in relation to self and other. New contextual frames become possible in this meta-communicative process. In this case, monks took responsibility, becoming more able to treat each other as persons, neither idealizing nor denigrating the Superior, perhaps making it less likely that the new Superior would become a 'coat that everybody would climb into'.

Of course, in consultancy work, questions of contract, trust, and task are key. It takes time for consultants to engage organizational members in processes where they will take the risks required for development. This community, in engaging in dialogue of this kind, is working not just on their own behalf but also on behalf of the Anglican Church; working on patterns that can characterize Christian life in its many forms, including the split between the sacred and profane.

Chapter 15

Joining the organizational game

Five questions to guide consultants

Margaret Smith

Christine Thornton's five questions serve as a tool aiding the consultant to recognize and avoid joining an unconscious organizational game. This game scapegoats staff and avoids addressing the underlying management issues. Here I use the five questions to analyze the story told in chapter three, *Persecutor, Victim, Rescuer*. In spite of these dynamics, the consultant was able to make a meaningful contribution.

The five questions

In organizational commissions, there is always a tension between the explicit objectives and the commissioner's unconscious expectations. Success relies on making the latter more conscious. The five questions, shown with their system of sub-questions, offer a structuring of enquiry into overt and covert cues and clues – data we automatically or systematically collect – about client expectations. They are more fully explored in *Beyond the theory of everything: Conversation, group analysis and five questions to choose theory in action with teams* (Thornton, 2019).

Here are the five core questions:

- Who wants the team to be worked with?
- What is the purpose of the work with the team?
- What is organizational context of this team?
- Who or what am I invited to be?
- What is undiscussable?

Chapter three, *Persecutor, Victim, Rescuer*, is a worked example of the five questions.

The system of five questions

1 Who wants the team to be worked with?

- Where has the impetus come from?
- Who has made the decision?
- How far are team members signed up?
- Is there anything in the decision-making process that is characteristic of team relationships?
- Who is your key contact?
- Will everyone in the team attend, and if not, who will attend?
- Will members have a choice about attending? How many people will be involved?[1]

2 What is the purpose of the work with the team?

- How has that purpose been arrived at?
- How does that purpose relate to the purpose of the team's work?
- What ideas of our work's purpose do team members have?
- Is the purpose realistic given the number, length, and frequency of coaching sessions?

3 What is the organizational context of this team?

What do we know about this context and the demands on it? What evidence do we see of these factors playing out with this team? How could we learn more?

Everything is a potential communication. Notice which patterns are striking and most often repeated:

- What comes through the organization's front door?
- What are the contextual demands and constraints on the organization?
- What else is going on in the organization?

4 Who or what am I invited to be?

This question is about use of the self, how you use your own bodily and/ or emotional responses alongside your thinking to understand what is going on, including:

- What feelings and thoughts do I predominantly have in the room?
- What feelings am I left with afterwards?
- What speech/action do I feel impelled towards in response to this team?
- How can I understand these impulses, and what is the most useful response to that?

Another word for this is 'counter-transference'. Its subtler, harder-to-grasp aspects give vital information about what might be happening *unconsciously* between you and the team members. First identify what you feel, and then notice whether your feeling mirrors something in the team, organization, or broader system. Consider:

- Are they expecting to get from you what they do not have themselves?
- Are they expecting from you what others expect of them?
- Is there any parallel in this organization to my experience of it? (e.g. does it reflect what customers expect or get, or mirror a threat?)
- Are they communicating some feelings about the work or the state of their industry?

Working cleanly with countertransference requires consultation with a trained colleague or group of colleagues.

5 What is undiscussable (Argyris, 1980, 1990)?

Undiscussables are 'what everyone knows' about organizational life which everyone also 'knows' must not be spoken about. When looking for undiscussables, questions to attend to are:

- What is the gap between what we say and what we do?
- What is not being said?
- Round what topics is there a shift?
- What statements are impossible to disagree with?
- When does the group deaden, or get over-lively?

You can ask people:

- What you are holding back on?
- What are the unwritten rules here?
- What do you say about it to your best friend?
- What would a visiting alien make of it?

Highlight paradoxes, incongruities, and gaps; explore implications; attend to developing members' capacities to express the undiscussables.

Though the five questions are particularly useful at the opening 'contracting' stage, *all* organizational work requires continuous re-evaluation and re-contracting as the team or organization shifts and develops, especially if your work is successful.

Christine Thornton bravely presents an old case in order to outline learning about working in organizations (pages 31–39). She captures some realities of the consultant's experience that may feel familiar to many practitioners in this field. Asked to provide some management development training to managers, she describes a CEO without curiosity about why the managers were 'difficult', or about what her own part in this might be. She just wanted someone to sort out a 'problem' team who were not behaving in the way she wanted, after what was for the managers a major and traumatic change.

Familiar too was the description of the consultant as someone who was able to recognize and name what was undiscussable in the organization. The chapter recognizes but understates the importance of the consultant just being there as a witness and as the one who could create enough containment for the managers to be able to think in a context where some were seen as not as good as others. This was quite an achievement.

The questions she poses at the beginning are useful ones. The first: 'Who wants the team to be worked with?' was useful for me when I worked with organizational leaders who would ask for an intervention for the team they were managing. It was very rarely that they asked for consultation. More usually, the request was for stress management, help with a 'challenging patient' or staff mediation, depending on the team dynamic. I learnt very quickly that to take these requests at face value was joining their organizational game; complying with the request was often to scapegoat staff members for problems impacting on their work but outside their sphere of control. What helped me to gain my bearings was a paper by the family therapist Mara Selvini Palazzoli (1984) who conducted a research group of consultants who pooled their 'mistakes' from consultancy work, to produce some guidelines both on pitfalls and on good practice. One practice suggestion was to view the person who made the request for the intervention as the loser in an organizational game. In *Persecutor, victim, rescuer*, the Human Resources Director (HRD) might be viewed as the loser in an organizational battle between the CEO and the managers. She could not square the circle in the organizational game and asked for help with this impossible task. In her eyes the consultant was inevitably doomed to fail in her task too.

Thornton rightly shows that the question 'What is the purpose of the work with the team?' highlighted the tensions between the CEO and the managers. Her subsequent work with the managers achieved a considerable amount for them but was not what the CEO or HDR were looking for. That would have been impossible. It is under these circumstances that consultants can be left with the feeling that they have failed.

It would have been interesting to have heard more about the pressures faced by the CEO, and how these linked with the task of the intervention, articulated as to get the management team 'in line'. We could then think about tensions between the pressures experienced by the management team where their attention was on resources and day to day management of services provided for the victims of crime. Unfortunately, this CEO did not seem to have the resources herself to pay attention to this.

The answer to the third question: 'What is the organizational context of this team?' is useful in drawing attention away from the problem and towards what was happening in the wider setting. The vignette implies that there had been a hostile merger where different agencies, run by these 'difficult' managers were brought under one umbrella because of cuts to funding. If this was the case, these managers would have lost their autonomy and their experience might be analogous to grown up children returning home after living independently, with all the tensions that can bring.

Bramley (1990) suggests that when consultants work with staff groups, the role that they get drawn into is often one which is needed but missing in the organization. What was missing in this organization from the managers' perspective, was someone who could contain them and help them to develop their capacity to work together as a team in a constructive way. It is to the consultant's credit that she developed enough trust to be able to create a holding environment which allowed this to happen.

The fourth question is: 'Who or what am I invited to be?' For the CEO, it was to fix her problem which she saw as her management team; the consultant's task was to sort out the managers. The HRD wanted something that was not possible. Roberts distinguishes between three aspects of the primary task. The first, the normative primary task is the official task the organization asks the consultant to undertake. This was to provide training to managers. The existential primary task is what the consultant believed she was doing, to improve communication and reduce hostilities, and this was acknowledged to have been achieved. The third was the phenomenological primary task which is often unconscious and can only be inferred from behavior (Roberts, 1994a). In this case, the phenomenological primary task of the HRD was for the consultant to create conformity. What they were asking for was a fix for their impossible problem but it may be that, as much as anything else, the HRD needed support and containment in a role where she felt expected to square the circle between the CEO and the Managers. What the consultant did achieve was better relationships between managers who were the beneficiaries of the training; many were able to take in what was on offer.

I liked the final question: 'What is undiscussable?' because it takes the consultant immediately to the heart of their task, to work with what is operating below the surface of the organization. It generates fear, anger, or anxiety in the staff involved and blocks communication. The task of the consultant is to make conscious these aspects of the organizational dynamics by tuning into their countertransference. Being unable to express powerful feelings limits the capacity of the organization to communicate in a way that can resolve its dilemmas. By coming from outside of the organization, Thornton was able to see its task in the wider context and recognize the dynamics that were being enacted through the Drama Triangle of victim, perpetrator, and rescuer, which could not be thought about inside the organization itself. One aspect of this dynamic was an unconscious game which the organization was playing, seeing people as either OK or not OK (Berne, 1964). The HRD invited the consultant to provide training in order to change the managers by upskilling and improving communication. This would move them from being not OK to being OK, that is engaging in adult to adult relationships. However, what she really wanted was compliance, which involves parent-child relationships with her and the CEO in Area. This game, compliance, puts someone in the role of a child expected to conform. However, what happens to people put in this position is that they comply some of the time but rebel at others, the very opposite of what is being asked for. Thornton recognized that this was an impossible task. As Foulkes said, 'In order to see things whole, we have I believe, to see it in relation to a greater whole so that we can step outside of that which we want to see' (Foulkes, 1990b). From the vantage point of being outside the organization, we may also wonder what this organizational dynamic is playing out for our wider society, fed daily by the media stories of victims and perpetrators, some of whom may have passed through the services this institution provides.

Barnes (1994) talked about the importance of starting by taking a history of the organization as a part of the initial process of negotiating entry so that the intervention can be thought about in the wider historical context within the organization. What was also undiscussable in the task assigned to the consultant was the loss of autonomy that the Managers had experienced. The CEO seemed blind to the mourning and shame this stirred up in the managers. This reminds me of families where a child is seen as troublesome after a central figure in their life dies or is lost through a traumatic divorce. The child's experience is often that the pain of their loss is felt to be invisible. For Managers who are told to make changes, this implies that their former way of working wasn't good enough. Shame may then prevent them valuing the good things that they have achieved in the past. I have found that when invited in to work with staff who are resistant to organizational change, it is only when they are able to mourn the loss of what they had to give up and celebrate their former achievements that they are able to think in a constructive way about the future.

Thornton emphasizes the importance of having a holistic approach to organizational interventions where she works with the leader as well as the team. Using the vignette, she provides an illustration of what can happen when this dual approach is not taken. This is in line with Palazzoli's research, which recommends that in order to avoid seeing their work 'die quiet and unnoticed deaths', consultants should respect the hierarchical order and start any intervention by engaging the team at the top of the organization. We will also need to circulate information within the organization as widely as possible and promote alliances where both parties gain from working together around specific issues (Palazzoli, 1984). The dilemma for the consultant arises when this is not possible. Then we are in a position where we have to choose either to withdraw or to work towards what is achievable with those people who are willing to engage.

In this organization, the seemingly self-protective wall around the CEO meant that the organizational game, victim, persecutor, and rescuer, and any parallel process between this and the organizational task, to support victims, could not be thought about. The consultant may have felt that she was playing with one hand tied behind her back. However, what was achieved through her containing and thoughtful engagement did improve communication, something which Foulkes said was the route to change. Thornton's intervention, which achieved what the HRD requested, could never achieve the impossible, but (to misquote Winnicott) it is an example, of 'good enough consultancy'.

Note

1 Larger groups have additional dynamics requiring careful management.

Section VI

Praxis, power, and ethical issues in team working

Section VI on ethical issues continues to give insight into practitioner thinking processes and focuses on the dynamics of power in organizations.

Ewa Wojciechowska opens it with a 'social dream' (Lawrence, 2004) linked to the turning of blind eyes, a constant pressure on the reflective practitioner in human services. Exploring the dynamics of power and associated inhibition, her exploration of boundaries in chapter 16 shows us how taking the risk of opening our eyes and refraining from 'managing' responses can be richly productive for the quality of mental health services and the well-being of professionals.

Gwen Adshead and Ian Simpson bring their many years of experience leading departments and consulting to mental health services to a consideration of the contextual politics, ethics, and values of this work today. Their chapter 17 highlight the boundaries of the work and some of the dilemmas facing practitioners; their dialogue reflects both common analysis and differing strategies.

The validity of differing experiences and perceptions is a central tenet of group analysis, and in chapter 18 Vincent Leahy and Abdullah Mia share their experiences of working with difference and power dynamics in many organizational settings. They face the difficulties and limitations squarely, offering real-life descriptions of dilemmas and impasses, alongside analysis offering sage advice.

Chapter 16

Turning a blind eye

Some thoughts on personal and professional boundaries in groups in mental health settings

Ewa Wojciechowska

I awake from a terrifying dream. Convinced that the dream is real, I now hold in my hand the title of this chapter. It is my eyeball (which has been taken out by a shard of smoky glass) and I watch as it bounces on to the floor, under the furniture and out of sight.

Introduction

2017 saw an apparent increase in situations met with the 'turning of a blind eye'. The three wise monkeys are evoked: 'see no evil, hear no evil, speak no evil' in response to wrongdoing. Disclosure of serious sexual wrong-doing by a high-profile film producer has prompted vigorous public debate as to how men conduct themselves with women. It seems that a tipping point has been reached. But the tipping point was a long time in the reaching, as it emerged that many people had known about this man and his behaviors over many years. On the face of it, this represents several blind eyes being turned. There will be various reasons for this. Some will simply have not believed what was being said; others may have had some personal allegiance; probably the most influential factor though, will have been that to go up against this man was 'career suicide'. Collision with power often has a paralyzing effect on those involved and makes it more difficult for issues to be addressed.

I have explored previously (Hartley and Kennard, 2009) the management of personal and professional boundaries as the facilitator in a residential mental health unit; how to assist the staff in making sense of their work with difficult patients, in difficult times, in organizations struggling to survive and to do a good enough job. Here, I want to develop this theme further, considering some unconscious processes which play a part in boundary transgressions, and offering some thoughts about how group analytic and other ideas might help us. I shall illustrate this with the use of vignettes.

Boundaries

> 'Visitors to the Grand Canyon note that they are protected from falling into the chasm by a guard rail placed strategically at the edge of the canyon. This safety measure allows children (and adults) to play and enjoy themselves while being at minimal risk for catastrophe. Although (professional) boundaries in general are more flexible than a guard rail, in some areas, such as sexual contact, they are just as unyielding'.
>
> (Gabbard and Lester, 2003)

Foulkes (1964) advises us to always notice what is *inside* the boundary and what is *outside* and why?

But when is a boundary not a boundary? How elastic can it be? Why do people choose to ignore or deny the importance of a boundary? What needs are being served? What are the unconscious processes at work? How people manage boundaries gives us important information, to be utilized in the analysis of the person or group.

There is an important distinction between *boundary crossings* and *boundary violations* (Myers and Gabbard, 2008). The former occur when normal boundaries are crossed in some way which may be beneficial to the client, while the latter involve transgressions that are harmful *to* or exploitative *of* the patient or group member. These may be sexual or non-sexual. They are usually repetitive and the therapist discourages any exploration of them. By contrast, boundary crossings can be benign and even helpful breaks in the frame, if available for analysis. See also pages 241, 242–43.

An example of boundary violation

A young nurse, well qualified and brimful of ideas of how to improve life for the patients, arrived at the hospital. Over the next 6–12 months, things moved quickly. She became Deputy Ward Manager and took under her wing a young (and severely disturbed) patient. She made herself available to this troubled young woman for private conversations and the like and brushed aside any attempts to explore the nature of their relationship.

One day she absconded with the patient to join a faith group overseas. She was subsequently sanctioned by her professional registering body.

Personal and professional boundaries

'I don't know if I am bringing my real self or my professional self to this group. And what is the difference?'[1]

(A staff group member)

Within the *personal* boundary, we might think of private thoughts, hopes, fears, beliefs, attitudes, and internalized experiences – in short, all the psycho-social components which make up the person. *Professional* boundary refers to a defined task and role, within given values, behaviors, and ethos – a prescribed way of being for the carrying out of a particular role or task.

The 'personal' impinges on the 'professional' and vice versa, both in the present and the past. People often talk 'of taking their work home', but less often about taking their home to work; just as work may flow into non-work time and contexts, so vice versa. Work in the human services field is very largely carried out through the making of relationships and the subsequent examining of these. There are always slings and arrows to be borne, and the advice is often heard: 'don't take it personally': but, what do we mean by not taking it personally? How else would we take it?

Managing the boundary between the personal and the professional, and between individuals and the group, is crucial for the psychological well-being of the mental health professional and our success or failure at work. We come under very close scrutiny, and every aspect of self presentation is commented upon. This can be very wearing, and while on a good day we take it in our stride, on a bad day it can threaten to be overwhelming. It follows that to do this work successfully, one needs to be of a robust disposition and able to tolerate these impingements without retaliation or collusion. One needs to grow a second skin and to be aware of the 'slippery slope' referred to by Gabbard (2005), down which many people have slid!

Being one's real self, being authentic and being able to remain professional are matters to be worked at, to be renewed, every day. My own earlier experience at Henderson Hospital (see also page 80) taught me many things, one of the most important being how to wear different hats and occupy different roles while walking the tightrope of the personal-professional boundary.

Dynamic administration

The group-analytic concept of dynamic administration, where the conductor takes full responsibility for all aspects of the setting up and maintenance of the group, is the cornerstone of a successful group. The establishing of boundaries allows the group to feel safe and contained.

The conductor creates and maintains the necessary environment for the group's work. On the face of it, something like arranging that the same room be available at the same time every week ought to be simple. Experience tells us that it is far from that. Most practitioners versed in this work have had experience of the given room suddenly being required for another meeting, or patients or residents appearing outside the window perusing the staff. Privacy is absolutely basic and the conductor has to be at one and the same time diplomatically but firmly insistent on this precondition. Every aspect of the group's life, including absences, departures, late attendances and extra group communications such as phone calls and messages are referred to generically as boundary issues, open for discussion and enquiry.

Boundaries which are clear in purpose and 'patrolled' sensitively and effectively are the sine qua non of effective therapeutic work. At the same time, this establishing and maintaining of boundaries is a dynamic process. And it is more than possible for boundaries to ossify and become either too rigid or too porous and ineffective (Barnes, Ernst and Hyde, 1999, p. 85).

An example of boundary sabotage

I was called in to an NHS mental health team, in the throes of transition between one Trust and another, and about to lose staff and premises. They were under huge stress, unable to plan ahead and in fear of losing their jobs.

I would arrive to meet with them in their hospital setting, a huge Victorian building teetering on the brink of being unfit for purpose and find, sometimes, the door to our meeting room locked, no key to be found, and no one in sight. If I did manage to gain entry, the room would be set up with heavy tables which would need to be moved in order to sit in a circle.

People would invariably arrive late, often clutching sandwiches, and the membership was different from week to week, making the task of providing a safe and contained space impossible.

My countertransference was to feel what they were feeling through the communications over physical boundaries of space and time – lost, lonely, powerless, and inadequate. Their work lives were being radically transformed and so this group's boundaries were (unconsciously) sabotaged, communicating to me very clearly their own group state of mind.

Pulls across the boundary

We are familiar with the 'door handle question', when someone being escorted to the door asks a vital question or discloses an important feeling which cannot then be addressed; or in a group, someone brings up a hugely significant revelation just before time runs out. These are unconscious attempts to pull us over the time boundary and re-enactments of earlier deprivation and resistance to thinking.

Here, reflecting, boundary incidents are relatively easy to spot. However, in the moment, day-to-day, they are much less so, and can cause great confusion and/or discomfort for teams. For example, the inevitable emotions generated within the work, are experienced by a person who may have personal resonances to the situation. One of the most common examples in the helping professions is the re-enactment of the Drama Triangle, a term borrowed from transactional analysis (Thornton, 2016), the oft-played out scenario of persecutor-victim-rescuer where the staff member is drawn to become the rescuer, and re-enacts an internalized childhood experience in fantasy to work through her own unmet needs.

An example of time boundary stretching

A young nurse, in her first post, came to my group in tears. She had been unable to have a debriefing after an emergency community meeting during which she had been subjected to a torrent of verbal abuse from a patient. The meeting had been extended to two hours under the direction of the consultant psychiatrist, with no apparent resolution.

My response was anger on behalf of this nurse, who as a relative newcomer would have found it very difficult to challenge the psychiatrist. My anger informs my next step: where do I go with this? What might I say? How will it aid the group? I explore with them the consequences of not holding the time boundary.

The debrief time for processing their reactions to the meeting had been annihilated, resulting in the distress of not only this nurse but others who were present. I comment that ideally there needs to be a balance: the therapeutic work itself, and the thinking and processing in order to do it responsibly.

I'm seeing it in the context of the whole: what happens when time is stretched? Something else has to give; boundaries become distorted, leading to a breakdown in containment. A group analyst sees the group-as-a-whole and then the person, so if significant people are missing, she will see the gaps and the holes into which projections fly.

The psychiatrist responsible for the stretching of the time was absent and therefore could not be held to account for her actions, leaving the group frustrated and unable to resolve the situation.

She is highly regarded by the staff and one of the very few long-term staff remaining after much organizational turmoil, therefore far too valuable to offend or lose. Her behavior in extending the painful meeting was uncharacteristic, illustrating the pressure on thinking we can encounter when working with very disturbed patients.

In situations of heightened emotion everyone experiences increased pressure on the capacity to think. A dependency situation may easily be created, which makes boundary crossings more likely.

Regarding unconscious processes in groups, Foulkes (1971) spoke of 'the astounding conformity of the group . . . with its leader, which is a phenomenon of complete submission to the conductor's conscious and unconscious opinions, which always needs to be borne in mind and actively resisted'. Protecting a leader, or a group conductor, even when they behave in an erratic or even abusive manner, is a powerful imperative.

Institutional work

Institutions are notoriously difficult places to work, but many of us spend long periods doing just that.

We cannot do this work without to a greater or lesser extent getting 'bent out of shape'. So there has to be a facility for the protection of staff. Just as it is the task of the staff to contain the anxiety of patients and students, so it is the duty of the institution to contain the anxieties of staff.

Where staff fantasies and patient realities collide

In a secure facility, support and development was provided for the staff of the so-called 'sex offender unit' including a new weekly staff group, whose purpose was to encourage enquiry and reflection. This was greeted with a mixture of reactions – enthusiasm, curiosity, apprehension and, in the setting up phase, an unmistakable skepticism about this 'new-fangled' idea, especially from older staff who favored a 'no-nonsense' approach to work with this particularly difficult population. Nonetheless, the group was established and began to meet regularly.

For some time, members were very guarded in what they said, but the conductor was left in no doubt as to how he was seen. Best case he was there to 'psycho-analyze' them – whatever that meant – but whatever it was, it wasn't good! More likely, or so many of the group thought, he was there as a 'management plant' to report back on the 'weak links' in the team.

The group proceeded in a somewhat cat and mouse manner for several months, before reaching a point of crisis. Session 44 began with a period of silence – not uncommon for this group – but the quality of the silence was different on this occasion. There was a growing awareness of the team leader and his slightly agitated state. This man commanded great respect within the team, and his utterances were often taken as bulletins from on high. Never was he challenged.

In part, the silence was saying to him 'If you need it, here is a space for you to speak into'. And eventually he took up that invitation. What was troubling him, it transpired, was that the previous evening he and his wife had engaged in sexual play which was largely centered on the (consensual) enactment of a rough sex/rape fantasy. He spoke of this in some detail in a monologue (coming near to tears) making clear that what he was left with was a discomfiting mixture of excitement, arousal, transgression, and shame. Following this lengthy statement, the group fell back into silence.

During these moments, the conductor became more than a little anxious – thinking 'all it would take now is for someone to say (something like) "you fucking pervert" and this group is sunk'. But he resisted the temptation to intervene. The continuing silence felt like an age while everyone awaited the next move. Eventually, someone spoke – a relatively new member of staff. And what he said was 'me too', proceeding to give account of a similar event in his life. The group took hold of this and almost immediately began to access a deeper level of functioning, without recourse to the earlier unyielding, rigid defenses. They were able to begin to think about the similarities/differences between staff and patients.

This vignette illuminates various aspects of group life, but I want to call attention to just a few.

There are essentially two modes of relating available to people; one is by identifying with others, and the other is by projecting into them. In extreme circumstances, staff will (unconsciously) create a situation wherein the inter-group dynamic is dominated by mutual projections, as if all the mental health resides within the staff group and all the mental ill-health resides within the resident group. Something like that had happened in the earlier life of this unit, and the governing principles were moralistic rather than based on a professional curiosity. So, with things unfolding as they did in Session 44, a re-think became inevitable within this staff team. It had become possible to explore ways in which projective processes were skewing the work. For some staff, the very thought that they could be in any way like 'them' (the patients) was repugnant. But, for others, the dawning realization that one's own emotional responses could be used as a potentially rich source of information for the work was liberating. It provided a framework in which the work could be thought about and rendered less overwhelming.

The crescendo in Session 44 did not arrive out of a clear blue sky. The first 8–9 months of the group's life were undoubtedly defensive, but at the same time a culture was developing. Attendance was good, and despite hesitancy and reticence, the idea of a group was not being attacked. All of this contributed to a group climate within which skepticism had given way to thoughtfulness.

Foulkes (1975) cautioned against the use of plunging interpretations and this is an example of less being more. Groups will not be rushed. Any attempt to 'herd' them can reasonably be expected to fail. This demands great forbearance on the part of the consultant.

There are situational considerations too. This was happening in a service solely for men who were violators and transgressors. The personal statement in the group referred to transgression, not violation. From another point of view the distinction here is between reality and fantasy but in this case the fantasy was sufficiently near to reality to provoke enormous discomfort.

Although there are commonalities between a therapy group and a mental health staff group, the two are not the same. For example, members of a therapy group are enjoined not to meet outside the group sessions. With a work group it is very different. The moment the staff group finishes, most workers will be on the 'shop floor' engaging with patients in the usual range of activities, often in intensive, interpersonal situations (see also page 187.

It can be hard for staff to maintain each other's privacy in these circumstances. 'Leakages' can arise from lack of caution about protecting colleagues' private information, self-disclosure, or being 'played'.

When survival anxiety spirals out of control

In this psychiatric hospital, there is much upheaval: after the loss of the CEO who had been a much loved and constant figurehead, there was a period of instability and poor decision-making by a leadership team selected hastily and without due process; this led to a bad CQC rating which had an enormous impact on the staff.

A patient with a diagnosis of borderline personality disorder was angry and impatient with her progress in the unit (run on therapeutic community lines). She bypassed all the relevant staff and groups and approached a relatively new senior manager in the 'leadership team', with no direct clinical responsibility for the unit, and it transpired, little idea about how a therapeutic community worked. Instead of referring her back to the unit staff, the manager agreed that the patient could stay in the half way lodge, attached to the hospital for patients getting ready to be discharged. This had not been agreed with the 'responsible clinician', but for reasons subsequently explored in reflective practice groups, they agreed. This led to various unintended and destructive consequences for the team. The patient became a very 'special' case (Main, 1957) with 24/7 cover from unit staff, depleting their cover and undermining the very fabric of the unit.

There were some serious organizational problems in this hospital: a breakdown of clear lines of authority together with overwhelming anxieties about survival. Staff colluded with the manager's disastrous decision because they were frightened of challenging the leadership team, who had been sending off on 'gardening leave' staff who raised objections to their decisions.

A strong boundary helps to contain anxiety, generated from within or without; and it is up to the team leader to manage communications over the boundary. This team was temporarily without theirs, as he had been dispatched to another ward to manage a crisis. Anxiety can spill over from the wider organization into the team (and vice versa) and divert the team from its task, as in this case.

My role was to help the staff group analyze these unintended consequences and bring the situation (eventually) to an end, by re-admitting the patient to the unit and reuniting the staff.

Conclusion

> 'The eye sees only what the mind is prepared to comprehend.'
> (Robertson Davies)

The central strand of this chapter was to explore further the many ways personal, professional, and group boundaries can be crossed and to demonstrate how I as a group analyst might think about these events. I must 'patrol' these boundaries, being vigilant at all times as to how and when they are being used or abused and be curious about their meaning.

Interplay between external and internal pressures creates a force field around the boundary and can lead to inappropriate relationships between people, poor decisions, and other destructive consequences such as illustrated in the vignettes.

As the Hollywood film producer eventually discovered, boundaries which are transgressed can have catastrophic consequences. The reverberations from this tipping point have led to the downfall of many other prominent figures in society, reaching as far as the Swedish Academy, which awards the Nobel Prize for Literature. The prize has been withdrawn for 2018 following allegations of sexual misconduct and other boundary breaches.

We often refer to 'hindsight' when reflecting on actions taken and decisions made which have unintended consequences. I believe that in the analysis of the group by the group, including the conductor, we are able to cast a clearer and more truthful eye on our conduct in the here and now.

Grateful thanks to Graeme Farquharson for his significant contributions.

Note

1 See also the discussion on page 187.

Chapter 17

Values in practice

Dilemmas in reflective practice

Ian Simpson and Gwen Adshead

In this chapter we discuss the values and objectives of reflective practice (RP), widely used with teams in public service settings; we reflect on how to be a skillful RP facilitator. We begin with some historical context, and then discuss RP as a way to improve staff competence and resilience. In the second section, we briefly explore what makes for 'good' and 'bad' reflective practice and how organizational cultures develop. In the third and concluding section, we discuss boundaries and ethics in reflective practice; especially the boundary between the RP group and the organization in which it takes place.

Most of our joint experience has been in work with staff teams in healthcare organizations. We acknowledge here the contribution of the many participants in our RP groups whose generous participation has influenced our thinking and taught us a great deal. Where we describe the kind of material discussed in RP groups, our examples are fictitious, and no actual groups or organizations are discussed. The only exceptions to this are those examples which are in the public domain for obvious reasons.

History and the idea of reflection

We suggest that the RP story has its roots in both the democratic therapeutic community (TC) movement and the communitarian ideals of the 1960s. In both these contexts, the assumption of fixed hierarchies was challenged; especially the assumption that those who were ranked lower in organizations or businesses neither could nor should speak. The TC movement and communitarian ideals assumed the opposite: that everyone in a community should have a voice, (even if theirs was not the final decision or choice), and that listening to all empowers members of organizations to work better.

Naturally this was met with some resistance, as the first Northfield experiment showed (Harrison and Clarke, 1992). People with power are always loath to share it with others, and there may be good reasons for this as well as bad. Organizations that manage high levels of anxiety and risk under public scrutiny often feel safer with strict dominance hierarchies: although at times these organizations also realize that it is important to flatten hierarchies in order to get people to cooperate and experiment with ideas that may improve work life and function.

RP may also have its roots in changes in attitudes to managing risk and outcomes when things go wrong. It makes sense after a disaster of some sort for people to come together to review what happened and what could be done to improve things in the future. This type of activity was introduced in the UK after a spate of public disasters in the 1980s; and although its role in preventing mental illness has been shown to be limited, it is clear that people valued a chance to come together to think and learn from their errors. It then made sense to have such meetings in anticipation of serious incidents, rather than always reacting to them. Further, regular team meetings might help to build a sense of team cohesion that enhanced resilience: this was especially relevant to those organizations that manage human distress, injury, and high risk of trauma and death.

The contribution of group analysis to RP

Early psychodynamic study of healthcare organizations reported that staff who care for those in distress or who have been injured have strong emotional reactions to those people which are not addressed by their professional training (Menzies-Lyth, 1988a; Miller and Gwynne, 1972). All too often, healthcare professionals are encouraged to be dispassionate or detached and to believe that having feelings at work is unprofessional. This approach may have some limited utility in acute medicine and surgery: but is incoherent in services that offer long-term care, and where staff and patients build up relationships over time. As staff struggle to empathize and understand the people they are attending to, they find themselves responding to affect storms and semi-psychotic thoughts with complementary strong feelings and black and white thinking as a defense against feeling hopeless and helpless. When working with people with complex psychopathology, strong emotions can pull people out of professional roles so that boundary crossings and violations are more likely (American Psychiatric Association, 2001).

Both Spillius (1990) and Thorndycraft and McCabe (2008) suggest that staff feel and fear 'contamination' from exposure to psychological disorder,

which disturbs work function at the level of the individual and team relationships. This disturbance is made worse by organizational denial and
minimization of distress and disturbance caused by the work; especially
when the demands of the work become 'toxic' (Carson and Dennison,
2012) causing high levels of burnout and psychiatric morbidity in workers.

RP groups based on a group analytic understanding provide a space
where staff can share and explore the conflicts and anxieties that arise in
interpersonal relationships in the work. An understanding of groups and
group dynamics can help staff make sense of equivalence and mirroring
processes between their part of the workplace and the organization as a
whole. It is a fundamental group analytic principle that individual, group,
and social contexts are strongly interdependent. In healthcare organizations, both the institution and staff members working there must be containing and contained themselves to optimize therapeutic potential. RP
is essential to the development of self-awareness, which in this field is a
prerequisite for professionalism, both at the level of the individual practitioner and in the staff team as a whole.

The primary task of reflective practice

The primary task of RP is to help staff become more self-reflective, so they
can understand and perform their professional roles better. But before RP
can start, the primary task and context of the organizational system needs
to be studied and understood; both the manifest task of the organization
(as it is portrayed in the public domain) and the latent task (how it works
in practice). For example, a mental health service has a manifest task of
caring for people with mental disorder but also has a latent task of removing from communities people who make others anxious.

Second, it is essential to help staff members gain some basic understanding of unconscious processes, like splitting and scapegoating, that
can affect them. It helps staff to have a meta-perspective on conflicts in the
staff team, and relationships with patients. This understanding is especially important in organizations providing long-term care (where boundaries can become blurred with time) or in secure services which restrict
people's liberties in the name of public safety, because of the risks that
staff will exert power over patients in ways that are exploitative or abusive
(Carlyle and Evans, 2005; Riordan, 2008).

A thorough evaluation of the team and the context within which it
functions is helpful before any RP starts. On pages 141–43 and 196–97 there
are questions to consider. A questionnaire could be circulated to all team
members, exploring expectations and agreement with the process. Similarly, a meeting with the team, perhaps including individual sessions with
team members, should be arranged to check out expectations, explore the
hierarchical structure, look at the differences in professional backgrounds,

different ways of working, who should be in the RP group, and so forth. The appropriate and relevant tasks and boundaries for the team can thus be discerned and this in turn enables the facilitator to understand more fully the internal and external institutional dynamics and to 'hold and contain' these in their own mind and in the minds of the team members.

What is good reflective practice?

'Good' RP means different things to different people and in different contexts. At a simple level, 'good' RP is that which enables staff to carry out their primary task at work; which might include exploring dissent and conflict between themselves and their patients; and themselves and their organizations. There are different ways to think about RP, and so different ways to deliver RP, depending on context. For example, RP is different in an oncology ward as compared with a ward in a secure hospital as compared with a team in a prison. The common factors are (probably):

1   A safe place to sit and think without interruption
2   Organizational agreement to let staff sit and think
3   Some degree of protected time that happens regularly and at the same time
4   A facilitator who understands what the task is, and what it isn't
5   A facilitator who can let a conversation develop and allow the group to sit with some anxiety
6   A facilitator who can show compassion for the people and the task
7   A facilitator with a thick skin and a sense of humor.

Ineffective ('bad') RP will shut staff up or encourage them to act out the splits in teams through emotion and judgement. RP is not therapy, so it is vital not to treat members as patients. Some members will want to be patients, and it is not uncommon for a group to offer up one member as stressed and unwell, as an exclusive focus. This is tempting as a displacement activity, not least because the group member may actually be distressed and in need. However, the RP group is not staff support or an alternative to occupational health, and the facilitator will need to engage the group to think about how to stay on track, while being empathic about stress.

'Good' RP will enable people to speak honestly about what they think and feel about their work. This trust naturally takes time to develop. It must be acknowledged that no space can be perfectly safe, any more than the team can offer perfect care; it is helpful to discuss at the beginning what might be disclosed outside the group, if necessary. It is also helpful to remind members of the primary task from time to time.

Evidence that RP is working well: regular attendance by a range of staff; willingness to be curious about what is happening in the institution and in the group; creative dialogue that people remember across sessions; an enhanced tolerance for distress and mistakes. As part of the process, people get to know each other better, and it is therefore harder for projections to stick. This is an important reason that RP groups be multi-disciplinary and across different levels of authority. It enables a healthier dialogue when managers and clinical staff share the reflective practice space. It is harder to blame 'the management' for everything when 'they' are sitting next to you, sharing *their* anxieties about their work.

Boundary management in RP

A big challenge for facilitators is determining what can be spoken of in the RP group, and how best to manage the boundary between the group and the organization in which the group is operating. Much depends on the context of the group, how it was set up, and what the expectations are. See also pages 141–43 and 196–97.

Difficulties often arise when the expectation of RP is unrealistic, driven by severe organizational problems or past trauma. Not uncommonly there is a hope that somehow a weekly or even monthly staff group with an outside facilitator can resolve problems that relate to inadequate resources, poor line management, or general poor practice in the organization. The team may be feeling helpless and powerless and this can create a 'rescue fantasy' with powerful and unrealistic projections onto the facilitator; who in turn feels helpless and powerless. However, if this can be identified prior to engagement it can be worked with.

In some cases, managers see reflective practice from a very different standpoint than that of clinicians or outside facilitators. For instance, a manager who considers that reflective practice should be exclusively concerned with clinical problems, and decrees that interpersonal and organizational dynamics may not be discussed, leaves us with a real dilemma in terms of our professed task. If we adhere to this injunction, we are not facilitating reflective practice but case management; the work becomes focused on the patient (individual) and not the staff (group/team). As such it concentrates on what is wrong with the patient, ignoring what makes staff anxious. It becomes a social defense against anxiety rather than a tool for exploring staff group dynamics (Menzies-Lyth, 1988a).

Sometimes a facilitator hears something amiss that s/he thinks should be made known elsewhere in the organization. Should the facilitator disclose it, and if so, to whom and how? Much of this can be discussed in the group, and it often emerges that this kind of dilemma mirrors either the organization's work, or some other problem in the organization. It is sensible to have a plan for this before starting RP, a person or persons in the organization who will hear a 'quiet word'.

Even more commonly, a group member or some other professional approaches the facilitator for a 'quiet word' or 'something I want to talk about but can't bring to the group' (usually something one wishes they would bring to the group). Sometimes however it will be something worrying about the organization or someone in senior management. At this point the facilitator has a 'quiet word' with a person that they have hopefully identified beforehand.

Ultimately the facilitator 's obligations are (probably) to the organization's purposes: and secondarily to the RP group itself. But there is also an important duty to survive and maintain thought in the face of pressures not to think, and this is often the most complex task of all, requiring careful decisions. The facilitator has a role as the institutional memory of the organization, and so may sometimes also need to be a secret-keeper; sometimes on the other hand s/he may be a means of communication for the members, enabling an organization to hear something difficult.

Sometimes an RP facilitator needs to hold and contain individual members with issues they feel unable to express freely within the group. Things cannot always be talked about openly; for example, if group member tells you that a colleague is not fulfilling her or his duties adequately but does not want to address this directly with the colleague or the team leader. When the issue is too potentially destructive to raise in the group openly just now, the facilitator hopes that it will emerge in a subtler way, if the group is 'safe enough'. If this does not happen, the facilitator may be left bearing and struggling with a tension that arises both from the unspoken conflict and the associated secrecy. It makes sense for facilitators generally not to help secrets to develop, but to help staff find a way to explore such issues without individuals having to be named or exposed.

Facilitators must hold these situations, containing the anxiety levels in the team and enabling an opportunity for working through, in the hope that the individuals will gradually begin to say what they need to say to each other. Sometimes many team members are absent, so that we are working with a 'virtual' group. But this does not mean that effective or important work cannot be done. On the contrary, in the 'virtual' context, the team can be 'held and contained' and 'held in mind' without everyone being present at any given time, as the regularity and continuity of the reflective space is maintained.

The lived experience of the facilitator may be to be ignored, unheard and dismissed by everyone. They may even be left sitting alone at times. It is important at those times not to give up, but to continue to think, seeking to identify the defensive process and its origins. Sticking with the task of reflecting, even when it feels foolish, enacts a powerful commitment to thinking and is in itself a modeling intervention. The wise facilitator carries a book with them, or paper and pen to write reflections, for these lonely moments.

Political and ethical questions are inevitably raised when we facilitate groups with teams obliged to operate in unsafe conditions. This raises the wider boundary issue of whether to act if we clearly see this happening. Should we do more than facilitate? Should we abandon our professionally neutral stance and address this at another level in the organization? Should we actively encourage the staff to do something about it themselves or can we trust the reflective process to find solutions? These are questions that do not have simple or easy answers: the dilemmas themselves need reflection about the dynamics impelling us to act.

RP is a risky business, where confidentiality and professional boundaries have to be respected. We know from experience that if we go outside the boundaries of the work, approaching managers further up the hierarchy, it can only succeed if they are appreciative of the merits of reflective practice and are prepared to handle any issues identified with sensitivity and common sense. In other circumstances, to attempt such a move would be counterproductive, resulting in either a defensive or overcontrolling/punitive response towards staff in the team. Back channels can be useful but should be treated with caution.

If it appears that unprofessional practice is being directly caused by reduced/inadequate resources, RP facilitators may feel that they have a duty to act, rather than turn a blind eye, or keep a 'dirty secret'. We may feel that we have a professional duty, arising from our own identities as therapeutic agents, to stand up for the care of patients. What is less clear is how best to do this; and there is an ever-present concern that such ethical 'dilemmas' are *also* a manifestation of a dynamic that is going to undermine the RP process.

The internal dilemma: collusion or protest?

There may be occasions when the RP facilitator finds it hard to maintain a positive sense of purpose and considers that the RP is not working effectively. This is common when the wider organizational structure appears distanced from the realities of the clinical work and its effects on staff. Facilitators can be left with deep despair, frustration, and resentment at our powerlessness. We may hope that a reflective space for staff is helpful, even at the worst of times, but these experiences can immobilize us. Sometimes the most we can achieve is to validate and affirm the awfulness of it all, and to take away some of the trauma, functioning as a sort of therapeutic dustbin/container.

If the wider organization is a consciously or unconsciously undermining or abusive context, facilitators may face a very difficult dilemma: whether to continue with the RP group, (hoping that it helps to contain staff in such an intolerable situation) or to close it down.

When we experience this pervasive sense of helplessness, projected by the team and intensified by our own natural anxieties, we are invariably left feeling inadequate, demoralized, and frustrated. This also arises when supervising colleagues doing reflective practice with teams, who report how distressed and helpless they often feel leaving their sessions. In these circumstances it is best to acknowledge the feeling and feed it back. We can say to teams 'It's not your fault that you feel distressed, depressed and powerless in your current work setting'. We can also say that we might be more worried about them if they did *not* feel that way, and were colluding with a fantasy, by turning a blind eye or maintaining the deceit that things were ok. It is important to acknowledge that survival anxiety can make it almost impossible to think creatively.

When the context includes endemic intolerable distress and dysfunction, we have to consider the possibility that it may be inappropriate to attempt to establish meaningful reflective practice. If we refuse to engage, it sends a powerful message to the organization, and it is important to impart the reasons. We have experience of both closing an RP process because of its unsustainability; and also, of persevering, even when it felt hopeless to do so.

Chris Argyris (1980) describes as the 'undiscussable', those issues that the organization experiences as highly risky and threatening, particularly when those issues fundamentally question underlying organizational assumptions and policies. Examples in mental healthcare include serious incidents such as a patient death or professional boundary violations by staff. When these events occur, staff may find themselves wanting to talk about their experiences, but be silenced by employment processes and institutional investigations that demand strict confidentiality because they may prejudice legal proceedings. At times like this, the organization colludes in maintaining and reinforcing silence about problems; and may instruct RP facilitators not to discuss the issue under investigation.

This stance leaves the RP facilitator in an extremely tricky situation. We could go outside the boundaries of the group and try to convince managers that reflective practice is inhibited in its effectiveness in these circumstances, hoping they will see the value of reflection and change their position. If we do so, we will not always be thanked for exposing what is, in effect, a wider organizational dysfunction; we are in danger of being seen as 'subversive'. In any case an external facilitator may not be able to influence management. If they then ignore our input, we may have to 'consider our position' (i.e. consider leaving).

Alternatively, if we accept the silencing mandate, we may inhibit the functioning of the RP space, just at a time when teams are most distressed. Even then, many teams end up talking about the things they have been told not to, which positions the facilitator as a collusive boundary violator and makes the RP a receptacle for a 'hidden' collusive relationship that mirrors the initial problem. We may choose this option, but it sets the RP group against the organization.

Ideally, professional boundary violations are identified when they are still unenacted possibilities; see the case study on page 156. But the ideal rarely happens; facilitators find themselves having to decide whether or not to obey an organizational mandate that they think inhibits RP in a fundamental way. There is no obvious answer. For one of us, an injunction not to discuss something in RP would be a signal that RP cannot continue; for the other, it would be an issue to reflect on in the group and with the organization. These strategies are not binary or mutually exclusive; the RP facilitator must sometimes find and adopt multifaceted solutions to ethical dilemmas.

Personal and professional shame can lead to organizational silencing of reflection. The problem with the silence is that it leads to a loss of an opportunity to learn, and inevitably focuses attention on an individual now identified as 'deviant' and not the organizational failures. At time of writing, a young doctor has been struck off the medical register after a patient death, even though an independent legal review found that organizational factors contributed to the tragedy.

Conclusion

The provision of RP is a complex human business and as such must involve thinking and working with human values. Just as Robert Hobson (2013) asserts in relation to psychotherapy, reflection on values is an essential aspect of RP. Those who facilitate RP need to be psychologically 'literate' about values – their own, their group members', and the organizations'.

Chapter 18

Working with multicultural groups in organizations

Issues of power and difference

Vincent Leahy and Abdullah Mia

We discuss group analytic practice with multicultural groups in organizations, aiming to provide practical help by drawing on our experiences through vignettes. The vignettes act as anchor points for significant ideas about this work.

We hope this chapter embodies a containing space to explore the plurality of experiences and knowledges within any group. In discussing these spheres in organizations, we are also implicitly discussing the uses and abuses of power. These discussions are often daunting and painful, as the dynamics are often unconscious and highly defended.

The case for acknowledging difference

Difference has been central for us both, as second-generation immigrants. We are acutely aware of our experience of difference and the meaning of its relationship to power. Similarly, in organizations cross-cultural difference is omnipresent, despite attacks on or unconscious diminution of difference.

In our personal and professional lives working cross-culturally, we have reflected on what knowledge we have had access to, what expectations of us are, and what assumptions have been made before we speak. In considering our positions of visible and invisible difference, we know that enactments will

have a similar process regardless of which difference is in play. As participants and conductors, we have noticed patterns across a range of organizational settings; corporate, educational, health, public, and private sector.

People across organizational strata will more readily attend to the management of obvious difference, such as the impact of ethnic and gender
difference, though current equality legislation reaches further, acknowledging nine protected characteristics (see Equality Act, 2010).

1: Unacknowledged differences

When teaching diversity, I always ask members for their hopes and goals.
These mostly center on wanting to learn about how to work with ethnic minorities, or seeking a specific model to implement. Vice versa as a
learner in a diversity session, teaching consistently focuses on ethnic difference only.

This leaves me feeling why is it only about ethnic difference, and not the
broader range of cultural differences? I feel only obvious differences can be
discussed, and less visible differences are unacknowledged. The dominant
culture group often feel they do not have anything to contribute, silencing
their experiences. The general tone becomes one of negating difference.

**Key Point 1: Difference is everywhere, even if it's hard to see.
Be curious about your own difference. It holds important clues.**

The impact of these issues on a group's dynamics often become more
conscious when there is a grievance procedure or legal case. This is usually an unwelcome surprise with far reaching consequences. The low
threshold in proving workplace discrimination can be costly as well as
damaging to an organization's reputation. Organizations therefore need
to understand and work with deeper cultural group dynamics before they
reach formal grievance or litigation.

In this chapter we consider the frequently encountered work group,
functional but not necessarily achieving its potential. The experience of
members of the group, and particularly the leader, is a feeling they are
constantly dealing with disruptive issues that surface unexpectedly.

Working with difference

Our discussions have expanded and contracted much like an accordion.
Through reflecting together, we have become aware this expansion and
contraction is also what facilitators must practise, working within and
across cross-cultural contexts.

Facilitating many diverse groups have taught us that thinking and working cross culturally is an art. There is no single magic methodology, silver bullet, or critical approach to working effectively in multilevel complex groups. Bringing together concepts in group analytic theory, ethnography, and linguistics are invaluable ways of gaining insight, helping us understand and work with the subconscious tensions around difference that often hinder communication and the work of a group.

Sometimes difference may be so obvious and difficult that the group cannot overcome it, so that the work of the group is constantly hampered. Bion (1959) discusses the attacks on linking that occur when individuals avoid their emotional experiences and capacity to relate, arising from the pain of not knowing the 'other' person. In avoiding emotional discussions focusing on cultural differences, the group avoids thinking and giving meaning, undermining the organization's ability to understand difference.

2: Working with visible and invisible differences

Working with a senior education team, my initial experience was of their hostile mistrust of the process 'this is a waste of time' and 'what's the point of this?'. Members would avoid the group by attending other 'more pressing meetings'.

A particularly memorable moment was when a member of the group challenged my credentials. I realized that it was to do with her difference in the group, her 'Irishness', which I understood and shared, including a mistrust of imposed authority and 'Englishness'.

Working with the team leader I impressed the need to maintain the boundaries and hold the group in the process. Slowly the group members were able to explore their common purpose and share deeper information.

On a visible level this was a multi ethnic group, with African born, Asian, and British members. However other invisible differences emerged (e.g. sexuality, social class, and different Celtic nations) as core to this group's identity and communication.

Recognizing the Irish background one member shared with me partly explained the initial suspicion and challenge I encountered, paralleling my own knowledge of the use of anger as a defense in relation to power within the Irish community. Many group issues could be understood in terms of members' personal and social experience of powerlessness.

My own background was important in understanding some of the transference issues and power dynamics in the group. Discussing obvious differences eventually allowed them also to engage safely with feelings around other unrecognized cultural differences.

Key Point 2: Acknowledge the difficulties in seeing difference, and work beyond visible differences.

The task

The shared task is always seen, understood, and interpreted through the lens of individual and group cultural identity. Balancing the understanding of the shared task, the group also balances the tasks (and demands) set by internal departments and external agencies. The conflict this creates can also result in group members feeling threatened by the concept of difference. The group can feel so threatened by difference (in task and within the group) that their anxiety presents as a desire and need for 'sameness'. Indeed, where the task anxiety is intense the group's primary task can be supplanted by the 'anti-task' (Menzies-Lyth, 1988b) – where the various individuals work to achieve their own personal needs and values. The avoidance of discussing difference prevents the group from achieving the task, but also prevents them from utilizing the creativity that difference can engender in a group. Vignette 3 gives an example of this process, which can also be understood through Hopper's 'massification' (2012a).

When working with cross-cultural groups, as facilitators we begin by helping the group to focus on the surface issues and manage their anxieties in relation to this. Once the group is comfortable discussing this, we support the group to look at how difference within the group is discussed and utilized.

3: The challenges of professional difference

A multi-disciplinary team of healthcare professionals and prison officers, working with young adult offenders and currently without a leader, experienced constant undermining of their work from various parts of the organization, despite tacit support from the governor.

The team members agreed to begin to use a generic assessment, forgoing their specialist professional training and skills and minimizing differences between them, and also between them and the organization. Their professional individuality was diminished and devalued in favor of a unified front.

In the reflective practice group, the team did not voice differences in professional opinions. Instead they attacked differences seen in the host organization.

18 months later, now with a leader encouraging individuality and maintaining safety, the team began to discuss how their professional differences affect them within the team.

The group had been protecting itself at the expense of members' professional identity and difference. The real task had become survival.

Key Point 3: Pay close attention to groups whose anxiety can mask and disable professional expertise.

The typical group

The typical work group is atypical. Modern organizations and work groups consist of members from various cultural backgrounds working together on a task in a long or short term team. Within this, subgroups form on the basis of obvious similarities (e.g. like me–not like me, who shares some of my identity?). The cross-cultural reality of the group is far less observable and this is one of the paradoxes that illuminates a key insight into successfully facilitating cross-cultural groups. Difference goes beyond the observable surface difference, as facilitators we pay attention to how each person experiences their own difference in the group.

The facilitator role

When we work with a group, we keep the wider organizational context of the task in mind. The commissioning client expects a solution implied in the power relationship between me the 'expert' and the client. In contracting with the group, we highlight the potential for cross-cultural exploration.

Often problems can present as an 'organizational itch', something small but distracting and destabilizing. The 'itch' isn't the problem, it is a symptom; we observe it and consider the deeper causes, relating these 'itches' to the organizational task and purpose, and also the wider group's cultural differences.

When contracting with the group a key feature is to work closely with the leader, to help them develop an understanding of what is happening in the group, translating and interpreting projections of difference. These are often based in fears of the unknown, or of being misunderstood, and sometimes in historical experiences of differences being sublimated or abused.

Facilitators embody difference by being obviously outside the group. The group share the organizational context and relationships; as facilitators we do not. The group has its own relationships, and within these, subgroups. Being an outsider whilst within the group gives us information; paying attention to the transferential processes we experience is crucial to supporting the group achieve its task.

'Like me–not like me'

A key to understanding the ethnic, social, and cultural differences within the group is recognizing the 'like me–not like me' process, where individuals align themselves with those they perceive as similar. This process is often also paralleled by other members of the group, although this is often unconscious and unacknowledged. Often the group's 'sameness' can be projected into the facilitator. We have both experienced this, and it can be seen and felt as difference being sublimated, with any conversations about difference being dismissed passively or aggressively.

Members who experience difference are left holding a powerful paradox; protection from the group at a cost of their sense of belonging, or rejection from the group. Indeed, anxious belonging is the reason so many stay in jobs they dislike. To protect themselves from these feelings, group members will sublimate differences and assume they are inherently damaging. Sublimation of difference is a powerful defense enabling the group to focus on the shared task – most times. However, sublimation can also recreate individual's experiences of oppression (racism, sexism, and so forth). Being unable to speak about these creates anxiety, left unspoken and unaddressed; individuals' trauma can be re-experienced within the group and organization.

4: 'Your difference is better than mine'

An East European supervisor asked her English subordinate to act as a witness to a heated argument with another (English) supervisor. The subordinate refused, and grievance and counter-grievance were brought by the supervisor and the worker focusing on racism and aggression respectively

The senior HR manager could not make sense of the grievances, so brought in an external facilitator to investigate. The facilitator found the supervisor had acted in her fantasy of the UK as a society free of corruption, highly efficient, and valuing freedom of speech, unlike her negative perception of her home country. In her attempts to live by these values, she had not held the team to acceptable standards with respect to discriminatory language in the workplace. At the same time she honored core values of hard work and hierarchal power, part of her culture of origin.

When she chose to exercise her authority and expected her subordinate to witness and support her against the other supervisor, the subordinate experienced her demand as aggressive and an abuse of positional power. This was in addition to resentment by the work group at being held to high work standards by a foreign supervisor. The backdrop was a workplace culture that had become increasingly and overtly racist, partly as a result of the supervisor's idealization of 'Englishness' preventing her from addressing any prejudice. All of this took place against a background of Brexit, with social and political uncertainty and heightened 'casual' racism around immigration, particularly in relation to jobs.

The sublimation of difference, supported by two differing fantasies around Englishness could not be maintained as Brexit and use of hierarchical power came together to break the prevailing status quo.

Key Point 4: Pay attention to how the wider socio-political context impacts the team's difference and sameness.

Power and privilege

An important part of working in multicultural groups is constantly keeping the broader foundation matrix (Foulkes, 1975) – the social, economic, and political – in mind, whilst remaining constantly curious about what is being experienced in the group. Individual and group power is omnipresent in groups. Unconscious power is more available to individuals whose intersectionality – their own 'race', ethnicity, class, and gender – parallels society's hierarchy of power, privilege, and advantage. For some, power and privilege may be remote, as they do not consider themselves to be of a socio-economic class that would naturally be associated with easy and unconscious power. But for others, who do not feel they intersect with the dominant template in many ways, the experience of power in any setting will have a negative emotional impact or affect e.g. a sense of exclusion or inadequacy. This ambivalence around power may be consciously known but not expressed, or unconsciously suppressed and acted out in the group through projection, transference, or deflected conflict.

In thinking about power and privilege in organizations, we must also think about these projections in relation to the other protected characteristics and social class. These are unconscious, particularly in relation to racism and rarely discussed, due to anxiety. These discussions are often about the allegation of racism as opposed to the practice itself. The silence around racism is exacerbated by ethnic minority members being fearful of accusations of 'playing the race card'.

5: Difference has power

Working with a British multicultural leadership team led by a European national in a University department, I was struck by the insistence of all team members, when spending time together, on exclusively discussing performance and outcomes. There was a very powerful projection of unanimity in the group, with me as the outsider ('not-like-me'). I became aware that this might also be how others in the wider institution experienced this group.

Alongside this, paradoxically, I experienced a 'like me' process in the group, as members began to align themselves with my 'Britishness'. They hoped I would express their concerns to the leader. They were uncomfortable with the nature and manner of the leader's decisions and behavior such as her autocratic transactional style. A long-serving team member had left, and the team were unable to express their feelings about this. Exploring this individually uncovered a fear of a brutal response from the leader. In trying to explore this with the group, the leader emphatically closed the conversation down.

I was able to discuss with the leader how her approach was experienced by others; however, this was too difficult for her to allow into the group discussion. The damage to relationships in the group ultimately became irreparable, damaging the team, and the trust of the team within the institution.

Key Point 5: Talking about difference is difficult and requires thoughtful handling. Tread carefully.

In organizations the pressure to survive is central. Individuals are constantly required to make sacrifices, work smarter, deliver more with less, and accept as inevitable downsizing, restructuring, and frequently their own redundancies (see further pages 68, 73). A lot of resources are spent on ensuring employees identify with the organization's espoused culture and accept shared organizational values and procedures. Employees can conflate their survival with that of the organization, however the organization cannot guarantee the employee's survival. This conflict ensures continued anxiety which can become traumatic, and the neo-liberal logic of market forces ensures feelings of insecure anxiety and trauma continue. Employees attempt to relieve their unbearable feelings by placing them in an 'other' object, one that can hold the collective negative and then be sacrificed. Thus, the scapegoat individual or group becomes the means by which the bad feelings are got rid of and a fragile if temporary security restored.

In the process of constant sacrificing, the good is replaced by fear of annihilation and unbearable anxiety. The espoused values of the organization must be 'accepted', so the underlying reality becomes undiscussable (Argyris, 1980). The spoken values often mask any discussion about what is really going on and happening below the surface. This is a powerful force in an organization as it almost maintains the power dynamic around what can and cannot be discussed.

The availability of easily identified difference becomes the 'other'. The 'other' will often accept the projected scapegoating, attempting to mitigate this by becoming lesser and diminished, not wanting to emphasize their otherness for fear of further scapegoating. However, when rejected, the scapegoat will continue to receive the unconscious, unwanted projections of the group. This becomes intolerable for the individual and unconscious projections of 'otherness' break through the surface resulting in litigation or resignation.

Overt racism is rarer than institutional racism. Racially and ethnically different team members can be used to hold the team's projections of difference in themselves. This is further complicated if the racially/ethnically different team member identifies with these projections, drawing on earlier experiences of exclusion. This leads to racial scapegoating. Racial scapegoating can be identified by the facilitator through awareness of the subtle narratives relating to specific points of difference; these are often not personalized.

6: When difference is too much to bear

In a Muslim charity team, the CEO began experiencing indirect attacks towards her authority and position; i.e. a willful disregard for policies and directives. In the reflective practice group, the team discussed how in the last few months the organization was losing its religious focus, and expressed their disappointment.

We explored what had changed, and it transpired that the CEO had employed an ethnically different male staff member, whom the team suspected was gay. They had felt unable to discuss this, silenced by the depth of their fears about the philosophy of the charity.

As a facilitator, I needed to acknowledge that the Islamophobia, suspicion, and scrutiny they had experienced in wider society. These fears had been internalized and not discussed in the organization. They had been projected into the new staff member as the feared outsider. It was complicated further by the Islamic beliefs about homosexuality.

The challenges and complexities of integrating and understanding difference proved too threatening to their identity, and the group were unable to work through this together, resulting in the eventual suspension of the charity's work.

Key Point 6: Sometimes talking about difference can be unbearable and destructive. It may go against and disrupt the purpose of the organization.

Communication and language

Chomsky's (1957) generative grammar is a useful metaphor in thinking about communication in cross-cultural group processes. It helps us reflect on the communication – or sentence structures – we experience on the surface within the group. Comprehending at the surface level is not enough to understand the communication itself. For Chomsky, while two or more surface features – or sentences – may be similar on the surface communication, the deeper structure of each sentence is very different. For example, the active sentence – 'He did it', in contrast to the more complex but similar 'It was done by him'.

In basic terms, the complexity of the sentence corresponds to the number of transformations the idea goes through from the deep structure to the surface structure where it is communicated. Similarly, in communicating from a different culture, utterances around task and power for example will go through many transformations and complex associations of first and second language and culture before it is communicated in the group. In Vignette 7 we see the difference between the surface comprehension and the deeper transformations.

7: Differences unbounded

Following a departmental meeting, a member of staff had agreed to facilitate a discussion regarding cultural differences and their impact on the workplace and individuals. In doing so, the group began to discuss how difference can be sublimated and often not consciously acknowledged. An ethnic minority staff member spoke of how there were aspects of her life that she did not choose to show in the workplace, due to fears that it would result in negative treatment.

The team were horrified that someone would keep aspects of themselves private, and aggressively questioned the staff member's integrity.

The staff member had inadvertently made the unconscious conscious, and without appropriate boundaries, the team was not able to explore the differences safely. There was no conclusion to the discussion, which left the staff member feeling damaged, and concerned about further difficult interpersonal dynamics.

Key Point 7: Difference cannot always be safely spoken about.

Translation and interpretation

Communication and translation are central to the group-analytic approach (see chapters 1, 5 and 14). The facilitator has to be aware of the different 'communications' being expressed in the group, and to 'translate' them. Translation is saying something in another language without changing the meaning of what is being said[1]; it is the ability to use knowledge of the languages or ways of communicating, to articulate meanings accurately into the shared language of the group. Translation requires a methodical knowledge-based approach, accurately to understand and convert what is being said in one context and delivering the information accurately in another.

In contrast, interpretation requires an immediacy of simultaneous communication, in the moment, switching between what is said from a deeper personal level into a level that can be understood and engaged with at a shared surface level in the here and now. We have learnt that sometimes this has meant explicitly asking the communicator to share their thoughts in a different way, or at times even to interpret and convey the meaning for the communicator to the group.

As facilitators we consciously translate difference to the leader of the group, while interpreting difference within the group. Through both approaches, the group can hear and better understand their communication. This adds an additional lens through which reflective practice is conducted, being mindful of the group's safety in relation to the task, and then also in relation to the group's capacity to hold differences. It is here that our relationship with the group leader is essential, helping them partner and take an active role in the process of interpretation with and for their own group. Ultimately this enables the group's self-knowledge to deepen and secures their safety, not held solely by us as facilitators.

Conclusion

Group analysis provides us with a rich resource to understand enactments within organizations. Our experiences have led us to position difference as key to our understanding, but not our entire focus. This work is both political and deeply powerful, making it vital to create safety for leaders and the group alike. Working with difference is difficult, but let us be bold in facilitating this dialogue, based on connecting with our own differences.

Note

1 Editor's note: This is also true of the group analytic concept of 'translation' from unconscious/nonverbal enactments to verbal.

Section VII

Working with whole organizations

In section VII we turn to work with and between groups within a whole organization.

Chapter 19, opening the section on working with whole organizations, records a conversation with Earl Hopper about his insights linking consulting to organizations with group analytic theory. It introduces some important ideas, providing a more informal commentary to be read alongside his substantive contributions to theory.

Cynthia Rogers gives us a richly illustrated description of the internal process of the consultant as s/he enters an organization, and clear and astute advice on how to create the best possible conditions for change. Her chapter 20 explores the 'how' of the group analytic concept 'dynamic administration', particularly with regard to 'median' groups of up to 70 people.

Gerhard Wilke, one of our finest conductors of large groups, has written a concise and practical account of the core processes in large groups, and the key tasks of the large group conductor in chapter 21. It is illustrated with a story which underlines the broader societal value of a group analytic approach to dialogue.

I am honored to count Gerhard as a professional friend. When we began working together, we discovered considerable overlap in our thinking about organizations, rooted both in our group analytic training, and a shared pragmatism in praxis based in long experience. Three chapters in these final two sections of the book are the fruit of those conversations, particularly about 'translucent boundaries' and the necessary flexibility of the organizational consultant, and leader, in working with them.

In chapter 22 we discuss the relationship between the matrix, the systemic concept autopoiesis, and the formation of organizational identities, which regulate the behavior of the people within. We focus particularly on the dynamics of mergers in this chapter, with case stories suggesting practical ways to work with the challenges.

In chapter 23, we consider the impact of insider/outsider or 'us-and-them' dynamics between parts of organizations. Through the chapter we offer examples of how these can be successfully worked with. We close the chapter with ten key points for leaders and consultants seeking to 'tweak' an organization in the direction of greater coherence and mutual loyalty.

Chapter 19

A conversation with Earl Hopper

Earl Hopper and Christine Thornton

Earl Hopper is a distinguished group analyst, psychoanalyst, and sociologist, one of group analysis' most important theoreticians. He has written and edited many books and papers about, inter alia, the fourth basic assumption, trauma, the social unconscious and the tripartite matrix, and is the General Editor of the New International Library of Group Analysis, in which this volume appears. Rather than presenting a sequential argument, this chapter records a conversation with Christine Thornton sharing some of his thoughts about his long experience of consulting to organizations and how that relates to his theoretical writing.

Diagnosis, the matrix, role and culture

CHRISTINE: How do you use the matrix in the diagnostic process?

EARL: Well, 'diagnostic' is an interesting word – I don't always know exactly what it means in an organizational context – usually it boils down to matters of conflict, tension, which are not sustainable and are not containable in the organization. I always have in mind the tripartite matrix, and I am thinking to myself, foundation matrix, organizational dynamic matrix, smaller group dynamic matrix, and personal matrices.

And I have in mind that on my nose are the 'spectacle frame' and using a box of lenses, the way an optometrist does, dropping them in. Bion talks about binocular vision, well I always think that's just the start of it. Right eye, left eye, near vision, far vision, and doing all that, and then you have to check for whether you need other corrections, maybe you have a prism or you want other variations, you have something for summer, and this is the equivalent of those lenses, is what I am constantly doing.

CHRISTINE: You have to choose where you put the focus, and that decision has to be led by the – diagnostic process sounds too –

EARL: That's absolutely right.

CHRISTINE: It's a use of the self, to understand the span of the issue, a 'diagnostic process', though that sounds to me a little bit too purely intellectual.

EARL: Not in our field.

CHRISTINE: True. It's much more embodied and we don't necessarily get it all at once.

EARL: No.

CHRISTINE: The prism makes me think of Indra's net.

EARL: Ah yes. Well, why does it do that?

CHRISTINE: Because Indra's net is an image of infinite connection, with prisms of infinite reflection, mutual reflection, reflections of reflections of reflections of reflections . . .

EARL: Never-ending.

CHRISTINE: In Indra's net there would sometimes be a patch, where the prisms have – something sticky on them, so they stop reflecting.

EARL: A scotoma, that's what Bion would have called it – a blank spot, a blind spot. That indeed might be – the manager might have it, and you don't have it, and others have it, and that's a black hole, which destroys you if you get too close to it.

CHRISTINE: One of the things that happens a lot, is that people define the manager, the leader, as the problem, and some of the time that's true.

EARL: That sometimes happens, but it's never, or very rarely, only the leader. The person who is the so-called leader may have been really suitable for the role that developed in the organization, but it's the role that needs to be changed. And the whole organization might have to change in the interests of its own survival, or its own effectiveness, and that individual may or may not be suitable for the newly defined executive role. They may need to go to another organization, or be bought off – that's possible. You have to be able to say something like – 'you're a good man/woman, but you're the wrong person for this organization at this time. The need is for someone able to be more conciliatory, to bring together and make more cohesive these different sections of the organization, to move forward'. Say they are in old-fashioned terms a 'fight/flight leader', and there isn't any enemy any more. What is needed is an integrative leader. Take someone, a sparky fighting guy who set up a successful investment company but then was ejected when it was established. If I were a blind investor, I would probably invest in his new firm, a fighter, if he can raise the money, will probably make a quick success. Whether it will last forever is another question, but he might be really the wrong person for the last stage of institutionalization, of the other organization which he put together.

CHRISTINE: Yes, that makes complete sense. So, going back to the beginning of the process, and I agree with you that it starts with the first contact – often an email these days – the first phone call – what are the symptoms you look for?

EARL: Well, absenteeism or too much conflict in meetings, stuff like that. Those are all symptoms of something else. So how do you diagnose? Well, you diagnose partly by using groups as laboratories for understanding the human relations between the key players. So, you sit in on committees and look at what Yvonne Agazarian called the invisible group. It's not only a matter of basic assumption dynamics.

CHRISTINE: How do you find out about the culture of the company?

EARL: You sit in, you talk to people, and you are sufficiently experienced that you know what a culture is, and you have the tools that allow you to describe different kinds of sub-cultures. If you don't have some of that, you can't use the word 'culture'. Say you have a culture that rewards passivity and compliance. What we mean by culture is usually that the values, beliefs, and norms of the organization are patterned in certain ways, that they favor certain behaviors and ways of thinking and being, and dis-favour others. You have to operationalize it. I think one of the things you have to say at the beginning and make clear, is that you're not going to solve the problems. They are going to have to do it, and that is part of their problem.

Larger groups and the role of consultation

CHRISTINE: You described getting yourself to the right level first of all, as the person who makes the invitation may or may not be the person to work with. They may not exercise enough power to make a difference. Then, how widely do you intervene – to the whole organization? Is that your focus? Who should be included in the consultation?

EARL: Well you have to draw your line somewhere – let's say you're consulting to a big oil company with thousands of employees, you can't really get them together in one room.

CHRISTINE: I suppose that speaks to one of the bigger themes running through this book, something about the value of group analysis, the value of dialogue in large groups.

EARL: I have used large groups in organizations, Gerhard has used them. I have used organizational groups up to 300, and it is useful, but not necessarily useful in the way that a group analyst would ordinarily think, not reparative, though there may be some reparation. But people are very frightened, and rightly – they might lose their jobs, for instance. People don't want to give away too much, and I don't blame them.

CHRISTINE: I think group analysis as a discipline speaks to this kind of large scale issue. The GASI triennial events are important because at least we are trying to engage in international dialogue across all kinds of differences.

EARL: That's my feeling too. It's a good way, for example, ordinarily, of learning what's going on in the wider society. I think these large groups do tell you, if you listen carefully, something about people's preoccupations.

CHRISTINE: Taking this back to organizations then. Gerhard represents it as being about bringing the community together. But would you use a mixture of larger and smaller groupings?

EARL: And personal.

CHRISTINE: Yes, me too. And what about across?

EARL: Divisions? I have done it. It's useful. I just don't expect as much from it as maybe some writings would suggest, that we are going to have 'aha' insights. But it is really a good way of learning about an organization and I think there's something else. I really believe that giving people the space to put into words, some of the things they think and feel, is helpful. And feeling that thunderstorms haven't hit them, lightning hasn't hit them, nobody's died, nobody's lost their job, and it's taken off the pressure. Somebody's said this in the large group, what do we feel about that? It's very helpful. And if you can train some of them to listen better than they have been listening, then they become better managers. Managers often don't know how to listen, they can talk too much.

CHRISTINE: They think that's what's expected of them.

EARL: Yes, there's a lot of pressure on them to . . . they are very rarely put in a situation where they can just listen. And people try to please their managers. Then you can ask a question like 'I wonder whether there is a culture in this organization, where people can't say more openly what they think, without being fearful that they will lose their reputation or even their job?' Of course, people respond, 'Don't be ridiculous, of course we can speak' and I would say, 'Of course, in many ways you can speak', and then somebody says something that they have never said before, and it's not necessarily taken as critical or horrible.

CHRISTINE: It's about the degree of risk. Just a small risk, actually, to start. If people can step just a little bit outside of what's normally done, test it out, then you're more likely to get a sustained movement towards freer communication. Because that is part of the essence of what group analysts can offer.

EARL: I believe that is so important Christine, that it may be the only thing that the group analyst per se can offer to an organization: improvement in the communication, and the content and systems thereof in the organization hiring you as a consultant. I think we can do that.

CHRISTINE: I think so. It's the training. It's that long experience of sitting in groups – you learn it not even at a conscious level.

EARL: But it involves some teaching of managers and others to listen and to hear what's being said. Where we sometimes go wrong, is thinking that we can do much more than that. If we go in as group analytical consultants, we can see certain problems, we can see certain patterns of conflict, but we may not be able to do anything about it. We are not there to improve their accountancy systems. But we are there to facilitate their asking questions about whether their system of accounting is reflecting the process.

CHRISTINE: This is interesting, and sometimes I struggle with it. As a consultant you bring what you have been, and one of the things I have been is a manager so at times . . .

EARL: Very hard not to be a manager again!

CHRISTINE: I find myself asking how it is that they don't get decent management accounts.

EARL: The way you describe it is good though. Let's underscore something, the way you started that question: 'how is it that'. That's a valid group analytical question. How come? How has it come about? That's different from the statement 'you should have better management accounts' or the question 'why don't you have?' One is parental, and the other is consultative.

Social defenses and the ethics of working with teams in traumatogenic settings

CHRISTINE: Even in a relatively small reflective practice group, in a health service setting now, say, where things are extremely polarized and people are extremely fearful, there's an ethical issue about how appropriate it is to ask people to open up.

EARL: I agree. You know, this working with teams, which I used to do, but as the years went by I could see that we were asking so much from one another. What we are doing is saying 'for the next hour and a half we want you to step out of your formal role, just be people together' and then assume that they can just go back into their formal role – it's really not fair.

CHRISTINE: It's not that simple.

EARL: It's not, but that's what we are asking them to do. You know what I mean by 'populism'? in society generally, in terms of political populism, you assume that the greatest number of votes determines what's right and what's wrong. People are not in any role, they're just citizens. Well, it may be what a democracy requires, but it's not necessarily the best way to get work done. There's a conflict.

CHRISTINE: It's about the fourth basic assumption, about helplessness.

EARL: It is, mainly because it's about trauma. I think we can over-use the word trauma, just like we can over-use the word disappointment, but they go together. What about the military? How would you like to work in the military with a general and command structures, trained in a specialty and sent to particular areas, not that it works that way but on paper that's what they expect, and find that the only war that you are fighting is a guerrilla war, and you don't know where the enemy is? These are the kinds of wars that we are fighting now. Who are the enemy soldiers?

CHRISTINE: Whereas yours are perfectly identifiable, targets.

EARL: Very confusing.

CHRISTINE: Like the old TV show MASH.

EARL: That is a perfect example of the development of black humor in a combat situation.

CHRISTINE: And the value of that. One of the things that is not properly understood is that defenses are there for a reason, so that all this literature about opening up team communication . . . I don't think you necessarily do that with the police, or ambulance drivers, or firemen, for example. If they don't maintain fairly firm defenses, they probably won't be able to do their jobs.

EARL: And then there is the manic sexual boundary breaking in trauma situations. I have consulted in hospitals, for example, and other organizations too, where traumatogenic processes are ubiquitous, not contained or held or talked about. Then you can absolutely see that using sexuality as a manic defense against depression, loss, and meaninglessness, leads to these kinds of enactments. Like in MASH, where the black humor and the sexuality go together. If un-analyzed, it becomes a social defense. We could talk about that in terms of humor, black humor, or the use of sexuality. When you are working in an organization and uncovering it, once you know that, this is pretty typical. It's not that you are going to stop people behaving how they are behaving, but it's an indication that something is wrong. What I have found though is that if you start talking about it, the behavior does stop. Just as in psychoanalysis or group analysis, the symptom gets verbalized, and once verbalized, it becomes meaningful in a different frame of reference that no one usually understands anything about. So, once we start talking about it in those terms, people start saying 'actually it's very sad that we are in this war situation'. And that changes everything.

Take for example a psychotherapy agency where the leader is frightened of group reflective practice, but their staff really love the idea of exploring how working with the people they are working with somehow reverberates in their relations with colleagues and the dynamics of the organization. I get involved with conceptualizing this with them. It is a very female, feminine way of working. In the sense that there are no strict agendas for work, things are not linear, you can feel your way around the organization. This can change; an organization becomes linear as a typical response to trauma or crisis management.

On fear, envy and helplessness: the fourth basic assumption

CHRISTINE: And out of fear . . .

EARL: Out of fear. That's really very interesting. A hundred years ago, if you can believe it, my first publication, my Master's thesis. It was based on a participation observation study in a factory, owned by a British company, which was then bought by an American company. It was looking at manufacturing processes in terms of a revised model of frustration and aggression theory, trying to build on the sociologist's Alvin Gouldner's work on patterns of industrial bureaucracy, and also wildcat strikes. It was . . . 1957 I think, he published this stuff.

The most interesting thing was that people are under pressure and when they're under pressure systemically, they do things to create pressure on other people. That's a long time ago that he said that. The trick as a consultant is to delineate where the pressure is initiated and where you can intervene and modify. So, let's say certain kinds of foremen (these were in the old days) would recreate pressure on the employees, the people they were responsible for, because they were being put under pressure systemically by the executive decision making, that didn't include them.

CHRISTINE: They were being done to?

EARL: They were being done to and so in turn they did to. In St Louis, with Gouldner, we were starting to do work in small group laboratories, trying to conceptualize close and/or punitive and/or anomic supervisory styles in bringing about certain kinds of responses in terms of frustration and aggression. The idea being that close and/or punitive and/or anomic supervisory style would produce affronts to self-esteem on the part of the people working, and they would respond with aggressive feelings. And at times these aggressive feelings which could not be expressed directly towards a foreman, especially if their jobs were insecure, would come out by attacking productivity rates. Mistakes would be made, not 'on purpose' so to say. They would even be prepared to be self-destructive by being unproductive, if they were on the piece work payment system, which is what it was called in the 1950s.

So, I introduced into the study additional variations like the class of the foreman, the class of the worker, whether they were men or women, and I had different combinations, where you would assume that different pattern of self-esteem and normative orientation towards authority would be in play. In 1962 in Northampton, obviously women were a little bit more normatively submissive, the English were normatively inhibited about the expression of feeling, especially aggressive feelings. Anyway, that was my first publication and everybody at Leicester thought I was this little American kid, I was twenty-two years old, no one thought I would do any harm so they would let me get away with blue murder! I would drive two nights a week to Northampton, at the end of the afternoon, and had these experimental situations where we would alter male/female supervisors and the sizes of the groups. And that was my MA thesis, which I sent back to St Louis.

It's a long time ago, but I published part of that paper, in my book The Social Unconscious, Selected Papers (2003). The purpose of it was to show that you couldn't just talk about frustration and aggression, you had to contextualize it. As soon as you put women rather than men and class and varied these things, self-esteem was itself important in different ways depending on the context. It is so obvious! It was so obvious to me then.

CHRISTINE: And obvious now?

EARL: Should be obvious now. When consulting, for example, you might ask, what is it that you guys want to achieve? What is the difficulty to get to where you want to be? How do you imagine the future of the organization and your role in it? You release the creativity, but you also can release statements, putting into words so it's not mumbled as an autistic symptom, the sense of helplessness that so many people have in big organizations. And the fear that they're going to be wiped out.

CHRISTINE: How do we help people to access that feeling without being overwhelmed by it?

EARL: Well, I think that you can do it through group consultations and once you have it in your head, also individual consultations. It's not only group. And you can do it in larger groups than one thinks one can in an organization. Working slowly and supportively and acknowledging how difficult it must be to put so much into one's adult work life and often have a feeling that you can't do very much. That with global pressures decision-making is occurring in another country, even.

CHRISTINE: And what you were saying about frustration and aggression, I was thinking about shame and humiliation and the link between those and violence.

EARL: Are they similar?

CHRISTINE: It is a similar kind of process, leading to destructive enactments. This is the organizational version.

EARL: Very similar, very.

CHRISTINE: What I wanted to ask you though, is, when people are afraid, when you're working with an organization where fear or anxiety is the dominant affect, how you make decisions about what level to make a comment? Because I think that is quite tricky to judge, what level people can bear. The language is important as well, what kinds of words we use . . .

EARL: What you said just now. What people can bear to hear and think about.

CHRISTINE: But how do you make that judgment?

EARL: Just that way. By trusting my feelings about it. And, some people are better at it than others. It takes time to help young people under-stand that being an expert, imposing their point of view intrusively in a very troubled situation from which people's welfare derives is very dangerous and they actually have to be very gentle, and very sensi-tive – you have to be very very careful when you are working with these systems. People have their feelings hurt very easily. They have a lot at stake. So, you have to be very caring. It's something that clini-cians who are very caring often with their individual patients don't always understand, that it's even more so out in the real world. Would you agree with that?

CHRISTINE: I would agree with that. Because a work setting is public, you're there with your colleagues so the experience of being shamed or humiliated is very powerful.

EARL: Very powerful.

CHRISTINE: If we don't think through how the analytic thinking can be used in this particular setting then I think we can make some real howlers.

I just want to go back to what you said about class, though, because I think this is important. I want to tell you a story, from almost a hun-dred years ago, when I was running an advice center in the early 1980s. A colleague came back from representing one of our clients at a Social Security Appeals Tribunal. He was full of glee, because in his dirty and disheveled clothes, accompanying the client who was wearing a suit, the Tribunal Chair had thought that the client was the representative and my colleague was the claimant. For him it was a game; he thought it demonstrated his working-class credentials. I was outraged. Because he was more concerned with that than the client's real needs. It's not important in itself what you wear, but you wear what will help the work, not prejudice it.

EARL: Well Winnicott for example, which is partly where I got it from, was very formally dressed with patients. He was quite informal in his style, but he always wore a coat and tie. My own analyst was Italian, he had a certain sense of style. He always had on a suit, during the week, sometimes three- piece. And on Friday, he wore a sports coat.

I don't think I saw him in all those years without a coat and tie. Maybe once at a summer barbecue.

CHRISTINE: I think it's a minor aspect of dynamic administration.

EARL: Well, I think of it that way, it's a bit of boundary maintenance. You're making a statement, this is work and I'm taking you seriously and it's formal. My patients tease me because I'm usually pretty smart. I usually have a coat on. They tease me a lot about it. When you work in an organizational setting, it also helps to dress the way the others dress. It's a gesture of some kind.

CHRISTINE: It's also a short cut at times, in exactly the way that finding their language is a shortcut. You're bringing a different angle, you're bringing something new. But the experience needs to be near enough to what they recognize to be tolerable. If you dress like a scarecrow the chances are they might give you a pound.

EARL: These are communicational gestures.

CHRISTINE: Exactly.

EARL: Some organizations seem to have a culture of envy, though I don't like that expression 'culture of envy', Everything becomes a matter of envy, say during wage negotiations which are not just rational discussions about what can be earned, what can be afforded, the politics of it. These are understandably conflict-laden and should be, there is conflict of interest, but something more . . . There's a bitterness and a resentment which colors the discussions, so that people, often people of goodwill, end up feeling tarnished through the discussion. Organizations can get that way.

CHRISTINE: What leads to that?

EARL: I was thinking about that. There are these pockets of envy which are connected to pockets of creativity. So that wherever anything good seems to be happening, where there are signs of life and energy, equally you can find destructive forces or people who carry this sort of envy and jealousy and seem to undermine or begrudge others' success, and the people associated with it.

CHRISTINE: it's reactive?

EARL: it makes me wonder, I don't have an answer, but I certainly observe it. Sometimes for a while an organization is successful because that doesn't exist there, and then it changes. I don't know why it happens, I see that it does.

CHRISTINE: How fundamental is envy? I am thinking about the tension between group identification and personal identification. I like the fourth basic assumption because, as you argue, it's more fundamental. Bion's basic assumptions are all about envy. The fourth basic assumption is not, and it's more fundamental for that reason.

EARL: It's about helplessness.

CHRISTINE: Helplessness, and the fear of annihilation.

EARL: That's what I think.

CHRISTINE: Whereas envy is a defensive reaction to that.

EARL: This is my signature statement.

CHRISTINE: Yes. And I agree with you. Translating that into organizational terms then, what is the genesis of envy?

EARL: Helplessness.

CHRISTINE: Do you think our seeing envy (and fear?) as secondary rather than primal is because of the strong sociological strand in group analysis, which gives a broader base from which to consider meaning?

EARL: Yes.

Chapter 20

Creating thinking spaces in organizations

Dynamic administration in groups large and small

Cynthia Rogers

Introduction

Group analysis is a flexible consulting method that creates spaces where people can think together. The aim is to facilitate authentic free-flowing conversation. It offers a way of conceptualizing and relating. Individuals are seen as informed by their experience and constantly influencing and being influenced by others, including by their wider professional or sectoral context. The group analytic consultant uses a tripartite paradigm: a psychoanalytic conceptualization, a systemic perspective informed by complexity thinking, and an awareness of the psychosocial forces at play.

What makes this level of thinking possible?

In the example opposite, the group analytic model blames neither employees nor owner but looks at the interplay between the two. Group analysis sees transference at play in all our relationships. Knowing the client's personal history can illuminate motivation and identify the potentials for

The owner of a design company considered himself benevolent, open, dem-ocratic, and on good terms with his employees. In design, holding onto your talent is an important driver. The company had grown to about 50 people who stayed because he created a sense they were valued. He continued to hold all responsibility, which was stressful. The structure allowed the owner to believe that he had created a benevolent work family, where he could avoid conflict, feel indispensable and be in charge. This served as a distrac-tion from the fear that if he was not benevolent, the people he depended on would leave.

Senior managers were interviewed about their concerns, their under-standing of the present dynamics and their ideas for solutions. It became clear that because there was no hierarchy of decision making, relationships had become competitive. Others' new ideas were dismissed. People were not happy but were unable to say so. Once dissatisfaction came into the open, change became easier for the owner to contemplate, and managers and owner shared agreement that change was necessary. The choice then facing the owner was:

• To stay unambiguously in charge and deal with the conflict.

  OR

• To bring someone in, with real authority, to deal with conflict and install appropriate lines of decision making.

The owner chose the second option and an experienced and respected grandfather figure was introduced. This enabled the owner to delegate, reorganizing the reporting structures to be self-supporting and freeing him to be in charge of what really mattered. The owner had a mental model of good fathering and was comfortable with the idea of a grandfather. The two were able to model working together non-competitively, establishing a culture of co-operation and respect. Not everyone chose to stay, but those who did were making a more mature, realistic commitment than the previ-ously idealized, not altogether functional co-dependency.

misunderstanding. In the adjacent example, had the owner had a big brother who always knew best, it is highly unlikely he would have opted to bring someone in. The dynamics of the organization came into the relationship and the consultation where it could be discussed without retaliation or reward. Shortcomings were acknowledged as facts. Unhelpful dynamics were framed as inevitable but needing attention. The consultant did not try to do everything herself (as the client was wont to) but without losing face, brought in a partner with different expertise. She resisted the client's tendency to draw her into being either the 'expert', on a pedestal from which she would inevitably shortly fall, or an interfering yet inattentive, self-absorbed parental figure. Perhaps most important was sharing her ideas and her understanding of the dynamics, so a true collaboration could evolve. She stayed occasionally involved to help maintain the level of thinking achieved through the intervention.

Creating thinking spaces

Group Analytic thinking comes from engaging emotionally and intellectually with concerns and ideas. The network of relationships is the consultant's tool. Like any delicate instrument, it needs to be well supported. The consultant creates thinking spaces underpinned by careful dynamic administration, (Foulkes and Anthony, 1957; Behr and Hearst, 2005) which give the best conditions for authentic conversation and for a successful consultation. Christine Thornton (Thornton, 2010, 2016) provides comprehensive, practical practice checklists for dynamic administration in consultancy. Dynamic administration demands intelligence and creativity, beyond simply being diligent about arrangements. It requires the consultant to anticipate potential difficulties, reflect on practical arrangements, and think about structure, in the light of theory about unconscious processes and relational dynamics.

Getting off to a good start: initial contracting, building relationships

Even where there is apparent goodwill, consultation can be set up to fail. Anticipating unhelpful dynamics is essential. Group analysts are alert to power dynamics such as being brought in to reinforce an unsustainable model, over the head of the Director, or by the team member losing the current argument. Sometimes the invitation is made at the level where the pain is felt rather than where things can change. Participants uncomfortable with change may resist engaging.

Building secure relationships from the start creates the thinking spaces that promote a successful outcome. In the initial discussions with a commissioner, gentle questioning can encourage an awareness of the interconnected relationships and suggest a non-blaming approach to problems. This frees the consultant to develop their intervention and build relationships with others, vital for a successful outcome. Some questions to have in mind, and perhaps to ask, include:

- Whose idea is it?
- How is the request framed?

- What is the purpose – improve service to clients, reduce burn out, develop staff?
- Why now, is it linked to other changes e.g. reduction in staff?
- What previous attempts have been made to tackle the issues?
- What happened? If unsuccessful, how were they thwarted?
- What are the expectations of the consultation, and how realistic are they?
- How will the organization protect the time for the group(s)?
- How will we judge the success or otherwise?

How relationships are built with the participants sets the tone for the consultation. For example, including people in thinking about how to work together breaks down expectations that you will tell them what to do and challenges the idea of an omnipotent consultant. Again, there are questions to hold in mind.

- What agreements with each other will help the work be effective?
- How do they want to deal with differences between them, including hierarchical differences?
- What agreements does the group analyst needs, e.g. arriving on time?
- How will they judge the success or otherwise?

Engaging with significant figures and defining the purpose of the consultation

The purpose of the consultancy is usually initially defined by the commissioner but should also be shared by those involved. Where a senior manager is unwilling to be involved or passively fails to support the consultation it will be difficult. It can be tempting to leave the senior manager out of a consultation for simplicity's sake, but it is not wise. Group analysts are looking for maximum communication and expect to engage with the complexity of power and difference. They are less concerned with the needs of individuals in isolation than they are with the network of connections that meet the needs of these individuals. Engaging with multiple simultaneous relationships pulls the consultant in different directions but allows her/him to engage with the concerns of staff, senior managers, and CEO, offering support without conceding undue influence.

I wouldn't start from here if I were you . . .

A senior manager commissioned a consultation to support a team who were perceived as under-performing. The commissioner was not expecting to be involved, but it became clear that her concerns had not been clearly heard by, or not well communicated to, the team. Indeed, the team were unclear why they were being asked to meet. This lack of clarity led to a reluctance to attend and difficulty in thinking with purpose. Had the commissioner engaged with the team in a thoughtful way before, or as the work commenced, there could have been a shared purpose. The consultant could have started by asking for the team's thoughts about their senior manager's view of them, how that view had been created, and what they could do to change it.

Keeping the work on course: the consultant's stance and responsibilities

Group Analytic thinking is complex but appears superficially simple. Quality conversation is the aim, and it is helpful to make this explicit. Group analysts locate difficulties *between* people rather than in the individual. In organizational consultancy, this means conceptualizing organizational difficulties as interpersonal and constrained by the organizational culture. The consultation explicitly embodies this way of thinking, minimizing the fear of humiliation and undermining the tendency to scapegoat. Group analysts take this way of thinking for granted, but it is breathtakingly new to those used to a blame culture.

Participants deploy defensive maneuvers to give themselves a sense of control and safety. In practice this safety is illusory. One person will talk a lot while another will stay silent. People take up roles for the group; e.g. the helpful member, the group historian, or the one who is critical of both management and the consultant. The consultant challenges these positions. The person who is talking too much might be encouraged to consider 'whether the group is exploiting your goodwill?'. The person who says too little might be kindly challenged 'is it very difficult for you to talk? It is hard for the rest of us because we miss out on what you think'.

Groups work best when operating at an optimum level of creative chaos, the point where people think by drawing on their feelings as a result of participating in the group experience. (See also chapters five, seven and 12.) This can be arrived at whilst also reducing the anxiety levels of the participants. There is a common misconception that raising anxiety spurs people to action. In my experience, it induces caution and withholding; there is no place for a silent withholding consultant, stimulating anxiety and then interpreting it. The participants will reflect back the lack of spontaneity and resist sharing their concerns and experience. If the consultant is experienced as genuinely interested and engaged, the participants, taking their cue from the consultant about appropriate behavior, will be similarly engaged.

Attendance and starting on time are important. Making it an authority issue is counter-productive. Explaining why it's essential for everyone to be there at the beginning is more effective. When the consultant takes an authoritarian attitude, there is likely to be rebellion. Conversely, if the consultant seems unsure of their authority, collusive risk avoidance arises. 'Busy', 'important' people who absent themselves may need to be told they are needed and missed.

In a thinking space, ideas are valued not judged. The consultant will be interested in the ideas expressed, whether or not he or she agrees with them. Accepting or refuting ideas too quickly closes down thinking. The consultant intervenes in ways that model and prioritize curiosity about the emerging ideas and interpersonal dynamics. Ideas that are counterintuitive or challenging to implement are encouraged.

While the participants' role is to engage in authentic conversation, the group analyst is looking for hidden dynamics. The formal structures are not always those that have the real influence on behavior and the shadow system of informal relationships may emerge. The consultant will be alert to the dynamics of the organizational dysfunction arising in the group. For instance, in a consultation to a team working with a housing crisis one might expect difficulty in finding a room to operate from; it gives the consultant a lived experience of what it is like not to have a stable base. Group analysts expect the culture of the occupational groups to come into the consultation. Staff working with the elderly may well have issues around counter-dependency whilst detached youth workers may find it irresistible to detach from the consultation.

Providing the appropriate structure and setting

The starting point from which to establish trust will differ depending whether the consultation is to strangers or people in existing relationships. When dealing with a group of people who have existing relationships, they are influenced strongly by the existing organizational dynamics and the fact that they have to work with each other the next day. A consultant is called in when the dynamics are not allowing the thinking that is needed. The challenge is to modify the existing dynamics to allow a thinking space.

Dynamics of Procrastination

Called into a professional partnership where the future direction of the partnership needed to be decided but progress was being thwarted through procrastination, the consultant agreed to work not on the direction of the partnership, but on what prevented the partners from reaching an agreed view, and how to free them to make a decision.

Meeting with strangers who share some professional allegiances is an opportunity to have new thoughts, and is incidentally closer in praxis to therapeutic group analysis. A consultation to support doctors in general practice illustrates the value of being able to work with both individuals and groups, large and small, using the same consistent conceptual framework. The structure of each intervention could be carefully considered and designed in the light of the profession's values and sensitivities, to create a space where the relevant issues could be reflected on emotionally and intelligently so as to influence practice.

Consulting to a profession

The commissioner requested a group analytic consultation because professional stress had gone beyond individuals or sectors and now permeated the culture of the whole profession. The intervention needed to influence every level of the profession. The challenge was to create a network of relationships and a narrative that could challenge the assumptions driving despair and empower those on the ground, as well as those in positions of authority, to act. The commissioner was both an influential figure and someone prepared to be an active participant. A dinner was held for those 'experts with influence' in the profession. We shared our concerns and aspirations but more importantly listened to their ideas, as they tacitly bought into the project. The ideas were piloted at a national conference using a goldfish bowl and large group discussion.

The consultation

The consultation was fiercely group analytic but infinitely flexible. Workshops such as 'A masterclass in reflective practice' were held. These used median and small groups to address: managing change, practice dynamics, developing interpersonal resilience, and intelligent self-reflection (Rogers, 2018). Median and large groups are essential tools where an organizational consultant is interested in influencing the organizational culture, see also chapters 21–23. A median/large group can address issues as they operate within the culture of the workplace. It allows focus on the individual, the individual as a member of interconnecting small groups and the individual in their wider context.

Open monthly workshops were established where the median group was central and real experience of managing stress was discussed. Witnessing people saying something can be done, and perhaps even suggesting what might be done, is different from the perennial, 'something should be done'. Some participants joined reflective practice groups and analytic groups designed especially for doctors. Coaching was provided for individual practitioners and a workshop for practice managers.

Event titles directly connected with the concerns of the professionals, stressing what they would gain from coming rather than problematizing the issues or individuals. The considerable body of knowledge accumulated by group analysts, psychoanalysts, and those working in the health service (Wilke, 2005; Ballatt and Campling, 2011; Cooper and Lousada, 2005; Brooks, Gerada and Chalder, 2011), not necessarily readily accessible to the profession, was discussed in the workshops and at a lecture day.

A general election was imminent and provided a focus for doctors to articulate to all political parties what could be done to support the profession. Four one day-conferences were held. The format was a large group introduced by a 20-minute orienting provocation (see below), a small group and then another large group for the 70–100 participants.

The approach stimulated real thinking and new ideas and the discussions were noted verbatim by scribes with an anthropological orientation. The ideas and challenges from each event were carefully curated. Reports and papers were written. Finally, there was dialogue in a small group between the commissioner and some of those who had conducted and contributed to the work. Group analysts are not looking for a long list of good ideas and intentions but one or two truly new thoughts that might make a real difference to how we do things. For example, three ideas:

1 That doctors need to assert that they are not Harold Shipman and address the lack of trust in their profession (O'Neill, 2002).
2 Taking control of the discourse is essential if the doctors' arguments are to prevail. If doctors engage with the language of cuts they will only ever be discussing how deep.
3 Using the language of decluttering. There are no good arguments against decluttering. The lives of these professionals were cluttered by the need to demonstrate their professionalism in a bureaucratic way. Might they responsibly articulate the need to declutter?

The outcome of the consultation

The dialogue in the profession moved from denial, through anxiety, to quiet determination and indignation. Group analysts met with a small percentage of the profession but the ideas spread through the network of connections. Individual GPs were supported and some discouraged from leaving the profession. Most importantly the commissioner was able to articulate coherently the concerns of the profession to those with the power to act.

Consulting and dynamic administration with median and larger groups

Median groups vary in size but imagine something between 17 and 70+ people meeting, where everyone can see and be heard relatively easily. Like a community meeting, it is most useful when cultural shifts are required. A median group mediates the impact of institutional decisions on individuals. Participants tend to dislike the unfamiliarity of sitting in a median group but feel better if they understand why it is the appropriate setting (Rogers, 2013, 2017). See also pages 203, 207–209.

Practical culture change

In the NHS, working excessive hours is routine and difficult for one individual to resist. Staff may be afraid to put their heads 'above the parapet'. In a median group staff can come to an understanding of what needs to be done and there is a chance that one or more will be emboldened to act, setting an example by going home in a timely fashion, challenging the established culture.

Participants are encouraged to speak for themselves, not others, and not to hide behind a role. A conversation in a median group will usually have multiple threads, pursued at multiple levels simultaneously. Participants can feel for a while that their comment has dropped into a void. A median group will reflect the real world with hidden alliances and unacknowledged conflicts. Through learning how to participate actively, one acquires valuable skills for workplace negotiations. The consultant will be interested in the changing landscape of alliances and subgroups but avoid commenting in a way that fixes the moving relationships or privileges one view of sub-grouping over another. An organization implementing essential changes needs a culture shift and culture carriers; median groups influence and help people digest change.

Median groups to develop strategy

A major charity employed groups analysts over decades to conduct median groups as a primary management tool. Bi-annual weekend meetings used median groups to work sequentially through.

- Where are we now?
- Where do we want to get to?
- What do we need to do to get there?

It produced a consensus where the volunteers bought into the decisions and the directors were empowered to act. Even the inevitable isolation and resentment that the directors felt could be addressed constructively.

Using a provocation in median and large groups

In a median or larger group where people do not meet regularly or know one another, a provocation can be helpful. It is a 20-minute input of ideas followed by a median/large group where the provocateur feels free, but not obliged, to comment. A provocation is particularly useful when an organization invites a consultation because it is tired, has lost its way, and seems unable to respond to the stress it encounters. In constructing a provocation my attention is focused on – What is the culture? Why is it the way it is? Why is it articulated the way it is? What sustains it? What ideas can I offer?

As the participants in a median or larger group listen to the provocation the early stages of the group matrix forms. The individuals associate in their minds to the ideas, identifying with some and questioning others, without feeling they have to respond immediately. The seeds of differences and commonalities are sown in the room. Thus, the scaffolding that participants can use later to exchange ideas is built up. A good therapeutic alliance is likely if the participants feel understood. This might mean acknowledging both the received wisdom and mentioning issues that are more difficult to voice. A consultant with a simple conceptual frame new to participants, putting their concerns into words, looks as if they have something to offer. Confidently challenging existing negative predictions will also get people's attention.

Conclusion

Whatever the context, the dynamics and practicalities of each consultation is thought about analytically. Where the consultant creates a secure setting, and encourages authentic relationships, genuine thinking spaces emerge. The participants operate from a well-supported secure base to explore their relationships with others in the organization, all the while forming more mature patterns of relating and interdependence (Glenn, 1987).

Chapter 21

Large groups the group analytic way

Gerhard Wilke

Organizations are not machines but living communities, with both a formal structure of roles and status positions and an informal relationship matrix, similarly indispensable in making things work. Some modern management trends, such as the 'learning organization' (Pedler, Burgoyne and Boydell, 1997) and the embracing of 'emotional intelligence'(Goleman, 1999) acknowledge the reality that emotions and experiences are the great untapped source of data in every organization. It is in this arena that the group analytic consultant can free up communication across the organization, through large groups.

In large groups, all staff, or in larger organizations, representatives of all sections, meet face to face. With the help of a facilitator, they tell each other stories of mutual help, cooperation, and conflict between departments and the top, middle, and bottom of the organization. These exchanges make explicit the link between the formal and informal organization and its past, present, and future. The uninhibited telling of stories reveals what is going on and what is missing in the organization, enabling its members to face up to what needs to be done next and modify culture – how we do things – together and apart.

In everyday life, stories function from childhood onwards to convey complex social meanings. Storytelling surfaces the 'unnamable' and the 'unknowable' in human exchange. Stories, fairy tales, and myths help evolve a sense of self in each member of a community an identity integrating a feeling of 'who I am' and 'who we are'. This involves developing an awareness of how we do things in our in-group, and how other groups do them differently. Only by embracing the dynamic between what is familiar and reassuring and what is unfamiliar and unsettling, can each of us know what it means to belong, to have some inner security from a shared history. History is itself a story that helps us make sense of life events and gives them their meaning.

Starting with these assumptions, it makes sense to begin by telling my own story, how I became a Large Group Conductor. My generation of post-war Germans was morally burdened by the murderous inheritance of the Third Reich, a regime that not only destroyed the country but also plunged the whole of Europe into war, genocide, deportations, repatriations, and a descent into a human hell. The committed supporters of the Nazi regime, their compliant followers, and their silent resisters were my generations' parents. In the eyes of the world they were laden with so much collective and individual guilt that it was impossible to have a straightforward parent-child relationship after 1945. However, the parent generation was not just complicit with the Nazi Terror, it was also traumatized by experiences before and during the war. The implication? We in the next generation, or more precisely, the chosen children within traumatized German families, unconsciously took on the task of compensating for the guilt of our forefathers by feeling ashamed of who we were, with an over-developed sense of duty and, to a degree, the loss of self-determination. We wanted never to become perpetrators, as we feared our fathers had been; our imagined fathers, filling the memory void underneath the conspiracy of silence about what really happened in the war.

The Large Group on the Introductory Course of the London Institute of Group Analysis changed my life. The group, of 180 people, was conducted by Lionel Kreeger. He would simply say that the group had started and wait for the free flow of associations. The scene struck me as totally unbelievable. After a short period of frustration and bickering about the setting, the group began to think together, descended into fear and confusion, then recovered its wits and explored what feelings lay behind the pressure to speak and remain silent. In the very first group session we noted that we were meeting twenty years after the 1968 student protest movement. The Large Group reminded some people of sit-ins, spontaneous protest gatherings that had quickly turned into events where people taught each other and thought 'collectively' about social reform, quarreled about reform or revolution, and split into different camps. The 1968 radicals were united *and* divided, just like the Large Group we were sitting in.

As the group progressed I got in touch with my innermost inhibitions about a large group mass and its leader. In my mind these were always fused: I could only imagine it as a mindless and potentially dangerous social formation, a social monster that would give rise to an abusive leader and end in war and destruction. I felt this, long before I ever read a word by Bion. As the weekly Large Group sessions gathered momentum, it became clear to me that this setting was a space in which unconscious aspects of history, societal traumas and the vexed problem of what holds a community together, could potentially be explored and understood. Indeed, issues like the passing on of guilt and shame to the next generation, the cost of a totalitarian system to the parent generation, the un-mourned dead of two World Wars, the flight or evacuation from a homeland, and generally the unconscious aspects of societal upheavals and crisis emerged with amazing speed in this group, and could be named and worked with. I had to admit to myself that not all large groups are dangerous; also, that a large group gathering does not inevitably produce a charismatic seductive leader, who tells the crowd what it wants to hear and unifies it against internal and external 'enemies'. The benign nature of the conductor, and the accepting culture that grew in the group, enabled me to imagine that I could dedicate my group analytic work to the systematic exploration of socially unconscious processes in between groups and their link to the whole society and its history.

By contrast, ten years later, I sat in a large group with over 300 members in Germany. The theme of the Conference was Boundaries, about four years after the Berlin Wall had fallen, and the country re-unified. For an entire week, the group was pre-occupied with perpetrators, victims, and bystanders as subgroups within the Large Group – except when an annoyed sub-group-majority ganged up against the conductor to commit patricide. The Large Group conductor conceptualized it as a transposition of the oedipal struggle between father (conductor), mother (group), and the sibling horde. The casualty of looking at the large group only through this lens was that the miraculous external social and historical developments in Germany and Europe, as well as the multiplicity of feelings and social and cultural divisions and connections in the group, never came into the dialogue. The group exchanges and the interpretations focused only on the oedipal struggle between the generations and the split into German perpetrators, Jewish victims, and helpless bystanders.

That was a lightbulb moment for me: leading a Large Group requires the conductor to think group analytically about the matrix of the group and the foundation matrix of the surrounding society in a very conscious way. You cannot simply transfer what is known from individual psychoanalysis into an 'as if' societal setting; you need to use an understanding of social processes.

What is important for a group analytic conducting style of large groups?

The conductor of the large group embraces the three roles recommended by Foulkes for the group-analytic 'conductor': Dynamic Administrator, Analyst, and Translator. The conductor's work is to widen and deepen the communication at the level of the individual, the sub-group, the group (matrix) as a whole, and its connection to the societal, cultural, and historical context (foundation matrix). Symptoms of dis-ease are not an expression of individual pathology alone, but simultaneously an expression of what is taboo to think, say, and do in society. This emerges in the free-floating communication in a large group session. Psychic conflict in the large group results from lost connections, disturbed communication patterns, and disrupted mourning processes – all of which relate to the absence of a task or sense of direction and the suspension of the containing rituals of everyday conversation.

Without all the taken-for-granted, non-conscious expectations in everyday social exchange, the member of a large group experiences disorientation and fear: fear of being swallowed up in the mass, of being rejected and expelled or of not being heard or seen. By conveying trust in the large group, accepting whatever is spoken and enacted, the conductor can help the group find its own way of overcoming the 'dis-ease' between the speaker, the listener, the silent bystander(s), and the often moralistic and judgmental chorus. The Large Group is a form of theater and as in Greek tragedy, enacts the psycho-social-triangle of perpetrator/hero and victim/anti-hero and chorus/merged or fragmented mass. The exchanges in the large group mirror the foundation matrix of society itself, holding us-and-them divisions. Individual members and emergent subgroups name and work with social defenses, translate symptoms of trans-generational traumas and find ways of seeing and making sense in interaction with each other and the conductor. The exchanges illustrate what holds the group together as a temporarily coherent community, and what causes it to fragment or fuse under stress. If we understand organizations as living communities, the large group is a powerful tool for organizational praxis and learning from the experience of working together.

Dynamic administrator

The first role a large group conductor must embrace sensitively is Dynamic Administrator, thinking about the creation of the setting for a Large Group. The construction of a setting often involves compromises with the shape of the room, the size of the chairs, local traditions or Health and Safety Regulations. In a hotel, for instance, the conductor must seek permission to build the setting, and/or supervise the construction by staff. The conductor needs to build an alliance with the staff, who become co-owners of the setting and can function as guardians of the group boundary when the session has started. In consulting work, a fundamental issue is to name the event. The session needs a name that is sufficiently familiar for the participants. In a Scandinavian Engineering Company large group work was used to bring various merged parts of the global organization face to face to explore cultural differences and commonalities and to arrive at a better mix of global and local ways of working. They legitimized it by comparing it to a Viking Ting – a community meeting.

Socratic Dialogue, where people sat in a circle to dispute and search for a deeper philosophical truth and meaning in life, foreshadowed the group analytic way of organizing and leading Large Groups. In an organizational setting, the large group brings together people who are not equal. They usually come together to understand why things are stuck or why conflicts are not resolvable. Before a session I therefore try to get a sense of what kind of 'stuck'. If the organization feels depressed, traumatized, split, or disorientated, I try to sit everyone in one circle. This helps members of the organization to re-connect with the whole of the organizational community, not just their own team. If there is a split, say between management and staff, doctors and nurses, or engineers and sales, two concentric circles are better as the underlying issue of fight-flight is 'bodily' present through the setting. Large Groups in Psychoanalytic Institutions also require, at first, two circles because they have often evolved a split culture, comprising active and passive 'citizens'. Frequently there is a conflict between three generations, or between different sub-committees and the leader-group. In that case three concentric circles are preferable as the arrangement embodies and expresses issue of authority, power, the status hierarchy, and the unconsciously associated defenses of anti-authoritarian protest, generational conflict, and sibling rivalry.

In consulting work with whole organizations, using large groups involves working with a large number of participants. In this case, I prefer many concentric circles, evoking the core issue – how do we share a sense of one organization, whilst retaining a sub-identity and loyalty to our sub-group? How do we communicate and co-operate across the boundary of the top, the middle, and the bottom of the organization? Perhaps most importantly, how can we make visible and conscious that the organization has a formal and an informal structure – both indispensable to make things work. With professional organizations and psychiatric institutions, I usually spend the first day working with the various subgroups and the next day with the whole, large group as a community. The thinking behind this is to strengthen the confidence and identity of the sub-group, before engaging with the 'threatening or unfamiliar' others in another department or at the top of the organization. Over the years, it has become clear to me that intergroup relationships within a larger organization are best worked with by respecting rather than abolishing sub-group boundaries. The importance of this issue is explored further in the vignettes on pages 218–20 and 247–50.

Analyst

The second role a large group conductor must embrace is that of the containing Analyst. The large group conductor is above all a participant observer who cannot maintain a neutral and objective position. Analysis of what goes on in the group at any moment involves some revelation of the analyst's observation, feeling, and thought. Analysis comes into play when the conductor relates her/his own experience to what s/he guesses might be going on for the whole group. One of the prime functions of the conductor is to model a mind-set of acceptance, holding and searching for meaning and sense. In such a group, I link observation and analysis with an invitation to hear what sense others make of what is going on. As in real life, the conductor is more likely to get his/her authority legitimized by the group when s/he reveals that s/he is not an all-knowing god, but human and open for other views, thoughts and observations.

Translator

Last but not least, the Large Group conductor is Translator. This role involves observing, noting and translating boundary events into words to make them available for dialogue. In other words, creating a secure enough environment for enactments to take place and be understood through dialogue. What do enactment and translation look like? To illustrate, a story.

An architect whose parents are concentration camp survivors asked me to participate in a project designed to highlight the fact that the second largest Jewish Community in Germany did not have a synagogue, 45 years after the end of the war. The local politicians had given the community a piece of land in the sixties and promised large subsidies for the construction of a community center and place of worship. Underneath the ground lay the bunker for the Nazi elite, designed to let them carry on their work whilst the Allies bombed the city. A surveyor's report showed that the cost of removing the bunker would be greater than the building of a new synagogue. The community was reluctant to settle in a place associated with the mass-murder of their relatives. Nothing happened for almost thirty years. The community built a car park on the land, made money to finance a rabbi and a community center. Then a new head of town planning wanted to re-open the case for a synagogue in the city. She and the newly elected president of the community, herself a survivor, decided it could and should be built on top of the bunker – built on the heads of their persecutors – to signify that the Jewish community had survived the Nazis. Public awareness was raised through an unusual architectural project. Final year students from two architecture schools, in Germany and Israel, were invited to visit the site, interviewed the Jewish community, the townspeople, and the planners. After the consultation they had to submit designs for a new synagogue. With the designs in first draft form, the two student bodies met for a workshop. Integral to this event was a large group, to reflect on the emotional and historical sensitivities involved in the project. We met in the cafeteria of the university. The seating area for the students was part of the entrance hall of this university and built like a Roman amphitheater in the shape of a triangle, with three downward steps to sit on and an empty space in the middle.

After a short introduction, I wondered what the effect on the group would be of sitting in an oedipal triangle. Suddenly, the caretaker of the building stormed into the hall and somehow sensed that I was the group's leader. He started shouting at me: 'Do you have official permission for this illegal assembly? Wait until the Director gets to hear of this . . . Get out . . . I will call the police . . . Don't move . . . It is disgusting . . . I never know what is going on in this place'.

I did nothing and waited.

There was a very brief, silent stand-off between the caretaker and the group. Most of the group turned away and stared into the empty space in the center of the seating area. Suddenly a German professor stood up shouting:

> 'Of course we have permission, you stupid fool. Stop bothering us. Do your own work and leave us to do ours'.

The caretaker went off in a huff as the professor sat down. The group looked stunned and was silent for a while. Another staff member started speaking about whether in modern Germany, building a synagogue was any different from building a mosque or a church. Another person said he was going to design an empty building which could also be a fire station, what the inhabitants did with it was their business. They, not he, had to give meaning to the space. He was willing merely to design it. The word fire-station was a trigger for some students to say that this project was different, that a synagogue in Germany at the end of the twentieth century could never be viewed as a neutral construction site. Too many of them had been consumed by fire during the Nazi reign of terror. All these statements were verbal illustrations of how in a large group, the 'chosen traumas' (Volkan) or 'adopted foundation-myths' (Wilke) of national groups speak through individual contributions and connect us all in the here-and-now with the past, that shapes how we feel, think, and act.

The group carried on working and splits were opening up. One sub-group argued that the design for the synagogue should resemble a modernist, functional, and rational construction. A second sub-group defended the idea that the building should be built like a holocaust memorial. These two paradigms established themselves very firmly and were not shifted for a long time. Towards the end of the session a third perspective emerged. An in-between sub-group thought that both the modernist and memorial perspective needed to be reflected in the design of this building. Eventually, I suggested that the architecture of the different opinion-sub-groups in the group seemed to be shaped by the influence of their home and school experience. The sub-group who wanted to build a memorial to the holocaust victims had parents who had talked about their war time suffering or their collusion in the murderous war. The sub-group who wanted to exclude the history of persecution from the design of the building came from families who had remained silent and left children guessing about the real-life experience of their parents. The in-between group of students seemed freer to choose their response, feeling that they had nothing to hide or feel ashamed about, as far as their families are concerned.

Though it was intellectually satisfying to find a neat fit between the design and inner history of Germans and Jews via family and school, the really significant event of this large group was enacted beyond its boundary. While we were working on the emotional dimensions of designing a synagogue in Germany, the caretaker assembled his team and started to move furniture around us in a bizarre and mindless way. This lasted through most of the session. Amazingly, at the end, all the furniture was back in its original position, and the noise surrounding and uniting us as a group, stopped. Everyone looked full of dis-ease. I was left with just sufficient sound-free time to summarize the major patterns which had emerged during the session. The faces of the participants led me to think that the inner and outer group were connected. I said that the caretaker and his team had dramatized the traumatizing historical scene between the Nazis and their enemies – the Jews and Intellectuals. By moving the furniture, they embodied the mindless sub-group that attacked the thinking and reflecting group. Having failed to expel us, they wanted to reduce all of us to their own state of mindlessness. They had also reminded us of the raw power of the unspoken in post-traumatic societies like Israel and Germany. It was the group boundary and our capacity to go on working despite the noise that stopped them descending fully into a fascist state of mind (Bollas, 1991). Our contribution to containing their envy and rage was to maintain a 'gap' between us and them and tolerate their disturbance. They had not really become perpetrators and we had not become victims, nor bystanders. Thus, the group ended.

The dis-ease between the group of intellectuals forming the work group inside the boundary, and the group of alienated employees embodying a very primitive group outside the boundary, re-enacted the trauma between perpetrators, victims, resisters, and bystanders. The 'synchronicity' (Jung, 1982) of the encounter showed that the group process always has the potential to widen and deepen civilizing and de-civilizing forces. The inner sub-group struggled with reparation, mutual tolerance of difference, acceptance of an authority figure and the integration of a social order; the outer sub-group displayed a valence for disturbance, loss of social control, and subservience to a pathologically disturbed leader.

Foulkes (1948) perceived the individual, the sub-group, and the group as a transpersonal group matrix, linked to the foundation matrix of the society. Building on this, group analysts such as Kreeger (1975) and de Mare, Piper, and Thompson (1991) take a positive view of the potentials of the large group; this was my own experience in Kreeger's large group.

Pat De Mare and his colleagues (1991) posited that the large group frustrates the satisfaction of libidinal needs resulting in hate. Sub-groups contain the hate and turn it into the desire to speak. Through a dialogue between the subgroups hate is transformed into frustration, which in turn is the pre-condition for thinking and linking and therefore meaningful communication. De Mare et al. concluded that large groups can build a matrix between differing subgroups and develop the capacity for fellowship (Koinonia). Large groups therefore provide an ideal setting for working through inter-group conflict to democratic pluralism and conflict resolution through dialogue and compromise (see also pages 185–86, 229 and 232. The business benefit of speaking about the gap between strategic intent and lived experience can be seen in the vignette on page 218, describing my work with an international law firm.

Volkan (2009) has pointed out that group identities, a shared sense of 'we' is vital for the stability of every person's identity. So, when different national or professional sub-groups meet in a multi-national setting an us-and-them dynamic must develop, before any crossing of group boundaries and search for common ground and shared language is possible.

Under threat from another sub-group, a sub-group emphasizes its 'we' identity, losing any sense of moral responsibility for the 'other', the stranger. Members start splitting and adopt territorial maneuvers, designed to defend the threatened honor of their belonging group. Subgroups will use each other to demonstrate their own superiority. Such a crisis state typically emerges in the large group just as in the history of nations, when members flee under the protective 'ethnic tent' (Volkan, 2001) in order to restore their lost pride. In such situations the leader makes the difference between the belonging group becoming defensive and aggressive in a malignant or a benign way.

In the large group setting the conductor can make all the difference, when splits threaten to get out of hand. The conductor's interventions can push hostile subgroups in the large group into more conflict, or into first attempts to reach out and re-connect. Promoting connection is best done by linking any statement with the implicit task of any analytic large group – to study how it is able or unable to build under one 'group roof' a network of sub-group relationships with enough of a sense of shared communion to tolerate different views.

Conclusion

A group analytic conductor of a large group must embrace three roles: Dynamic Administrator, Analyst, Translator. The conductor's work is to widen and deepen the communication at individual, sub-group, group-as-a-whole, and cultural and historic levels. Symptoms of dis-ease are not merely an expression of individual pathology. Psychic conflict in the large group results from lost connections, disturbed communication patterns, and disrupted mourning processes. By modeling how to trust large group process, the conductor helps members find their own way of overcoming the 'dis-ease' between speaker, listener, and silent bystander(s), making dialogue, exchange, and interdependence possible. The large group then, like society itself, create a relationship matrix that holds and facilitates working through, collective mourning, adaptation, and re-creation.

Chapter 22

Whole organizations, mergers, and the matrix

Translucent boundaries and 'tweaking' culture creatively

Christine Thornton and Gerhard Wilke

Because of its flexibility and ability to respond to nuance, group analytic praxis is valuable for 'tweaking' culture in larger organizations, and for harnessing resistance to change to achieve better outcomes. In this first of a pair of chapters on working with whole organizations, we explain how the group analytic concept 'matrix' relates to *autopoiesis*, a concept from systems theory, to offer a coherent framework for understanding whole organizations as social systems. We offer examples of how group analytic thinking about translucent boundaries was applied practically in particular consultations, including an extended vignette about an international merger which also illustrated the anthropological lens of tribalism ('us and them' thinking) with which we open the next chapter.

The matrix, autopoiesis, and identity

Only the smallest organizations are a single group. Most consist of interlinked groups which must cooperate to achieve the common goal. The key task in leading or consulting to a larger organization is to influence relationships between these groupings. The words 'tweaking' and 'influence' are chosen carefully. Serious leaders must give up the illusion of control and learn that their role is to create a working environment within which positive change can emerge. Serious consultants can then help them, without recourse to triumphalism or manipulation. As with work with parts of organizations, such as teams, there is no manual. Group analysis offers a way of thinking that enables practitioners to make praxis choices in the particularity of the organization and its situation.

The group analytic concept 'matrix' (Foulkes, 1990a and b; Bhurruth, 2008; Nitzgen and Hopper, 2017) provides a coherent framework for consulting to whole organizations, elaborated through links to complexity thinking and ultimately to Bohm's (1951, 1980; Bohm and Hiley, 1993) quantum theory, seeing the universe as a flowing, unbroken wholeness. Conversation is central to praxis, and this is richly explored by Stacey (2012) and his colleagues; see chapter five in this volume.

The matrix links personal, group, and cultural patterns giving a rich understanding of identity as dynamic, consisting in patterns of relating (Dalal, 1998; Thornton, 2004). Here we explore this by reference to the work of two Chilean scientists, Humberto Maturana and Francisco Varela. Their theory of *autopoiesis* was developed as a new systemic understanding of biological phenomena, not immediately applied to the social world. However, used as a social metaphor, it illuminates the matrix and also the work of Gregory Bateson on the ecology of systems as 'wholes', mutually determining/determined complete fields of relations. For whole system work, intuition, experience, and generational dynamics are vital (Wilke, 2014). We take up this theme in the next chapter.

Autopoiesis (Maturana and Varela, 1980) focuses on the relationship between 'system' and 'environment' which Maturana and Varela saw as a false dichotomy, using the provocative word 'closed' to challenge the dominant view of open systems including systems-environment interaction. They argued that living systems have the capacity to self-create or self-renew, through three characteristics: autonomy, circularity, and self-reference. The most important product of any system is its own organization and identity.

Identity is maintained by subordinating all changes to the maintenance of the system *as a given set of patterns of relating*. These are circular, so that change in one part is always reflected in changes elsewhere, creating continuous patterns that are always self-referential. The system cannot enter into interactions that are not specified in its defining pattern of relating. Therefore, a system's interaction with its 'environment' is a reflection of its own organization, and always aids its own self-production.

'Autonomous' and 'closed' do not mean 'isolated'. The autonomy and closure are *organizational*. Living systems 'close in on themselves' to maintain stable patterns of relating, and this process of 'self-reference' is what makes a system a system (Morgan, 1997).

Maturana and Varela offer a provocative interrogation of the nature of system boundaries, addressing the problematic question of where a system begins and ends by positing a false dichotomy of system and environment. All systems analysis eventually runs up against the 'Russian doll' issue – wholes within wholes. They argue that there is no beginning and no end, because the system is a closed loop of interaction. Chapter six concerning 'parallel process' opens and closes with an example of how a particular pattern of relating can be seen at personal, group, organizational, and societal levels. Here is another example:

I worked with a lobbying organization which had just experienced a cata-strophic explosion. The new CEO came from a very different kind of organi-zation, and her senior leadership team (SLT) had orchestrated a vote of 'no confidence' and tried to get her sacked. The Board had backed the CEO and subsequently relationships between CEO and her team had completely broken down. This lobbying organization operated in a country faced with a national crisis of authority, with no clear national leadership talent on any side, and where similar 'palace coups' were rife.

Many conflicts had been stirred and all parties were adept at supporting their positions through political maneuvers. All the SLT were highly gifted intellectually, but unskilled at interrogating and using their feelings to improve the relevance and quality of their decision making. The consultancy question was whether they could repair relationships enough to work together again; I listened carefully to everyone and brought them together to listen to each other: the outcome was a fragile peace within the team. Perhaps the most important piece of work was with the leader so that she could mourn the high hopes she had brought into the company, and bear to work with her colleagues again. A year later she succeeded in bringing a major policy pro-ject to fruition, working with these same colleagues.

In the example, we see the reflection or equivalence (Hopper, 2007) between a lack of confidence in leaders and highly conflictual relationship patterns, at a national and an organizational level. But which came first? There is no conclusive answer to this, but the repetition of patterns of relating at many levels is the essence of the matrix, in the example perhaps intensified by the organization's focus on national politics. Maturana and Varela regarded the human brain as closed, autonomous, circular, and self-referential (Morgan, 1997). The brain does not process information from an environment as an independent domain, nor represent the environment in memory; it organizes its environment through perception, as an extension of itself. This has obvious links with developmental psychology (Stern, 1985) and with many versions of psychoanalytic thinking. For the brain to make 'true' representations of its environment, it would need an external point of reference – to be able to see its world from a point outside itself. Thus, it is seriously questionable that the brain by itself can represent reality.

This is very difficult for us to get our heads around, since we can *only* per-ceive through the brain. We see living systems, including organizations, as entities, because we see them from our own point of view, rather than from 'inside', understanding their logic from within. 'Outside' is the usual open-ing position as we begin working with an organization. Perhaps the notion of working *into* organizations gets us closer: as group analytic consultants, trained to attune to the internal rhythms of an organization, we are drawn into the organization's patterns of relating. We then come 'out' and reflect on those experiences, sharing our reflections with the clients. We go 'in' again, repeating the process many times in the course of a consultation. We are both 'in' and 'out', moving between; 'into' captures some of these dynamics.

Autopoiesis recognizes that systems have environments but insists that relationships with them are determined *within* the system, by the existing patterns of relating. Group analysis suggests that patterns are more important than attributing cause and effect (see chapter 6).

The matrix consists of patterns of relating and these create identity, whether at an individual, group, or organizational level. This fits well with the concept of autopoiesis. In group analysis, identity is understood as a developmental *process*, not fixed but adaptable (Dalal, 1998; Thornton, 2004). However, organizations, like people, can become too fixed in a particular self-identification. They then interact with 'environments', enacting dramas which are projections of their identities, resulting in frustration, failure, and sometimes extinction, as with the companies who defined themselves as making typewriters, resulting in extinction. The following vignette gives an account of how three law firms successfully softened outworn self-identities to incorporate a new additional identification as an international law firm.

A few years ago, we worked with a leading international law firm, led from Germany and the UK, coming together from the merger of three firms. The firm grew in a few years from having roughly 35 partners to having 550, facing formidable challenges in bringing together the best practice and habits of the very different German and two British firms. One British firm was concentrated in London and based on City work; the other in the Midlands, previously a challenger to the old established London firm. The German firm had several devolved regional offices and, like the Midland firm, worked with a much broader range of industries and clients than the London firm, which focused on high end City companies and felt superior to the others.

The senior partners of the firms recognized each other as senior elite lawyers. They were highly paid and used to working with the leaders of business and government in the UK, Germany, and the European Union. Despite the overlapping client base, there were sharp differences in the cultures of the three firms. London-centric English partners struggled with the spread of business and government in Germany and the Midlands. German partners struggled with the indirect ways of speaking of all the English partners. There were different patterns of professional education and training. People might speak good global business English, but behind the shared words were often very different cultural assumptions. The English preferred a centralized Headquarters and global market thinking, the Germans recognized that in their country business was done regionally. In England people served corporations, in Germany the focus was more on family owned firms and connections with significant players in local, state, and federal agencies.

There was a long history in all three firms of identifying leaders through conversations among leading partners, rather than headhunting or selecting to an abstract brief. This tradition proved very helpful as people had a deep-seated respect for free floating dialogue to find workable solutions. With the help of a small team of consultants, embodying different skill sets and assumptions about how human social systems work, the firm decided to set up a dual English-German leadership pair in each Department and at the Senior Partner level to run the firm after the merger. We as a team of consultants encouraged this so that all the cultural differences could be kept in mind when making strategic and operational decisions. This decision went against conventional wisdom, that in a merger one side is bound to come out on top and it is better to work towards this end, avoiding a consensual mish mash. It was clear to the leaders that the German partners would not accept being subordinate to the British firm, nor the British to their old enemies. There would have to be a genuine alliance of the three cultures to make the new whole work.

The group analytic dimension of this consultation was to turn Bion upside down. We thought of 'pairing' not just as a group defense, but as a generative principle to give birth to a new baby – in this case 'parental', 'containing', and 'firm' leadership, in charge of a frighteningly fast process of expansion as well as the difficult process of connecting three very different cultures – aristocratic, bourgeois, and petty bourgeois.

Once the leader pairs of all the Departments and at the Senior Partner level were formed, the consultants offered them reflection groups. Those leader pairs considered what was growing together, where there were splits and when and how to end the dual leadership arrangement and choose a single lead partner. We helped each pair have robust discussions about priorities, ways of working, and how cultural differences played out in their relationships. It was never a matter of ending one way of doing business and simply adopting a new one. It was necessary to work through the differences and examine what would help the whole firm for the future. It enabled people to end their exclusive attachment to 'their' original firm and achieve a triple loyalty to the whole firm, their section, and their cultural belonging group. Gradually the leaders who emerged were those who cared about the success of the new firm as a whole. They could respect the loyalties important to people's identities but were determined to overcome communication patterns that obstructed working together. The emerging single leaders eventually ended a range of working practices to make way for elements of the new federal culture. We helped them achieve a dialectic integration of us, them and all of us together.

When the sub-sections of the firm had evolved this new culture and let go of their old ways, it became clear that the integration of the whole organization as a distinct new culture had been smartly steered by the two senior partners, with the help of a sense of fairness, tolerance, and care. The seniors patiently watched and supported the efforts of the partners and consultants in bringing the three cultures together. They kept their nerve, despite being repeatedly mocked as wasteful and conflict-avoidant in the legal press. As the new sectional sub-cultures developed, they realized that the new firm was simply too big to be held together by them and by policies alone. They were able to acknowledge openly to the entire management group that they were pioneering an entirely new organizational form.

Previously integration was the responsibility of the senior partner, chief executive, and finance director. The troika, as it was affectionately and mockingly called, had to end. A forum was created for delegates, representing ten partners each, to meet regularly to reflect on organizational integration, including cross boundary co-operation and open communication channels between top, middle, and bottom. Our experienced consulting team helped, comprising people who knew about law, business, group dynamics, and culture. The section leaders and consultants then created a mini 'parliament', a large open group of 50 leading partners, selected from across the firm, to meet once a quarter; its purpose was to guide the future development of the firm and adjust strategy in the light of current market conditions and partner and customer experience.

A leading partner commented on the consultancy:

> 'You enabled us to talk about the things that mattered. You got us out of the trap of mistaking strategy for reality. We learnt that strategies are not a guarantee of security and function primarily as an anxiety management device. It also became clear to all of us that we have an evolving culture, embodied and lived and adapted by the partners. It is not acceptable anymore to think that we can re-engineer our culture. We learnt to have real and honest conversations and that this is what keeps us safe and is our best insurance policy against decline and complacency. It also makes us more open to the real needs of our clients as we have all learnt to listen and ask open questions'.

This merger was no conventional, top-down 'driving through' of change. It involved a careful building of enough agreement among the group of senior partners, pragmatically dealing with pressing issues. It required open and direct conversations about a number of tough issues, across sub-divisions and up and down the hierarchy. The lawyers worked in a pluralistic fashion to handle conflicting interests and viewpoints. Instead of simplifying the problem or looking to a magical leader to sort everything out, leaders and sections in the firm moved forward carefully, step by step. The consultants' contribution was to work with the leading partners and pay attention to the tasks, the team, and the network of cross-boundary relationships that held the whole community together.

This story shows how investing in the social capital of your community pays dividends, paying attention to dissent and cultural diversity rather than dismissing its significance. No preaching 'one family', as if the whole community did not have meaningful sub-divisions. Only when dissent and difference is invited into the dialogue, linked to cross-boundary 'representation' in meetings and projects, can an organizational community move on from reacting to events to creating a joint future.

The firm's leaders thought politically, acted strategically, and communicated with social and psychological awareness, which made it straightforward to end the consultancy. Separation was both sad and joyous. The group of five consultants had modeled working together in a thoughtful way; this was experienced as helpful and adopted as good practice. In other words, the consultant group embodied a good object the client could make use of in future transitions, separations, endings, and new beginnings.

Another example of a successful consultation to a whole organization can be found on pages 247–50. In that case, leader and consultant had to be 'killed off' so that the renewed organization could go forward. Chapter three demonstrates that problems between parts of organizations cannot be solved by consulting to only one part.

Translucent boundaries

The idea for this pair of chapters began with conversations between us about 'translucent boundaries' in organizational work, meaning the need to see boundaries in a different and less rigid way when working organizationally. For example when, as often happens, an organization needs to loosen internal territorial behavior, rigid boundaries on the part of the consultant may be actively unhelpful. Attending to the informal conversational structures and using opportunities to suggest new ways of viewing things is at least as helpful as the more formal parts of our consultant role. See further pages 242–43. These 'boundary crossings' should not however become 'boundary violations', where the more fluid boundary primarily benefits the consultant, not the client. See page 152.

Barry Oshry (2007) has catalogued some of the ways in which organizational 'identity' can ossify, describing pervasive unproductive patterns resulting in misunderstanding, tension, conflict, and breakdown. He observed certain universal patterns that emerge irrespective of sector, scale, or type of organization; symptoms are polarization, antagonism, and destructive conflict. Oshry argues that our primary lens for understanding our experience is personal. We think that we are dealing person-to-person, or group-to-group, when in fact we are also dealing context-to-context, established organizational divisions and team hierarchies or subgroups. We explain difficulties through the characteristics, skills, qualities, intentions, and beliefs of the 'problematic' individuals or groups. This leads to personal 'solutions' – so coach, retrain, fire, or side-line the problematic individual is the prevailing dictum. Oshry challenges this, and his systemic approach mirrors the group analytic concept 'location of a disturbance' in which a problem gets located in a scapegoat, dysfunctional individual or group, who embodies the symptoms, relieving everyone else of their shared responsibility for what is going on.

Oshry identifies four common forms of 'social blindness': spatial blindness, seeing our own part of the system but not the experience of others or the whole picture; temporal blindness, seeing the present, but not the history leading to this point; relational blindness, seeing ourselves as autonomous and denying our reliance on work relationships; positional blindness, being stuck in reactive behavior patterns as 'burdened tops', 'torn middles' or 'oppressed bottoms'.

'Translucent' means 'letting light through' and this is a good metaphor for what we do as consultants. We bring a different perspective which may 'shed light' on organizational blind spots previously hidden. We can design or participate in programs which bring together individuals from different parts of an organization, so that they 'shed light' on each other. Here is a second merger story:

A federal grouping of several regional housing associations providing affordable homes in the UK came together in a new national organization. By contrast to the story in *Persecutor, victim, rescuer* on page 31, this merger was given considerable thought by a talented internal organizational development specialist. She understood that the merger was not complete on 1st April simply because the legal process was completed then. She won support for action learning sets bringing together managers from *different* parts of the new organization, representing as many as possible of the original agencies in each group. The explicit aim was to learn together about how to tackle the many operational issues arising from the merger and implement better service standards. As the method was a form of conversation, and the structure of the days allowed time for informal conversation too, the result was members of different internal 'tribes' (previous agencies) getting to know and form attachments to people in other 'tribes'. They soon realized how much they had in common and it was far easier to accept the reality of the new organization.

I was invited to work with the level above the groups, the Regional Managers Team (RMT), tasked with making the new merger a reality and raising practice standards across the country. This team sat immediately below the Senior Management Team (SMT) and carried operational responsibility for all the work of the new Association. These five people, strangers at the outset, wished to become a team and so a pure action learning methodology was inappropriate (Thornton, 2016). I worked with them regularly over 3–4 years, consulting them at each stage about their needs and evolving ways of working which they took up and used. They were a committed and creative group with widely different approaches and strengths. The acknowledgment and acceptance of these helped them became a powerhouse team with a strong sense of mutual support and shared responsibility. In the meantime, the action learning sets allowed their reports who managed localities or larger services to experience the commonality and shared strategic purpose of the unified organization. An important part of the design was the regular meeting of the consultants leading all the groups, which enabled a free flow of information between groups. Problems could be identified and addressed while still small. The RMT, and their people in the action learning sets, ultimately carried the Association merger through to successful completion despite conflict at more senior levels.

It is interesting that the internal commissioner in this case designs the program. She is not of great seniority but has won the respect of leaders for her savvy in organizational development. The depth of the value of her design was not necessarily fully understood at the top of the organization, but her standing was such that they were willing to back it; a gamble that paid dividends.

It is perhaps worth stating that not all workplaces need all change all the time. Many work situations require a blending of automatic competence with expert assessment of the singularity of each situation. For example, an operating theater needs stability of staffing and an acceptance of role specialization, as well as a reliable system of support to ensure its highly specific needs; firefighters need to rely on automatic responses for many tasks while thinking carefully and quickly about the specifics of each callout.

Conclusion

Because of its flexibility and ability to respond to nuance, group analytic praxis is valuable for creating new conversations to loosen outworn patterns and create the conditions for positive change in larger organizations. In the next chapter we continue with these themes, offering some practical advice to leaders and consultants.

Chapter 23

Translucent boundaries, leaders, and consultants

How to work with whole organizations

Gerhard Wilke and Christine Thornton

Leaders and consultants are boundary workers. Organizations are living communities; only rarely single groups, they are usually complex collections of groupings needing to relate to achieve a larger, shared goal, though often the groupings seem to exist mostly to war with each other. As with all communities, there are politics and 'insider-outsider' (us-and-them) dynamics. Taking up the themes of the last chapter, we open with a consideration of insider-outsider dynamics (us-and-them or 'tribal' thinking) within organizations, focusing on how leaders and consultants need to harness these powerful forces to create favorable conditions for change. The remainder of the chapter is structured around 10 key principles for leaders and consultants in working with whole organizations. The advice we offer is deliberately blended: leader and consultant must consider the same issues, and the role of the consultant is to help the *leader* to create the best environment for productive work.

Dynamics between parts of organizations are largely ignored in the business literature, which places too much focus on individual actions. In social psychology research, three models of comprehending inter-group contact prevail:

1 The *personalization* model (contact will work if it is based on people who know each other)
2 The *common in-group identity* model (the original in-group distinction can only be overcome if the new shared in-group becomes the primary object of attachment and loyalty)

3   The *mutual differentiation* model (rather than overcoming existing group loyalties, build on them, structuring contact so that sub-group and whole new group identities can be tolerated and made to function in a complementary way).

Finding value in all these, we favor the third. A multi-layered identity model is more likely to help the whole group form, storm, norm, and then perform. The leader's role in this approach is to name the differences and remind everyone of the larger, shared goal and task, focusing dialogue on the goals and work rather than the differences.

Offices without walls, teams without clear role descriptions, conflicting expectations and a flattened hierarchy can be perceived as modern and efficient, but also as a great source of anxiety for many in our organizations. Without clear physical, hierarchical, and role boundaries, all have to deal with permanent tension between cohesion and coherence. The merger vignette on pages 218–220 illustrates this. Holding the connection between integration and differentiation in mind is key to survival while retaining the capacity to think, work, and act intelligently.

Us and them: the insiders and the outsiders

Humans are social and psychological animals, and also classifying beings. Classification systems rely on the distinction between the familiar and the unfamiliar, between insiders and outsiders (Elias, 2009), people like us (PLU) and not like us. Symbolic classification systems are the way humans order the social universe, the location of their group and the other groupings within the imagined cosmological order. Underneath each classification system is a philosophical assumption that gives birth to a trajectory of thinking, whilst simultaneously making a string of other thoughts taboo. For instance, if you think health rather than illness is the basic purpose of a hospital, you prioritize the restoration of health and prevention of death. Dying in hospital then becomes a problematic event, subject to suspicion and investigation. Similarly, if we prioritize finance, we priorities audit knowledge over work experience and professional values in organizations. Bringing the un-named assumptions into the light of day, naming the 'undiscussables' (see pages 41 and 153) is a core role of the group analytic practitioner. Modeling the communication of unpalatable but important ideas extends the range of communication available to our clients.

Some fundamental questions of sense and meaning arise consciously and unconsciously in all human groupings, including all groups in any organization:

- Who am I, who are we? Who are the others?
- How do we make contact, across group boundaries?
- How do we avoid war?

- How can we find a way of exchanging ideas and resources?
- What basic understandings do we have about sub-group boundaries within a community?

Each person needs to know that I am me and you are not me; that they are not like us. The trouble with these definitions is that we automatically look down on the out-group, 'not-us', ascribing our own worst qualities to the 'outsiders', deriving status and social superiority. 'We' belong to a civilized culture and 'they' are wild, as yet uncivilized (Leach, 1982). We see 'us' as more homogeneous than we are, and 'them' as more dissimilar from us than they are.

Group identifications are important determinants of human interactions, sometimes generating heroic acts of sacrifice, sometimes murderous acts against outsider groups; they shape how much or little we can cooperate. Points of potential contact and exchange become highly charged affairs surrounded by fears of pollution, invasion, and take over. Us-and-them divisions can govern the behavior of professional groups within multi-disciplinary teams, for example, between the various health professions in the UK NHS teams, or between sales and research in Pharma. How we handle personal and group assumptions about the us-and-them dynamic is a key determinant of cross-boundary working or conflict (Binney et al., 2017).

How to lead and consult to a modern organization: 10 key principles

Organizational leadership and consultancy can be conceptualized with the help of a number of group analytic ideas. The matrix suggests that investment in the social capital of the organization is essential at the level of the individual, the team, the division, and the whole organization. Here are the key principles discussed in the chapter:

Key leadership and consulting principles

1 Encourage exchange
2 Cultivate the art of conversation
3 Accept reality and name it
4 Stay humble and authentic
5 Engage creatively with paradox
6 Create meeting rituals
7 Work with cooperation and competition dynamics
8 Make a space for play
9 Minimize 'insider/outsider' blinkers
10 Accept the roles of politician and boundary worker.

I Encourage exchange

Traditional coaching is done in a private space; away from the group(s) that the leader relies on for delivery. Of value to the individual client, this approach does not help the organization translate the learning into an adapted way of working. Instead, consider what we might call *accompanying* or *live coaching*, or *live group analysis in action*. We coach leaders whilst simultaneously developing the sub-group(s) and the organization, recognizing that the capacity to lead and animate groups is linked to the collective wisdom and talent of the whole system. Accompanying a leader into real meetings avoids the unhealthy split between the cocoon of (sacred) coaching and the reality of (profane) working with and through *difficult* others. It is striking how shared reflection impacts quickly on the style of the leader, the engagement of the group, and the level of trust, open communication, and commitment between everyone involved.

In the context of a larger piece of organizational development, I spent a day with a Research Professor in order to observe how she led meetings and handled 'difficult people'. She had grown fond of the program and felt safe enough to challenge me to be more active. At the end of a meeting concerned with reviewing the progress of research projects, she turned to me: 'I am wondering whether we could hear your feedback to me now, in front of all of us. We have time as most of us will stay for the next meeting and some of us could carry on reflecting together on how we work and how I lead? We can put our agenda aside, if people agree'.

They did. I responded that the leader stayed in role, taking responsibility but that the meeting pattern was one-to-one performance reviews, her holding each project leader separately to account. The group was like a classic Greek Tragedy with a heroine, an anti-heroine, and a primarily silent chorus of witnesses. Although it was important that some dialogues between leader and led were witnessed in public, the group appeared detached and disengaged, a spectator group that muttered approval or disapproval, with little energy. The paradox was that a very competent leader seemed to shy away from deeper, direct questions and be satisfied with 'Everything seems to be going well' stories. Was it because no-one dared ask 'why do we have to hold each other to account like this, why not in a more developmental and less check-list-oriented way?' I suggested that the established meeting ritual could signify several unconscious processes: distrust between competing group members, a need of the group to be dependent and the leader to be in control. I ended by saying that the group felt like a mature team and seemed ready to experiment with a shift from 'one-to-one appraisals' in public, to involving the whole group in a discussion of what needed to be done to improve performance in each project.

I suggested a practical experiment, right here and now. I asked project leaders to evaluate their research projects without prompting, this time revealing what they were worried about and asking the others in the group to help. My working hypothesis was that this form of exchange would develop the connections between people and attach them more securely to the uniting purpose of the whole group. If each project leader could find help and reassurance in the group before taking a frightening or risky next step, a culture of shared responsibility and mutual trust could develop. The group adopted this change and the result, after a relatively short time, was to relieve the leader of the overwhelming burden of taking all decisions. Within six months, she was able to spend more time on research, publications, policy impact, and patient benefit.

Several things are worth noting here. The consultant is *opportunistic*, seizing the moment in responding to the leader's invitation. The invitation itself arose from the quality of their relationship established within the broader program, so that she trusted that the feedback would not humiliate her and could serve the broader purpose; her courage in taking the risk was well-founded. The feedback invited all to examine their underlying assumptions about 'how we do things around here', questioning what was most 'fit for purpose'. Rather than the leader struggling to incorporate 'private' feedback in a group setting, the resources of the whole group were engaged in the shared task with exponential improvements to efficacy and efficiency: the openness created strong mutual support and challenge. Members were empowered to engage with their real responsibilities in the meeting, with adult exchanges and reflection, rather than a 'monitoring' charade. This 'tweak' had important and lasting consequences.

The principle can be applied on a larger scale. Exploring shared experience in cross-boundary meetings moves things on, as we saw in the merger vignette on (pages 222–23). A culture of talking *to* each other more than *about* each other emerges and is sustainable over time. The informal gossip 'corridor' community and the formal and role-bound organization are then connected (Blackwell, 1998).

Leaders need to create spaces for others to have conversations. If social and mental boundaries are 'translucent', exchange can occur across them. Exchange, of words, data, or objects, is a linking activity that can produce mutual obligation, trust, and interdependence, the conditions for multiple loyalty and attachment relationships: to the team, the Department, the whole organization. It is a recognition of the multi-layered matrix of identity and attachments. Group analytic consultation can bring together large groups of people for purposeful yet free dialogue. It gives them permission to come together in normally unauthorized, unthinkable combinations in order to move situations on that have become stuck or self-defeating.

2 *Cultivate the art of conversation*

Group analysis is a developed discipline of conversation, and people speaking to each other is the means by which we co-create our social world. If we share our true perceptions, we influence each other: new metaphors and narratives are created with the power to change the way that we view things, and so the way we act. Faced with organizational challenges, leaders must model openness in conversation, sharing their ideas, dilemmas, and experiences to encourage others to do the same.[1] Opportunities for informal conversations are as important as formal meetings, connecting to the network of informal conversation that is an important component of any organization – where people express 'what is really going on' for them. By providing an appropriate and safe setting for indispensable conversations between key players, group analytic consultants are uniquely positioned to help organizations work with their internal divisions between top, middle, and bottom or across different subsystem with an us-and-them mind-set. In the drama of change and continuity, we can help an organization's leaders release the collective intelligence and passion of the whole system, locked up in the web of their sub-group relationships and informal conversational system.

3 *Accept reality and name it*

Leaders must learn to expect the disorder of reality, cultivating comfort with acknowledging 'how things really are' and not knowing all the answers. The heroic all-competent leader is a damaging fantasy, leaving a trail of destruction in its wake in many settings. The Research Professor trusted her colleagues and learned to find a way together through the complexity of their task. In the vignette on page 217 this had been destroyed, and could only be rebuilt gradually.

4 *Stay humble and authentic*

Modern leadership requires humility. Leaders' role are vital, but no one person can control the activity of an organizational 'living community' – at least not in a benign way. Twentieth century history is littered with malignant 'heroic' leaders, from Hitler to Milosevic. Authenticity is the core of good leadership, finding honest ways of speaking with others about the dilemmas and challenges in the work, and building a culture of shared reflection in understanding and tackling them. Attending to small details in creating a good work environment can release people's creativity (see also Rogers, chapter 20 this volume, Thornton, 2016). These 'tweaks' do not guarantee success, but they nudge things in the direction of success, allowing others to take responsibility and organize themselves. The task of leaders is to manage *contexts*. Implied is a shift from attending to resistance to change, instead focusing on creating environments which enable new thinking to emerge. Leaders influence, they do not control.

Thoughtful practitioners too know that they may only influence, not control, and modeling this in their relationships with leaders may be an important part of their contribution. We must keep the whole picture as far as possible in mind (Bohm, 1980). Particularly important are the boundaries between different parts of the system, and how these are conceptualized and therefore managed. The Reseaerch Professor succeeded in truly sharing responsibilitiy for the projects' success with her senior colleagues, by acknowledging her need for their help. This was a significant boundary shift. We know from Maturana and Varela (pages 216–18) that boundaries are mental contstructs which are capable of movement. Like leaders, practitioners must aim for small intervention which will improve the quality of exchange at the boundaries, making them more 'translucent'. All the vignettes illustrate this point.

5 Engage creatively with paradox

Paradoxes are otherwise known as tensions, contradictions or impossible challenges. They are often 'embodied' in two (or more) subgroupings who take up positions aligned with the poles of the dilemma. These are the daily headaches of many leaders, which can be turned into great opportunities for change.

In his classic *Images of Organization* (1997), Gareth Morgan makes a list of common organizational paradoxes:

Innovate	⟷	avoid mistakes
Think long term	⟷	deliver results now
Cut costs	⟷	increase morale
Reduce staff	⟷	improve teamwork
Be flexible	⟷	respect the rules
Collaborate	⟷	compete
Decentralize	⟷	retain control
Specialize	⟷	be opportunistic
Low costs	⟷	high quality

These paradoxes express approaches that apparently contradict each other. However, each pole may have value for an organization. In many places, the tension between these poles is played out between different camps: for example, the managers who emphasize low costs and the professionals who emphasize high quality. If a leader can bring these politics to the table, acknowledging the value of both perspectives, creative solutions can begin to emerge.

Group analytic practitioners do not seek to 'resolve' paradoxes. They cultivate contentment with contradictions and resist the desire of people within organizations to resolve them. Instead, we help people to explore the tensions between them, to generate the best specific solution in this organization now. We do not expect the solution to be 'good for all time'. Our position, both 'in' and 'out' of the organization is valuable in challenging the resolution of paradoxes (Thornton, 2016).

6 Create meeting rituals

Rituals mark important transitions. As we saw in the international merger story (pages 218–20) meeting rituals, where people come together from across the organization, can contain anxiety and open a space for a new form of relating so that people get to know their differences and thereby discover their communality (Foulkes, 1990b). Liminal points, like the beginnings and endings of meetings, are important moments for containing rituals (Thornton, 2016). For example, an action learning set meeting over seven years always opened with the group analyst asking 'What do we know about action learning?' The group then, half-serious and half-mocking, would rehearse the 'ground rules'. Meeting for a reunion years after the group had ended, members remembered how this ritual had profoundly embedded these ideas into their work practice: 'listen carefully', 'nice easy pace'. Similarly, in Switzerland, many organizations have the habit of asking at the end of a meeting how the German, Italian, and French speakers have understood what has been decided and how they, in their own sub-system, plan to translate the joint decision into local delivery. Sometimes an appropriate ritual will arise spontaneously.

7 Work with cooperation and competition dynamics

Group identification shapes the behavior and attitudes of people dependent on each other for how they work, think, and perform. When members of two different groups meet, two forms of behavior are potentially generated: pro-social or anti-social. Managing tensions between these two linked, not opposed, poles needs to be a focus for leaders. Leading, and consulting, is boundary work, in-between sub-group divisions and across status hierarchies. The leader, employees, and consultant must deliver across translucent boundaries, integrating the organization as a living community. We avoid here the currently fashionable word 'collaborative' because it has a denied shadow side. Collaboration can mean offending ones belonging group and getting sucked into the role of traitor.

It is useful for leaders, working across groups, to note whether people are in competitive or cooperative mode when they work together. This is particularly important in 'mixed-motive' situations where cooperation is necessary to maximize outcome and achievement, but where the temptation exists to act competitively in order to satisfy self-interest. In the research world, this dynamic is evident in collaborative research undertakings, especially in global networks, where success depends on the interaction between clinicians and clinical academics.

8 Make a space for play

In support of this piece of advice, we reproduce a fragment of dialogue from our contributors' discussion day (9 December 2017) which concerns its importance in connecting the formal and shadow structures in the organization, releasing creativity:

DICK – An idea I picked up from Stacey is that formal structure inhibits the kind of dialogue you might want to have to produce creative ideas. These dialogues are driven underground – like Goffman's 'underlife or shadow system' – and are just the discussions at the photocopier and lunchtime. Stacey was concerned with how you surface that dialogue, how you bring that into the formal system, and what prevents free flow of thought and ideas.

. . .(Laughter)

GERHARD – It doesn't have to be a challenge. I bring the work group and the gossip group together to learn that they are intertwined, but different.

DICK – We might disagree, but I would like to introduce Winnicott and 'play' – the sense of fun and thinking about why people want to be in organizations and be together – because it was fun to be there.

CHRISTINE T – Blimey, is that counter-culture now – there are so few workplaces where it is OK to play.

DICK – How to play, have fun, was a valuable part of being creative and being disciplined.

EARL – The difference between formal and informal.

GERHARD – This relationship needs to be made visible.

CHRISTINE T – In most organizations now, play is delinquent.

EARL – Yes!

GERHARD – And at top they play-act, they delude themselves as being gods. (Laughter)

CHRISTINE T Yes!

EARL – They are actually unconsciously playing. At the top of an organization, there are so many role games but split off. There is no reflective dynamic, it is not taken seriously.

DICK – Appearance and masquerades – how people give the appearance of doing something without doing it. Ticking all the boxes but nothing changes. (Laughter)

CHRISTINE T – Yes.

EARL – How do we differentiate the group analytic approach to consultancy?

GERHARD – Inequality and hierarchy are normal – which makes us different from our clinical brothers and sisters. (Laughter)

CHRISTINE T – Structures are essential, and . . .

GERHARD – Us-and-them are normal, we have to work with this reality and help them make connections that work.

Play cannot be forced, or it is not play. We are not speaking here of mandatory activities but simply of creating time and opportunity for people to get together and choose what to do together.

9 Minimize 'insider/outsider' blinkers

We tend to underestimate the importance of insider-outsider behavior. We focus on outsiders' strangeness, on their dissimilarity. We see our own behavior as caused by the situation, but that of the 'others' as caused by their flaws. Success is due to our own stable, engaged, and competent group and failure is located in the situation, the whole system, bad partners or other departments.

For example, in a health research context, clinicians and academic researchers cast themselves as the goody and the 'others' as the baddy. The leadership challenge is to overcome this split by pointing out that goodies and baddies live in the same society and earn a living from the same organization.

Contact alone does not guarantee positive working relationships and inter-group cooperation. Groups with the same culture but differing interests can be very competitive and aggressive. A joint activity with investment in the connection and shared super-ordinate goals is useful, significantly reducing the in-group pressure on guarding the boundary between us and them.

Cooperation is harder when the contributions of groups to the joint venture are perceived as unequal in terms of value and status. Where groups compete for limited resources, it tends to fuel conflict rather than cooperation. Joined-up bids can contain this problem.

Successful multi-center collaborations are helped by regular contact over time but also by independent contacts with different members of the 'outgroup'. These breakdown stereotypes and reveal heterogeneity in each group.

10 Accept the roles of politician and boundary worker

Like consultants, leaders work on the boundaries of organizations, in, across, and outside different subgroups. The interfaces between subgroups and status hierarchies is the place where change is possible. The leader at the boundary protects the group and its work, whilst linking it with the wider system on which it depends for exchange, development, growth, affirmation, and survival. A consultant can help the leader develop greater sensitivity and political savvy in this equivocal, intermediate role. Sometimes leaders with excellent political skills in the corridors of power outside the organization, neglect to use that savvy within it, assuming an unanimity of purpose that is unlikely to exist. This is a sure route to trouble, failure, and (on occasion) to being the victim of a political 'coup d'état'. The consultant's role is to help the leader shoulder the burden of political work at all levels.

In some settings, the contextual politics create further problems. For example, in the story below, a feminist politics rejecting masculine power and its trappings resulted in a cumbersome management structure accompanied by a culture in which it was very difficult for anyone to exercise authority. A focus on the abuse of power arose from the work of the organization, opposing domestic violence, intensifying resistance to the possibility of a positive use of authority.

The consultancy was designed to enable a major women's campaigning organization to change its constitution for greater efficiency (and so effectiveness). The lack of authority structure made it necessary to create a new internal group to commission the work; it was hard even to identify a single contact person for managing the administration of the work. Design and delivery of the consultancy, to involve a series of members' consultation events in many regional locations, was undertaken slowly, and the consultant worked with a self-selecting group of internal allies to develop a framework and skills for convening the consultations. The self-selection was important not only because there was no one with the authority to order anyone else's involvement, but also because it identified those who were prepared to take some risks. More than once the consultant was obliged to enact the exercise of authority in the face of feuding groups. Her reference group initially found this frightening, because of their fear that she would be attacked and destroyed. Ultimately, they found her willingness to 'put her head above the parapet', and her survival of the resulting attacks, liberating. They were able to 'lead' (this word could still not openly be used) the consultation. After more than two years' painstaking work the allies succeeded in persuading the whole federation to a structural change which though counter-cultural, made it far more effective. This happened at a time when external political opportunities were multiplying, with many opportunities both in developing better legal and policy remedies at a national level, and in providing local services. The change enabled the organization to capitalize on these with profound effect: women escaping violent relationships were better served.

The allies' experience of seeing the consultant survive attack, engendered their courage to 'stand up and be counted' in the service of an important change feared to be unpopular, was important. The willingness to take the work at a slow pace, allowing members time to catch up with the thinking, was vital.

The challenge for leaders and consultants in any organization is to name the hidden us-and-them tensions that exacerbate conflict. Different groupings within the same organization must find an agreed way to 'deal' with each other. Retaining sub-group loyalties, they consent to a larger attachment with the whole organizational community. The organization also sits within society (one at least), the reference point for cultural, ethnic, or national identity. Leaders and consultants must find ways to pay homage to various sub-groups' identities, building common ground so that the various players subject their sectional interests to a shared and larger symbolic order. This can best be reached through exchange and communication rituals.

Conclusion

Leaders are boundary workers, not so much at the top, but in the middle, between, above and below, inside and outside. They are also between past, present, and future. They are humble, and they are political. Boundaries keep things out and let them in; in an interconnected world with rapid change, they must be translucent to remain functional. Thinking about and influencing translucent boundaries and relationships across them is central to both leading and consulting work.

Note

1 Except for matters where confidentiality is essential.

Section VIII

The ending

Section VIII consists of a single chapter. Chapter 24 brings together some of my reflections on endings with those of Gerhard Wilke. It underlines the real world non-ideal character of many endings in organizational work. It offers questions, not answers. 'The end is in the beginning' is our watchword, and the ambiguities and complexities of 'good enough' endings are explored.

The end is in the beginning

Perspectives from two group analytic consultants

Christine Thornton and Gerhard Wilke

Christine

Endings are vitally important. How we remember past experiences is heavily weighted by how those experiences end. Given a choice between a short unpleasant experience, and a longer unpleasant experience with a slightly less unpleasant time *added* to the shorter experience, humans will overwhelmingly choose the latter. Utterly illogical, this has been experimentally demonstrated (Kahneman, 2011). We are hardwired to remember, and over-value, how things end.

We do not always know how long our engagement with an organization will be, and much of this chapter is devoted to the ambiguities of this situation. However, when our engagement is for a fixed period, we can work more explicitly with the end from the beginning. In these circumstances, it is very important to mark the midpoint of the work, so that awareness of the ending sharpens people's thirst for learning and change (Thornton, 2016).

I recently watched the film *Brooklyn*, a sensitive adaptation of the original novel (Tóibín, 2009). The poignant losses and insoluble dilemmas of the migrant are faithfully rendered, as are the limited options available to an immigrant woman; but the ending of the film is made 'happier' than the book. Events are unchanged, but the emotional tone of Aelis' return to her Italian-American husband is changed. The book ends on Aelis' profound regret at leaving behind for the last time Jim Farrell and her original home in Enniscorthy, with all its confinement and ambiguities. The film goes forward to her happy reunion with Tony. This satisfying of our thirst for 'happy endings' is not an unusual occurrence in film. But can any ending truly be untinged happiness?

All things must pass. We know this, and we also resist knowing it, at least in relation to ourselves. It is said that we cannot realize our own deaths, though at times we must needs tolerate the loss of those dear to us. Just as all losses reactivate at an emotional level earlier experiences of loss, so they also foreshadow the ultimate loss, of life itself. For many, perhaps most people this makes endings challenging, and it is important for the consultant to help enable a 'good enough' ending for clients, appropriate to the tone and the depth of this particular organization.

Good enough endings

At the end of a piece of work, the consultant must first discern when the ending has arrived, which is sometimes less simple than it sounds. Then we must enable the organization to make the ending it needs, sometimes and at most tweaking it in a direction which will be remembered more kindly by members (Thornton, 2016).

A good enough ending is not 'happy-happy'. All endings include ambivalent feelings and painful reminders of previous losses. Sensitively following the cues and clues about what is needed now, by these particular people, is the art. To attempt to over-control the ending and make it 'all-good' will be counter-productive, forcing underground some of the more difficult feelings that a group analytic containment can render shareable and thus bearable (Stern, 1985). Nevertheless, people find value and comfort in simple ending rituals that allow them to say what they need to say but would not normally say. A discussion of these can be found in an earlier book (Thornton, 2016). Or simple ending rituals may arise spontaneously.

> At the end of the final meeting of a peer learning group that has met for 20 years, someone asks 'Should we do something?' There is silence as group members search for what might be appropriate. Someone else says – 'I don't know – but I would like to thank you all. Thank you'. Members all thank each other and the first person adds – 'Yes, that was it!'

Endings in organizational life are rarely ideal. Companies and people end, or are 'ended', for many reasons. Reorganization, redundancy, company failure, merger, competition, envy, and bullying can all play a part alongside the more easily acknowledged reasons. It is hard to remember that an organization is an abstraction, a shared mental construct among a community of people. Once an organization exists, its stated purpose is only its second goal; its first goal is always its own survival. This seems to relate to our need to attach ourselves, to belong to something larger which lends us an important part of our identity. Within these constructs, to which we attach ourselves so strongly, sibling rivalries may be (re-)enacted with great ferocity.

Here are some stories of real endings. Which of them do you consider 'good enough'?

Miriam was the Research Director of an influential national anti-poverty organization. Staff were highly motivated and had competed to work there. Like most such organizations the search for funding was a constant theme. As Research Director Miriam had focused on achieving wider recognition and dissemination of its research studies. She had considerable success in publishing in more influential journals, popularizing through the media and organizing conferences and events which spread the word and incidentally created additional revenue. The CEO departed, and during a lengthy interregnum, the interim CEO appointed ignored the external part of his role. When the Board seemed unable or unwilling to tackle this, Miriam stepped into the breach, increasing her public speaking engagements, liaising with funders, and ensuring reporting was completed. She did not want the CEO role but wanted to ensure the survival of the organization. Again, she was successful: the high regard for the quality and originality of its research enabled her to hand on a relatively stable financial base for the next few years.

The Board appointed Sarah as CEO, and Miriam heaved a sigh of relief. She welcomed the opportunity to return to her true calling, directing research. However, Sarah was not similarly pleased. She responded coldly to Miriam's attempts to engage her in a collegiate relationship and was highly critical of the detail of Miriam's work. At first Miriam strove to please Sarah, until Judith, consulting to Miriam, commented that Sarah seemed not to wish for partners in the work, but subordinates, preferably less experienced than her. Miriam realized that the kind of relationship she had hoped for with the new CEO would not be possible. Although there were projects she wished to complete, she instead left to take up a similar role in a new organization. 'I left before I wanted to', she commented later, 'but at least I left in the way I chose'.

The consultant here, in response to Miriam's descriptions of Sarah's subtle but persistent bullying, frankly shares her analysis of the realities of the situation. Perhaps Judith is more concerned for Miriam than for the organization, particularly the potential impact of undermining behavior tolerated over time. As consultants, we often grow fond of those we work with, and Judith is aware both of Miriam's strengths – her intelligence, creativity, and capacity for hard work – and her vulnerabilities, her personal sensitivity, and need for acknowledgment and respect for her work. In a significant percentage of coaching situations, our clients may arrive at an understanding of their situation that results in their leaving the company. In this case, Miriam was able to continue to work in the same field, but in another setting.

Saoirshe had consulted to a third sector psychotherapy agency for four years. Their work was with struggling families, their approach was innovative and its efficacy had been demonstrated. Saoirshe met them monthly, in a reflective group for both therapeutic and administrative staff, about 20 people. She also consulted to the CEO and the Clinical Director. The CEO, Aidan, was not therapeutically qualified, though over time he became interested in the unconscious life of organizations, eventually undertaking training. Saoirshe helped the team hold the inevitable tensions between clinical and business leadership. This was always against a background of the Board questioning the cost of maintaining the team's reflective sessions, so that the contract was renewed for 6–12-month periods at a time. The team valued the reflective space and made good use of it to maintain the quality of their work, and to manage the difficult feelings evoked by the trauma in the work.

The Clinical Director departed and Theresa was appointed to replace her. There were high hopes of what Theresa would be able to offer. However, Theresa avoided meeting with Saoirshe and Aidan for as long as possible, and when a meeting was eventually convened, simply refused to engage. 'I don't know what it is for' was her repeated comment both about these leadership dialogues and the team reflective sessions, before *and* after explorations of purpose. It emerged gradually that Theresa saw the containing of the therapists' clinical work as solely *her* domain – her language was that of the protective mother of injured and traumatized children – whereas before this had been explicitly understood to be the shared (adult) task of the whole team.

Having worked closely with the previous clinical director, Saoirshe made several efforts to meet with Theresa to establish a working partnership; these overtures were ignored. Aidan then telephoned Saoirshe to say that the Board had decided to terminate her (Saoirshe's) contract in two months, and that she was not to mention this at the next reflective session because it would be too upsetting for staff. Saoirshe responded that it would violate her ethics to keep this secret. She advised Aidan to give them the news himself, but said that if he did not, she would. Aidan then emailed to say that the Board had instructed Saoirshe not to attend the next session. Citing their long and productive partnership, Saoirshe arranged to speak to Aidan, seeking to understand how trust between them had broken down. In the course of this conversation she commented frankly 'Theresa has no interest in working with me'. Aidan responded that Theresa had no interest in working with him either, and the floodgates opened. He described at length a working relationship so strained as to be non-existent, and the many failed strategies he had tried.

Saoirshe negotiated a 'stay of execution' so that she had 3 more sessions with the team. These were suffused with pain and anger at her departure, and Theresa's; Theresa was now on sick leave. Theresa was not confirmed in post. Shortly afterwards, Aidan announced his departure. At the end of the 3 months, the team had lost Aidan and Theresa, business and clinical leads, as well as the sessions with Saoirshe; in the final sessions staff were very sad and also very angry, abandoned with their very demanding work but without the people and structures that supported it.

Some time later a semi-retired senior colleague local to the agency phoned Saoirshe to say she had been approached by team members to undertake the work voluntarily; however, she ultimately refused the invitation.

Here a successful consultation, which formed an important part of the team's containment of very challenging work, was brought to a messy and abrupt end. Saoirshe's frank observation to Aidan (a boundary crossing) restores their working relationship so that he at least is supported through a similarly messy ending of his role. This example also illustrates a limit of group analytic consulting: it doesn't work with those who refuse to play. It would be over-simplifying to regard one poor appointment (Theresa) as the cause of the problems, but Theresa's resistance (as clinical director) was a catalyst, and her alliance with members of the Board who had always disliked the provision of reflective space to the staff team, led to its termination. It is relevant too that these events took place in a context where there were deep cuts to the family centers within which the agency provided most of its services; the team were also facing profound challenges to their working model and so their professional identities. There is no happy ending for this team: the good containing they have had has come to an end. Their attempt to replace it is, at least, a good sign.

This was a small scientific company holding the patents on a leading-edge technology which supported agriculture in the developing world, winning contracts from governments funding development. The company had a glorious history of three decades, running on familial lines. The Board had appointed a CEO, Damian, young 'talent' from a multi-national corporate to exploit the potential and the reach of the patents as fully as possible. The staff and existing leadership of the company were highly resistant to challenge, and 'closed ranks'. The conflict became so powerful and pervasive that the senior team ceased to be able to work together.

Two Board members approached and carefully assessed a number of consultants, appointing Meredith who agreed to an initial assignment concerned with whether the team could find a way forward together; an important element was the one-to-one work with Damian. Damian was extremely intellectually gifted, even by the standards of this gifted team, and as committed to the widest possible use of the technology as his colleagues. He had come to the company with high ideals and hopes, and was still reeling from the shock of his experiences.

The initial piece of work with the team was successful, and a fragile working alliance was achieved. Meredith's consultation to Damian was primarily focused on 'coming to terms' with his disappointment and hurt: a work of mourning.

Coming together again, the team showed itself able to work well at an intellectual level, but issues of trust persisted; Damian had recovered enough to flex his intellectual muscles and to respond more robustly to challenges within his team; he had also worked on building alliances throughout the company. 'Very cautious optimism' was the overt note but there were regular setbacks arising from mutual suspicion. Meredith recommended medium term team consultation to help maintain the changes.

This won little support from either the team or Damian; financial cost was cited but this did not seem to be the true reason. While there was genuine gratitude for the work that she had done, Meredith was associated with a very difficult period, and the extremely painful work necessary to resolve things. The team had had enough of it, and so declared their condition 'good enough' – which in the 'dog eat dog' world of competitive science, perhaps it was. Damian too, used to being a 'high flier' rarely in need of support from another, had ambivalent feelings, and the departure of the team member most strongly opposed to him allowed him to believe there were smoother waters ahead. Meredith's sense of how much better this team *could* have functioned limited her ability to understand when enough was enough, for them. Damian met Meredith one to one and 'lets her down', gently but unmistakably, so that she did not lose face. Even when we over-estimate the client's appetite for more of what we can offer, their gratitude for what they have received can result in a sensitive valediction.

As consultants, we always work on the boundary of an organization – 'into' the organization, neither fully in nor fully out. We *temporarily* inhabit the organizational worlds of our clients. It is our responsibility to be as aware as possible of what is needed from us now, and to explore these understandings with our client-colleagues. Understanding that what they need from us is our ending – realizing our own 'death' – can be hard, as it was for Meredith.

In two of these examples, the consultants, Judith and Saoirshe, 'cross' boundaries (see also page 152 in ways that are helpful to their clients, Miriam and Aidan. Endings are a time when boundaries may indeed become more 'translucent', more flexible, signaling that the former relationship is coming to an end. In the third example, Meredith, a highly experienced consultant, had higher outcome standards than the team itself, blinding her somewhat to their lack of appetite to attempt it.

Consultants working with organizations over the medium and longer term, like Saoirshe, find themselves being drawn more fully 'in' – a situation which highlights and exacerbates the dilemmas but does not change their essential nature. There are particular temptations in this situation; consultants share with the rest of humanity the need to belong, though we are usually also among those who find belonging most problematic. A long-term consultant has some of the benefits of belonging, without the heaviest of the costs. Also, a group or a leader we have worked with for a long time will usually be more rewarding to work with, because they have learned to work at greater depth (see also page 42). It is hard not to want that to continue. Sometimes we may stay past the point of true usefulness to the organization, but on the other hand a long-term engagement may be essential in settings where steady containment or profound relationships are central to the work in hand, such as a therapeutic community or a setting with a high degree of trauma. Keeping the question 'how much longer will I be useful?' alive with the client, who may be equally comfortable with the arrangement, and genuinely reviewing our involvement at 'exit points on the spiral' (Foulkes, 1975), is our responsibility.

Gerhard

Endings are a social process. Even after a person has died, they go on living in the minds of those left behind. Thus, in organizations, which are living communities, people remember losses as well as gains. As a group analytic organizational consultant, I think of the end from the beginning of any intervention. Even facilitating an away day, I keep in mind that the participants have to leave in the afternoon. In a longer term organizational intervention promoting better performance, cooperation, adaptation, or innovation, I keep in mind that the organization exists for a purpose, serves customers, and needs to function and to live within its means. In short, for me thinking at the start of an organizational intervention of the ending, introduces the reality principle into the work. The people who hire me are responsible for all that. My task is to explore the relationship networks and the group dynamic issues that restrain, hinder or block their performance and adaptability.

The ending of a consultancy focuses the mind on transitions like stepping up and stepping down or moving in and out of an organization. Consultancy is designed to open up transitional spaces and the consultant is a transitional object like Prospero in the Tempest, who re-connects what has been disconnected. Consultancy interventions must be thought about as transition work. Transitions start with an ending and a loss, before a new beginning.

The transition from the end of one generation's reign to the beginning of that of the next one, just like the transition from childhood into adulthood via adolescence, is an underestimated force in shaping what happens in history, in organizations and in every society.

I choose three-generational metaphors deliberately (grandparents, parents, children) (Von Friesen and Wilke, 2016), because our organizational age of permanent transitions, repeated restructuring processes and serial leader changes generates symptoms of post-traumatic stress disorder. These behavior patterns have generated organizational cultures characterized by symptoms of dislocation in individuals and teams, disembedding departmental and whole-organizational social structures (Giddens, 1999). This gives people the collective feeling of living in a universe of chaos and leaves them with a diffuse sense of 'existential anxiety' and of working in 'liquid Times' (Baumann, 2007) without containment. There are endless beginnings, endless thwarted endings and so a reservoir of incomplete mourning processes. We witness the unconscious search of organizations' members for 'as if' parents, who can offer containment and holding.

The three-generational principle gives us a model for 'normal' endings. These lived generational relationship matrices and their propensity to react to each other in a culturally confirming and adapting way, shape the dynamic in most consulting processes and can restrain or facilitate the work of the beginning, the substantive intervention and a good enough ending. Organizational managerial hierarchies can also be conceptualized as top, middle and bottom, as can accumulated experience and knowledge.

Typically, my consulting work with law firms, engineering or property companies occurs as a result of existential fear for the survival of the organization. Little wonder I have ended up thinking that the end is in the beginning. The reigning paradigm is the top team writing a strategy and determining a timeline for implementation of desired changes. The middle of the organization gets charged with the implementation of the intended or better envisioned changes and the bottom is the object of restructuring, reform, and improvement. At some point the change management process gets stuck or blown off course, and it is at this point that a consultant with a group dynamic outlook most often gets asked to help.

The help the client hopes for is knowledge of overcoming resistance and 'emotional intelligence'.

At the beginning the hiring manager, the consultant, and the affected employees can meet in an inquiry phase. A group analyst can help everybody to think about the change process from the end point backwards, and resist a top-down wish list, which can treat real human difficulties with contempt in order to reduce loss, resistance, and mourning to compliance, a demand to accept followership willingly and mindlessly. Instead group analysts bring the reality principle, enabling clients to face the world as it is and master it with inner resourcefulness and mutual help.

A caveat: before thinking about how to work with clients' endings, it is vital that the consultant be fully aware of her/his personal stance on endings. Choice of clients and ways of thinking and working will be rooted in very personal development, and our connection to socially unconscious processes in our society of origin.

A continental story

This story is about the relations between groups within an organization, and also the wider social and economic influences that affect us all; the cultural foundation matrix within which organizational life takes place. What happens to an organization when the world changes significantly and confronts all its members with its mortality?

An Institute of Psychology established in 1922 provided supervision, psychodynamic training, and organizational development services to the whole of the country's governmental, social, and health institutions, privileged by the state to be the sole supplier of these services. In the 1990s, the government could no longer ignore the neo-liberal ideology becoming ubiquitous throughout the world. Government jobs were advertised, and institutions were invited to compete for all public-sector work, encouraging competition and favoring market forces to dictate how and what got done and by whom. Foreign companies began to dominate the market for all consulting service, large consulting firms from the US and UK experienced in competing for and winning public contracts. The Institute was well established in the local context, but relatively small and completely inexperienced in competitive tendering.

The Institute's history fueled a culture of over-confidence and a belief in its own immortality. Silos had built up with each sub-group invested in its own superiority, and there was a divide and rule culture at the top. The management team consisted of the heads of each silo, coming together to divide up work and keep real cooperation to a minimum – real cooperation across psychological methods and theories being akin to treachery and betrayal. Only when they really, really had to, would the organization come together as a whole. They were ripe for attack and takeover in the market. In this situation they decided to call in outside help.

They asked me to help them reflect on the processes blocking change, and find new ways of working together, to help them survive and avoid the end of a great institution.

The work started with an exploratory research phase, and then an analytically led Large Group, held at the top of a mountain in a hotel. We met in the ballroom – which was big enough for all the 120 staff to sit together in one circle. After describing my research findings and how I would work with them, I let the group go into silence and did not set any goals or targets for the work, except survival. Silence increases the psychological pressure within a group and often leads to someone needing to speak about the issue that really matters to them and to others. It was a hot day and there was no air-conditioning; the windows were open. As we sat in silence, the sound of all the church bells in the valley came clearly in – marking the fiftieth anniversary of the end of the Second World War. Someone started crying.

She was sitting opposite me and at the other end of the room. Everyone lowered their heads and looked away from her – preferring to stare into the empty space of the floor in the middle of the group. Only when the bells stopped did people lift their heads. Then I asked her what the connection was between the sound of the Church bells, her tears and the fact that everyone, apart from me, had avoided looking at her. 'A few months ago', she answered, 'we had another consultant working with us. As a result thirteen people lost their jobs. I'm crying for them and I'm scared the same thing will happen after today. But I'm also crying because we were spared the suffering of the second World War. I remember my parents being frightened throughout, they feared being occupied by the Germans.' But my tears are also for the shame of Switzerland, because of the money that was never returned to the victims of the Holocaust and the fact that we bankrolled some of the Nazi war costs'.

In the conversations that followed, it became clear that many inside the Institute questioned the way things were working. The firm needed to see learning as a continuing process at the heart of their work. They had to re-learn how to connect with the world and each other, and get real about what they did and what was needed from them. They had to become more pragmatic and engage with clients with the breadth of their enormous experience so that they could remain more valuable in their clients' eyes than their marketing-savvy competitors. Above all, they had to learn to win tendering processes and secure their own jobs. In analytic terms they had to end their culture of dependency on the CEO and the fight–flight interactions between the specialties. They had to become a diverse and integrated community again. I chose to work through large groups as they open a transitional space, in which they could experience their institution as something whole, something divided, and something inter-dependent.

The group succeeded in helping the organization survive and stabilize itself, but it took eight years with two whole day meetings a year. A slow but cost-effective intervention, the total cost less than a whole consulting day offered by a small team from Ernst & Young or McKinsey. Each time we met, the whole organization mandated small working parties to address specific issues, then reported on and worked through in the next cycle of large groups. These working groups had to be cross-departmental and include the whole range of the skills available. All the work was informed by the analytical approach of free association and of expressing thoughts and feelings freely, subject to the working groups' tasks.

This approach, attending to relationship, task, and emotions, allowed the organizational community to process their fears and defensive responses evoked by the changes they had to embrace. There were unresolvable tensions of perspective between the different departments that could not be wished away but it was always possible in the large group sessions to work with them and arrive at compromises. By naming conflicts and bringing them out into the open, there was a sense of relief and a willingness to grasp the nettle together. Slowly, step by step, the culture of we are right/wrong, superior/inferior ended and became a culture of openness and inquisitiveness.

Naming things for what they are in front of others is a way of ordering and re-ordering the world we find ourselves in externally, and the world we belong to and identify with internally. The symbolic naming of how we see things does not in itself define the meaning of what is being perceived and said, but it allows members of a group and community to confirm or adapt the meaning of who they are, what they stand for, and why they do what they do. Naming can facilitate an end to self-idealization in order to avoid self-destruction and above all it makes organizational boundaries translucent, letting things in and out. An end worth having.

The organization began to behave like a Parliament in the Large Group, with groups working on different issues and submitting issues for approval, improvement or rejection to the whole assembly. The management team were not outside the other work streams – they behaved as simply another one of the working groups striving together to reinvigorate and recreate the organization. The management team, like any of the working parties, came to the whole organization group with the dilemmas it faced and invited the wider population to support them in choosing what to do. They did not assume they had a monopoly on the knowledge and wisdom. The organization was creating collective support for what was being done and the choices that were being made. There was no preaching and no bullying. By the end the organization had a sense of community while at the same time nurturing and sustaining healthy sub-group identities – these sub-groups were largely informed by the variety of professional expertise within the firm.

The organization also became more outwardly orientated, better at staying in touch with external reality. They created a Board of Governors linked to the needs of Civil, Social, Medical, and Academic services. The Institute had changed and yet stayed connected to its roots. What was recovered was the ability to be attractive in the eyes of the national civil society in the twenty-first century. As a last step in the process, the old boss stood down and I, the consultant who worked for that boss, was 'sacked'. What the woman who cried in the first Large Group had feared, that people would get sacked had been prevented, but the sacrifice of the CEO and the consultant integrated the leadership team of the next generation and facilitated their succession. The participants in the Large Group intervention had treated the consultant both as a transitional object and a substitute parent. The parent got kicked out of home and the transitional object became an internal object, which could be used in future crises. The end of the consultant's power and influence in the institution, helped the new power holders to cross the threshold into their own new age.

The Large Group work approach offered this organization a communal space in which the exchanges across departmental and specialty boundaries, ended up confirming the group's common social identity and everyone's sense of social location and psychological security. On the basis of this psychological re-grounding, the organization and its various subgroups found the energy for survival and renewal.

In the last session I attended in this Institute I could feel that moves were afoot, that both the CEO and I would be sacrificed to end the old culture and integrate the new. I accepted the fate of any large group conductor, to be put aside without a proper ending process, as a child puts aside its transitional object when it has outgrown it. This kind of end needs to be accepted by large group leaders as normal. Thinking back on this project, I conclude that the whole process intervention could be characterized as a repeated cycle of disillusionment, re-illusionment-dis-illusionment and renewed re-illusionment.

Organizations, like individuals, survive, thrive, grow, and die through existential crises. The challenge for leaders is to grasp that such existential questions can only be worked through locally and that they may take time to address. No amount of power point presentations, magical thinking or consultancy will find a shortcut. Furthermore, and this maybe is the hardest step, leaders cannot control or mandate the change process to middle managers. Success and a good enough ending of a change process, involving the whole organization, as described here, requires that the change starts in the Leader, the management team, and the consultant. The advantage of an analytic or group analytic consultancy approach is that such practitioners can work with mirroring, projection, transference, and counter-transference. It is these reflective processes that put the consultant in touch with what can and can't be named by the people involved, needing to be voiced or enacted by the consultant and/or the leader first.

This particular consultancy intervention started with tears and a sense of loss and mourning. Group analytic change consultancy is mourning work and the thought of ending is an integral part of the intervention, right from the start.

Conclusion: Christine and Gerhard

Right at the start of any consultation something must end, if an analytically inspired consultation is to succeed in helping the organization mature. The hope must end of an external savior, achieving unrealistic goals, or that change is plannable, controllable and without unintended consequences. In a democratic society and its institutions, change and the end point of a consultancy process can best be reached through participation, consultation, and compromise – in the full knowledge that the transition to some new way of working together starts with the end of the old one. The previous generation gives way to the new, and the adoption of new arrangements, ideas, and practices is preceded by an ending and a loss. This is the rhythm of life. Group analytic consultancy concerning change is therefore primarily mourning work, and the end is indeed in the beginning.

Note

1 My being German must have been relevant.

Section IX

Further leads

Section IX rounds off the book, with a brief afterword, a combined list of references for all chapters which provides the curious reader with bibliographical leads, and an index to help the reader navigate and make sense of the matrix of the book.

Afterword

Christine Thornton

Dialogue with the talented people who have contributed to this book has been tremendous fun – 'serious fun' – which is a good definition of 'high-performance teamwork'. We hope that it is an important contribution to the thinking about group analysis applied in organizations, and in the wider world. What it *isn't* is the 'last word'. If you would like to continue the dialogue, email organizationalgroupanalysis@gmail.com.

Bibliography

Adams, D. (1987). *Dirk Gently's holistic detective agency*. London: Heinemann.

Adlam, J., Lee, B. and Kluttig, T. eds. (2018). *Violent states and creative states: Structural violence and creative structures*. Vol. 1–2. London: Jessica Kingsley.

Adlam, J. and Scanlon, C. (2005). Personality disorder and homelessness: Membership and 'unhoused minds' in forensic settings. *Group Analysis*, 38(3), pp. 452–466.

Adlam, J. and Scanlon, C. (2011). Working with hard-to-reach patients in difficult places: A democratic therapeutic community approach to consultation. In: A. Rubitel and D. Reiss, eds., *Containment in the community: Supportive frameworks for thinking about antisocial behaviour and mental health*. 1st ed. London: Karnac, pp. 1–22.

Adlam, J. and Scanlon, C. (2013). On agoraphilia: A psychosocial account of the defence and negotiation of public/private spaces. *Forensische Psychiatrie und Psychotherapie*, 20(3), pp. 209–228.

Adlam, J. and Scanlon, C. (2018). Insult and injury: Reciprocal violence and reflexive violence. In: J. Adlam, B. Lee and T. Kluttig, eds., *Violent states and creative states: Structural violence and creative structures*. Vol. 1. London: Jessica Kingsley, pp. 45–58.

Agazarian, Y. and Peters, W. (1995). *The visible and invisible group*. 2nd ed. London: Karnac.

American Psychiatric Association. (2001). *Practice guideline for the treatment of patients with borderline personality disorder*. Arlington, VA: American Psychiatric Publishing.

Arendt, H. (1958). *The human condition*. 1st ed. Chicago: The University of Chicago Press.

Argyris, C. (1980). Making the undiscussable and its undiscussable and its undiscussable discussable. *Public Administration Review*, 40(3), pp. 205–213.

Argyris, C. (1990). *Overcoming organizational defenses: Facilitating organizational learning*. Boston: Allyn & Bacon.

Argyris, C. (2009). *Theories of action, double-loop learning and organizational learning* [Online]. Available at: www.infed.org/thinkers/argyris.htm.

Armstrong, D. (2005). *Organization in the mind: Psychoanalysis, group relations and organizational consultancy*. London: Karnac.

Ballatt, J. and Campling, P. (2011). *Intelligent kindness reforming the culture of healthcare*. London: RCPsych.

Barnes, B. (1994). Unpublished communication.

Barnes, B., Ernst, S. and Hyde, K. (1999). *An introduction to groupwork: A group-analytic perspective*. Basingstoke and London: Macmillan Press.

Bateson, G. (1972, 2000). *Steps to an ecology of mind*. Chicago: The University of Chicago Press.

Bateson, G. and Haley, J. (1954). A theory of play and fantasy. In: *Symposium of the American psychiatric association on cultural, anthropological and communications approaches*. Mexico City, Mexico, 11 Mar.

Batmanghelidjh, C. and Rayment, T. (2017). *Kids: Child protection in Britain: The truth*. London: Biteback Publishing.

Bauman, Z. (2000). *Liquid modernity*. Cambridge: Polity Press.

Bauman, Z. (2002). *Society under siege*. Cambridge: Polity Press.

Baumann, Z. (2007). *Liquid times*. London: Fontana.

Behr, H. and Hearst, L. (2005). *Group-analytic psychotherapy: A meeting of minds*. London: Whurr.

Benjamin, J. (2018). *Beyond doer and done to: Recognition theory, intersubjectivity and the third*. London: Routledge.

Berne, E. (1964). *Games people play: The psychology of human relationships*. New York: Grove Press.

Bertalanffy, L. V. (1973). *General system theory: Foundations, development, applications*. Harmondsworth: Penguin.

Berwick, D. (2010). *Dr. Donald Berwick's speech to the British national health service* [Online]. Available at: https://khn.org/news/berwick-british-nhs-speech-transcript.

Bhurruth, M. (2008). Matriculating the matrix: A different understanding of psychic structure, resonance and repression. *Group Analysis*, 41(4), pp. 352–365.

Binney, G., Glanfield, P. and Wilke, G. (2017). *Breaking free of bonkers: How to lead in today's crazy world of organizations*. London: Nicholas Brealey International.

Binney, G., Wilke, G. and Williams, C. (2005, 2009, 2012). *Living leadership: A practical guide for ordinary heroes*. 3rd ed. Harlow: Pearson Education.

Bion, W. R. (1959). Attacks on linking. *International Journal of Psycho-Analysis*, 40, pp. 308–315.

Bion, W. R. (1961). *Experience in groups*. London: Routledge.

Bion, W. R. (1962). The psychoanalytic study of thinking: A theory of thinking. *International Journal of Psycho-Analysis*, 43, pp. 306–310.

Bion, W. R. (1967a). Attacks on linking. In: W. R. Bion, ed., *Second thoughts: Selected papers on psychoanalysis*. London: Heinemann, pp. 93–109.

Bion, W. R. (1967b). Differentiation of the psychotic from non-psychotic personalities. In: W. R. Bion, ed., *Second thoughts: Selected papers on psychoanalysis*. London: Heinemann, pp. 43–64.

Bion, W. R. (1967c). A theory of thinking. In: W. R. Bion, ed., *Second thoughts: Selected papers on psychoanalysis*. London: Heinemann, pp. 110–119.

Blackwell, R. D. (1994). When everything needs to be thought about, more things become unthinkable: The psychoanalytic and group dynamics of thinking under political fire. In: *Psychoanalysis and the public sphere conference*. London: University of East London.

Blackwell, R. D. (1998). Bounded instability, group analysis and the matrix: Organizations under stress. *Group Analysis*, 31(4), pp. 532–546.

Blackwell, R. D. (2003). Colonialism and globalization: A group-analytic perspective. *Group Analysis*, 36(4), pp. 445–463.

Blackwell, R. D. (2005). Psychotherapy, politics and trauma: Working with survivors of torture and organized violence. *Group Analysis*, 38(2), pp. 307–323.

Blackwell, R. D. (2011a). Postscript: Poetry, passion and peace. *Group Analysis*, 44(1), pp. 114–119.

Blackwell, R. D. (2011b). Ships in the night: The 'Open Group' for clients on the waiting list. *Group Analysis*, 44(3), pp. 247–265.

Blackwell, R. D. (2014). Response to Elisabeth Rohr's Foulkes lecture. *Group Analysis*, 47(4), pp. 384–391.

Blackwell, R. D. and Dizadji, F. (2014). Demonised, blamed, negated, and disappeared: The victimisation of the poor in the globalized economy. *Psychotherapy and Politics International*, 14(1), pp. 5–16.

Block, P. (2011). *Flawless consulting*. 3rd ed. London: McGraw-Hill.

Boal, A. (1998). *Legislative theatre, using performance to make politics*. London: Routledge.

Bohm, D. (1951). *Quantum theory*. New York: Prentice Hall.

Bohm, D. (1980). *Wholeness and the implicate order*. London: Routledge.

Bohm, D. and Hiley, B. J. (1993). *The undivided universe: An ontological interpretation of quantum theory*. London: Routledge.

Bollas, C. (1987). *The shadow of the object: Psychoanalysis of the unthought known*. London: Free Association Books.

Bollas, C. (1991). *Forces of destiny: Psychoanalysis and human idiom*. Lanham: Jason Aronson.

Bourdieu, P. (1984). *Distinction: A social critique of the judgement of taste*. Cambridge: Harvard University Press.

Bourdieu, P. (1993). *The field of cultural production: Essays on art and literature*. New York: Columbia University Press.

Boxer, P. (1996). Personal communication with R.D. Blackwell.

Bramley, W. (1990). Staff sensitivity groups: A conductor's field experiences. *Group Analysis*, 23(3), pp. 301–316.

Brenman, E. (2006). *Recovery of the lost good object*. London: Routledge.

Bridger, H. (1985). Northfield revisited. In: M. Pines, ed., *Bion and group psychotherapy*. London: Routledge, pp. 87–107.

Britton, R. (1998). *Belief and imagination: Explorations in psychoanalysis*. London: Routledge.

Britton, R. (2008). What part does narcissism play in narcissistic disorders? (Chapter 3). In J. Steiner. ed. *Rosenfeld in retrospect*. London: Routledge, pp. 22–34.

Brooks, S. K., Gerada, C. and Chalder, T. (2011). Review of literature on the mental health of doctors: Are specialist services needed? *Journal of Mental Health*, 20(2), pp. 146–156.

Burkitt, I. (1991). *Social selves, theories of the social formation of personality*. London: Sage.

Butler, J. (2004). *Precarious life: The powers of mourning and violence*. London: Verso.

Campbell, D. (2010a). *Opponent of NHS reform driven by grim memories of 60s* [Online]. Available at: www.theguardian.com/society/2010/nov/19/nhs-gp-leader-clare-gerada [Accessed 24 Nov. 2017].

Campbell, J. (2010b). The Islands of the blest. *Group Analysis*, 43(4), pp. 413–432.

Carlyle, J. A. and Evans, C. (2005). Containing containers: Attention to the 'Innerface' and 'Outerface' of groups in secure institutions. *Group Analysis*, 38(3), pp. 395–408.

Carson, J. and Dennison, P. (2012). The role of groupwork in tackling organizational burnout. *Groupwork*, 18(2), pp. 8–25.

Chemero, A. (2000). Anti-representationalism and the dynamical stance. *Philosophy of Science*, 67(4), pp. 625–647.

Chemero, A. and Silberstein, M. (2008). Defending extended cognition. In B. Love, K. McRae and V. Sloutsky, eds., *Proceedings of the cognitive science society, 30th annual conference*. Austin, TX: Cognitive Science Society.

Chomsky, N. (1957). *Syntactic structures*. The Hague, Paris: Mouton.

Clancy, A., Vince, R. and Gabriel, Y. (2012). That unwanted feeling: A psychodynamic study of disappointment at work. *British Journal of Management*, 23(4), pp. 518–531.

Commoner, B. (1971). *The closing circle: Nature, man, and technology*. New York: Knopf.

Cooper, A. and Lousada, J. (2005). *Borderline welfare: Feeling and fear of feeling in modern welfare*. London: Karnac.

Cooper, C. L. ed. (1976). *Developing social skills in managers: Advances in group training*. London: Macmillan Press.

Cooper, V. and Whyte, D. eds. (2017). *The violence of austerity*. London: Pluto.

Craib, I. (1994). *The importance of disappointment*. London: Routledge.

Cronen, V., Johnson, K. and Lannamann, J. (1982). Paradoxes, double-binds and reflexive loops: An alternative theoretical perspective. *Family Process*, 21(1), pp. 91–112.

Dalal, F. (1998). *Taking the group seriously: Towards a post-foulkesian group analytic theory*. London, Philadelphia, PA: Jessica Kingsley.

Dalal, F. (2011). *Thought paralysis: The virtues of discrimination*. London: Karnac.

Dalal, F. (2017). Group analysis in the time of austerity: Neo-liberalism, managerialism and evidence-based research. *Group Analysis*, 50(1), pp. 35–54.

Davis, J. and Tallis, R. eds. (2013). *NHS SOS: How the NHS was betrayed and how we can save it*. London: Oneworld.

De Maré, P., Piper, R. and Thompson, S. (1991). *Koinonia: From hate, through dialogue, to culture in the large group*. London: Karnac.

Dixon, N. (1976). *On the psychology of military incompetence*. London: Random House.

Dorling, D. (2010). *Injustice: Why social inequality persists*. Bristol: Policy Press.

Dubouloy, M. (2011). Is recognition a requisite for citizenship for managers? In: L. Gould, A. Lucey and L. Stapley, eds., *The reflective citizen: Organizational and social dynamics*. 1st ed. London: Karnac, pp. 131–149.

Elias, N. (1991). *The society of individuals*. Oxford: Blackwell.

Elias, N. (1994, 2000). *The civilising process*. Oxford: Blackwell.

Elias, N. (2009). *The established and the outsiders: A sociological enquiry into community problem*. London: Sage.

Enteman, W. F. (1993). *Managerialism: The emergence of a new ideology*. Madison: University of Wisconsin Press.

Erlich, H. S., Erlich-Ginor, M. and Beland, H. (2013). *Fed with tears; poisoned with milk: The Nazareth group relations conferences*. Geissen Germany: Psychosozial-Verlag.

Foulkes, S. H. (1948). *An introduction to group analytic psychotherapy*. London: Maresfield.

Foulkes, S. H. (1964). *Therapeutic group analysis*. London: George Allen and Unwin. (Reprinted 1984, London: Karnac).

Foulkes, S. H. (1971). Access to unconscious processes in the group analytic group. *Group Analysis*, 4, pp. 4–14.

Foulkes, S. H. (1975). *Group analytic psychotherapy: Method and principles*. London: Gordon and Breach. (Reprinted 1986, 2002, London: Karnac).

Foulkes, S. H. (1983). *Introduction to group analytic psychotherapy: Studies in the social integration of individuals and groups*. London: Karnac.

Foulkes, S. H. (1990a). The group as matrix of the individual's mental life. In: E. Foulkes, ed., *Selected papers: Psychoanalysis and group analysis*. 1st ed. London: Karnac, pp. 223–234.

Foulkes, S. H. (1990b). *Selected papers: Psychoanalysis and group analysis*. London: Karnac Books.

Foulkes, S. H. and Anthony, E. J. (1957). *Group psychotherapy: The psychoanalytic approach*. London: Penguin.

Freud, S. (1923). The ego and the id. In: *Standard edition*. Vol. 19. London: Hogarth.

Freud, S. (1937). Analysis terminable and interminable. *International Journal of Psycho-Analysis*, 18, pp. 373–405.

Frosh, S. and Barraitser, L. (2008). Psychoanalysis and psycho-social studies. *Psychoanalysis, Culture and Society*, 13(4), pp. 346–365.

Frost, L. and Hoggett, P. (2008). Human agency and social suffering. *Critical Social Policy*, 28(5), pp. 438–460.

Gabbard, G. O. (2005). Patient-therapist boundary issues. *Psychiatric Times*, 22(12).

Gabbard, G. O. and Lester, E. P. (2003). *Boundaries & boundary violations in psychoanalysis*. Washington, DC: American Psychiatric Publishing.

Gerada, C. (2014). 'Trust me . . . I'm a leader'. A personal view from Dr Clare Gerada, *NHS confederation* [Online]. Available at: www.nhsconfed.org/~/media/Confederation/Files/Publications/Documents/trust-me-im-a-leader.pdf.

Gerada, C. (2016). Healing doctors through groups: Creating time to reflect together. *British Journal of General Practice*, 66(651).

Giddens, A. (1999). *Runaway world*. London: Routledge.

Gilligan, J. (1996). *Violence: Reflections on our deadliest epidemic*. London: Jessica Kingsley.

Gleick, J. (1987). *Chaos: Making a new science*. New York: Viking.

Glenn, L. (1987). Attachment theory and group analysis: The group matrix as a secure base. *Group Analysis*, 20(2), pp. 109–117.

Goffman, E. (1961). *Asylums*. New York: Doubleday.

Goleman, D. (1999). *Working with emotional intelligence*. London: Bloomsbury Publishing.

Gould, L., Lucey, A. and Stapley, L. eds. (2011). *The reflective citizen: Organizational and social dynamics*. London: Karnac.

Grace, C. (2016). Endings and loss in mergers and acquisitions: An exploration of group analytic theory. *Group Analysis*, 49(2), pp. 134–148.

Hamel, G. (2000). *Leading the revolution*. Boston: Harvard Business School Press.

Harrison, T. and Clarke, D. (1992). The Northfield experiments. *The British Journal of Psychiatry*, 160(5), pp. 698–708.

Hartley, P. and Kennard, D. eds. (2009). *Staff support groups in the helping professions: Principles, practice and pitfalls.* Hove: Routledge.

Heinskou, T. (2002). Organizational psychology programme at the institute of group analysis (Copenhagen): A training programme in group analysis and group relations. *Group Analysis*, 35(2), pp. 271–286.

Hobson, R. F. (2013). *Forms of feeling: The heart of psychotherapy.* 3rd ed. London: Routledge.

Hochschild, A. (2001). *The time bind: When work becomes home and home becomes work.* New York: Henry Holt.

Hofstadter, D. R. (2008). *I am a strange loop.* New York: Basic Books.

Hoggett, P. (2009). *Politics, identity and emotion.* London: Paradigm Publishers.

Hoggett, P., Wilkinson, H. and Beedell, P. (2013). Fairness and the politics of resentment. *Journal of Social Policy*, 42(3), pp. 567–585.

Honig, B. (1996). Difference, dilemmas and the politics of home. In: S. Benhabib, ed., *Democracy and difference: Contesting the boundaries of the political.* 1st ed. Princeton: Princeton University Press.

Honneth, A. (1995). *The struggle for recognition: The moral grammar of social conflicts.* Cambridge: Polity Press.

Hopper, E. (1991). Encapsulation as a defence against the fear of annihilation. *The International Journal of Psychoanalysis*, 72(4), pp. 607–624.

Hopper, E. (1997). Traumatic experience in the unconscious life of groups: A fourth basic assumption. *Group Analysis*, 30(4), pp. 439–470.

Hopper, E. (2002). *The social unconscious: Selected papers.* London: Jessica Kingsley.

Hopper, E. (2003). *Traumatic experience in the unconscious life of groups: The fourth basic assumption: Incohesion: Aggregation/massification or (ba) I:A/M.* London: Jessica Kingsley.

Hopper, E. (2007). Theoretical and conceptual notes concerning transference and countertransference processes in groups and by groups, and the social unconscious: Part II. *Group Analysis*, 40(1), pp. 29–42.

Hopper, E. (2009). The theory of the basic assumption of incohesion: Aggregation / massification or (BA) I: A/M. *British Journal of Psychotherapy*, 25(2), pp. 214–229.

Hopper, E. (2012a). Introduction: The theory of incohesion: Aggregation/massification as the fourth basic assumption in the unconscious life of groups and group-like social systems. In *Trauma and organisations.* London: Karnac, pp. 41–51.

Hopper, E. ed. (2012b). *Trauma and organizations.* London: Karnac.

Hopper, E. and Weinberg, H., eds. (2011). *The social unconscious in persons, groups and societies: Mainly theory.* Vol. 1. London: Karnac.

Hopper, E. and Weinberg, H., eds. (2017). The social unconscious in persons, groups, and societies: Volume 3: *The foundation matrix extended and re-configured.* London: Karnac.

James, D. C. (1984). Bion's containing and Winnicott's holding in the context of the group matrix. *International Journal of Group Psychotherapy*, 34(2), pp. 201–213.

Jones, M. (1968). *Social psychiatry in practice: The idea of the therapeutic community.* London: Penguin.

Kahneman, D. (2011). *Thinking, fast and slow.* London: Penguin.

Kapur, R. (2009). Managing primitive emotions in organizations. *Group Analysis*, 42(1), pp. 31–46.

Kapur, R. (2016). *Psychiatric rehabilitation: A psychoanalytic approach to recovery.* London: Karnac.

Kapur, R. (2017). Management of day to day organizational human relations: A Henri Rey perspective. *Psychoanalytic Psychotherapy*, 31(1), pp. 211–236.

Kapur, R. (2018). What's in the good enough introject? Emotional ingredients in settling disturbed states of mind. *British Journal of Psychotherapy*, 34(1), pp. 46–60.

Karpman, S. (1968). Fairy tales and script drama analysis. *Transactional Analysis Bulletin*, 7(26), pp. 39–43.

Kauffman, S. A. (1995). *At home in the universe.* New York: Oxford University Press.

Kennard, D. (1983). Democracy and psychoanalysis. In: *An introduction to therapeutic communities.* London: Routledge, Kegan Paul.

Kets de Vries, M. F. R. (2005). Leadership group coaching in action: The Zen of creating high performance teams. *Academy of Management Executive*, 19(1), pp. 61–76.

Knauss, W. (1999). The creativity of destructive fantasies. *Group Analysis*, 32(3), pp. 397–411.

Kraemer, S. and Roberts, J. eds. (1996). *The politics of attachment: Towards a secure society.* London: Free Associations Books.

Krantz, J. (2011). Reflective citizenship: An organizational perspective. In: L. Gould, A. Lucey and L. Stapley, eds., *The reflective citizen: Organizational and social dynamics.* London: Karnac, pp. 149–162.

Kreeger, L. ed. (1975). *The large group, dynamics & therapy.* London: Constable.

Lacan, J. (1966). *Ecrits: A selection.* New York: W.W. Norton.

Lawrence, W. G. (1998). *Social dreaming at work.* London: Karnac.

Lawrence, W. G. (2000). *Tongued with fire: Groups in experience.* London: Karnac.

Lawrence, W. G. (2004). *An introduction to social dreaming.* London: Karnac.

Leach, E. (1982). *Social anthropology.* London: Fontana.

Leal, R. M. (1982). Resistances and the group-analytic process. *Group Analysis*, 15(2), pp. 97–110.

Legislation.gov.uk. (2010). *Equality act 2010* [online]. Available at: www.legislation.gov.uk/ukpga/2010/15/contents [Accessed 3 June 2018].

Lemma, A. (2010). The power of relationship: A study of key working as an intervention with traumatised young people. *Journal of Social Work Practice*, 24(4), pp. 409–427.

Lewin, K. (1939). Field theory and experiment in social psychology: Concepts and methods. *American Journal of Sociology*, 44(6), pp. 868–896.

Lewin, K. (1947). Frontiers in group dynamics: Concept, method and reality in social science; social equilibria and social change. *Human Relations*, 1(1), pp. 5–41.

Lewin, K. (1951). *Field theory in social science: Selected theoretical papers.* 1st ed. New York: Harper.

Lorentzen, S. (2014). *Group analytic psychotherapy.* London: Routledge.

MacDonald, P. (2002). *The concept of therapeutic presence in nursing* [Online]. Available at: www.temple.edu/ispr/prev_cpmferemce/ . . . /2000.

Maher, M. (2009). Authority and control: Working with staff groups in children's homes. In: P. Hartley and D. Kennard, eds., *Staff support groups in the helping professions: Principles, practice and pitfalls.* Hove: Routledge, pp. 122–134.

Main, T. F. (1957). The ailment. *British Journal of Medical Psychology*, 30(3), pp. 128–145.

Mandelbrot, B. (1967). How long is the coast of Britain? Statistical self-similarity and fractional dimension. *Science*, 156(3775), pp. 636–638.

Mandelbrot, B. (1977). *Fractals* [ebook]. Available at: Wiley Online Library.

Marshall, J. (2001). Self-reflective inquiry practices. In: P. Reason and H. Bradbury, eds., *Handbook of action research*. 1st ed. London: Sage, pp. 433–439.

Maturana, H. R. (1978). Biology of language: The epistemology of reality. In: G. A. Miller and E. Lenneberg, eds., *Psychology and biology of language and thought*. New York: Academic Press.

Maturana, H. R. and Varela, F. (1980). *Autopoiesis and cognition: The realization of the living*. London: Reidl.

McMullin, E. (2002). The origins of the field concept in physics. *Physics in Perspective*, 4(1), pp. 13–39.

McNeill, B. W. and Worthen, V. (1989). The parallel process in psychotherapy supervision. *Professional Psychology: Research and Practice*, 20(5), pp. 329–333.

Mead, G. H. (1964). Social consciousness, and consciousness of meaning. In: A. J. Reck, ed., *Selected writings*. Indianapolis, IN: Library of the Liberal Arts.

Meltzer, D. (1968). Terror, persecution, dread: A dissection of paranoid anxieties. *International Journal of Psychoanalysis*, 49, pp. 335–342.

Meltzer, D. (1986). *Studies in extended meta-psychology*. Perthshire: Clunie Press.

Menzies-Lyth, I. (1959). The functions of social systems as a defence against anxiety: A report on a study of the nursing service of a general hospital. *Human Relations*, 13, pp. 95–121.

Menzies-Lyth, I. (1988a) The functioning of social systems as a defence against anxiety, Chapter 2. In *Containing anxiety in institutions: Selected essays*. Vol. 1. London: Free Association Books, pp. 43–99.

Menzies Lyth, I. (1988b). *Containing anxiety in institutions: Selected essays*. Vol. 1. London: Free Association Books.

Miller, E. J. and Gwynne, G. V. (1972). *A life apart: A pilot study of residential institutions for the physically handicapped and the young chronic sick*. London: Taylor & Francis.

Miller, M. and Gerada, C. (2017). General practice, mental health, and stress. Part 1: A dialogue. In: A. Vaspe, ed., *Psychoanalysis, the NHS, and mental health work today*. London: Karnac, pp. 187–212.

Mojovic, M. (2007). The impact of the post-totalitarian social context on the group matrix. *Group Analysis*, 40(3), pp. 394–403.

Mojović, M. (2011). Manifestations of psychic retreats in social systems. In: E. Hopper and H. Weinberg, eds., *Social unconscious in persons, groups and societies*. 1st ed. London: Karnac, pp. 209–234.

Mojović, M. (2016). Serbian reflective citizens' matrix flourishing in the leaking containers. *Group Analysis*, 49(4), pp. 370–384.

Mojović, M. (2017). 'Untouchable infant gangs' in group and social matrices as obstacles to reconciliation. In: G. Ofer, ed., *A bridge over troubled waters: Conflicts and reconciliations in groups and society*. London: Karnac, pp. 139–138.

Morgan, G. (1997). *Images of organization*. London: Sage.

Mori, I. (2012). *Britons are more proud of their history, NHS and army than the royal family* [Online]. Available at: www.ipsos.com/ipsos-mori/en-uk/britons-are-more-proud-their-history-nhs-and-army-royal-family [Accessed 24 Nov. 2017].

Mowles, C. (2015). *Managing in uncertainty: Complexity and the paradoxes of everyday organizational life*. Hove: Routledge.

Mowles, C. (2017). Group analytic methods beyond the clinical setting – working with researcher – managers. *Group Analysis*, 50(2), pp. 217–236.

Myers, M. F. and Gabbard, G. O. (2008). *The physician as patient: A clinical handbook for mental health professionals*. Washington, DC: American Psychiatric Publishing, Inc.

Nichol, B. (2000). *Bion and Foulkes at Northfield: The early development of group psychotherapy in Britain* [Online]. Available at: www.businesscoachinstitute.com/library/bion_and_foulkes_at_northfield.shtml.

Nietzsche, F. W. (2001). *The gay science*. Trans J. Nauckhoff. Cambridge: Cambridge University Press.

Nitsun, M. (1996). *The anti-group: Destructive forces in the group and their creative potential*. London: Routledge.

Nitsun, M. (1998a). The organizational mirror: A group-analytic approach to organizational consultancy: Part 1: Theory. *Group Analysis*, 31(3), pp. 245–267.

Nitsun, M. (1998b). The organizational mirror: Group-analytic approach to organizational consultancy: Part 2: Application. *Group Analysis*, 31(4), pp. 505–518.

Nitsun, M. (2009). Authority and revolt: The challenges of group leadership. *Group Analysis*, 42(4), pp. 325–348.

Nitsun, M. (2015). *Beyond the antigroup: Survival and transformation*. London: Routledge.

Nitzgen, D. and Hopper, E. (2017). The concepts of the social unconscious and of the matrix in the work of S H Foulkes. In: E. Hopper and H. Weinberg, eds., *The social unconscious in persons, groups and societies, volume 3: The foundation matrix extended and re-configured*. London: Karnac, pp. 3–26.

Norton, K. (1992a). A culture of enquiry: Its preservation or loss. *Therapeutic Communities*, 13(1), pp. 3–26.

Norton, K. (1992b). Personality disordered individuals: The Henderson hospital model of treatment. *Criminal Behaviour and Mental Health*, 2, pp. 180–191.

Obholzer, A. and Roberts, V. (1994). *The unconscious at work: Individual and organizational stress in the human services*. London: Routledge.

Ofer, G. eds. (2017). *A bridge over troubled waters: Conflicts and Reconciliations in groups and society*. London: Karnac.

Oliver, C. (2005). *Reflexive inquiry*. London: Karnac.

Oliver, C. (2008). The collapsed chair consultation: Making moments of significance work. In: D. Campbell and C. Huffington, eds., *Organisations connected*. London: Karnac, pp. 39–58.

Oliver, C. (2016). Response to 'Endings and Loss in Mergers and Acquisitions: An Exploration of Group Analytic Theory,' by Corina Grace. *Group Analysis*, 49(2), pp. 175–182.

Oliver, C. (2019). A contextual framework. In: A. Novacovic and D. Vincent, eds., *A group analytic approach to work with staff teams and organisations*. Abingdon: Routledge.

O'Neill, O. (2002). *BBC Reith lectures 2002 – a question of trust* [Podcast]. Available at: www.bbc.co.uk/radio4 [Accessed 15 Apr. 2002].

Osborne, H. (2015). *Early humans did not mumble and grunt: Language 'developed rapidly'* [Online]. Available at: www.ibtimes.co.uk/early-humans-did-not-mumble-grunt-language-developed-rapidly-1494573 [Accessed 1 Apr. 2015].

Oshry, B. (2007). *Seeing systems*. Oakland: Berrett-Koehler Publishers.

Palazzoli, S. M. (1984). Behind the scenes of the organization: Some guidelines for the expert in human relations. *Journal of Family Therapy*, 6, pp. 299–307.

Parker, D. and Stacey, R. D. (1994). *Chaos, management and economics: The implications of non-linear thinking*. London: Institute of Economic Affairs.

Pearce, W. B. (2007). *Making social worlds: A communication perspective*. Oxford: Blackwell.

Pedler, M., Burgoyne, J. and Boydell, T. (1997). *The learning company: A strategy for sustainable development*. 2nd ed. London: McGraw-Hill.

Pennycook-Greaves, W. (2003). Commentary on 'A Working Conference on Professional and Managerial Dilemmas working in and with Organizations: Building Bridges between Group Analysis and Organizations' by Marlene Spero. *Group Analysis*, 36(3), pp. 340–343.

Powell, C. (2009). The insider as facilitator: Conducting a group for hospital clinical team leaders. In: D. Kennard and P. Hartley, eds., *Staff support groups in the helping professions: Principles, practice and pitfalls*. London: Routledge, pp. 135–146.

Prodgers, A. (1991). Countertransference: The conductor's emotional response within the group setting. *Group Analysis*, 24(4), pp. 389–407.

Rance, C. K. (1987). Is it good or bad form to talk about a group-analytic intervention in organizations? *Group Analysis*, 20(4), pp. 379–380.

Rance, C. K. (1989). What has group analysis to offer in the context of organizational consultancy? *Group Analysis*, 22(3), pp. 333–341.

Rance, C. K. (1998a). The art of conversation: The group-analytic paradigm and organizational consultancy. *Group Analysis*, 31(4), pp. 519–531.

Rance, C. K. (1998b). Organisations in the mind. In: S. Hardy, J. Carson and B. Thomas, eds., *Occupational stress, personal and professional perspectives*. Cheltenham: Stanley Thornes.

Rance, C. K. (2003). Commentary on 'A Working Conference on Professional and Managerial Dilemmas Working in and with Organizations: Building Bridges Between Group Analysis and Organizations' by Marlene Spero. *Group Analysis*, 36(3), pp. 336–339.

Rapoport, R. N. (1960). *Community as doctor*. London: Tavistock Publications.

Rey, H. (1994). *Universals of psychoanalysis in the treatment of psychotic and borderline states*. London: Free Association Press.

Ricketts, A. (2017). Former PM adviser says Camila Batmanghelidjh was the victim of a 'conspiracy'. *Sunday Times Magazine* [Online]. Available at: www.thirdsector.co.uk/former-pm-adviser-says-Camila Batmanghelidjh-victim-conspiracy/governance/article/1444855.

Riordan, D. C. (2008). Being ordinary in extraordinary places: Reflective practice of the total situation in a total institution. *Psychoanalytic Psychotherapy*, 22(3), pp. 196–217.

Rizq, R. (2011). The perversion of care: Psychological therapies in a time of IAPT. *Psychodynamic Counselling*, 18, pp. 7–24.

Rizq, R. (2012). The ghost in the machine: IAPT and organisational Melancholia. *British Journal of Psychotherapy*, 28(3), pp. 319–335.

Roberts, V. Z. (1994a). The organization of work: Contributions from open systems theory. In: A. Obholzer and V. Z. Roberts, eds., *The unconscious at work: Individual and organizational stress in the human services*. London: Routledge, pp. 28–38.

Roberts, V. Z. (1994b). The self-assigned impossible task. In: A. Obholzer and V. Z. Roberts, eds., *The unconscious at work: Individual and organizational stress in the human services*. London: Routledge, pp. 110–120.

Rogers, C. (1987). On putting it into words: The balance between projective identification and dialogue in the group. *Group Analysis*, 20(2), pp. 99–107.

Rogers, C. (2013). Engaging with the median group. *Group Analysis*, 46(2), pp. 183–195.

Rogers, C. (2017). Provocation in large groups: Reflective practice and organisational consultancy. In: C. Thornton and P. Zelaskowski, eds., *Special reflective practice edition: Group analytic contexts*. Vol. 75. Group Analytic Society, pp. 38–40. Available at: https://www.yumpu.com/en/embed/view/5ZKB6kOpqotlhRrX

Rogers, C. (2018). Consulting to doctors in general practice – don't talk to me about work. In: A. Novakovic and D. Vincent, eds., *Group analytic approach to work with staff teams and organizations*. Abingdon: Routledge.

Rosenfeld, H. R. (1971). A clinical approach to the psychoanalytic theory of life and death instincts: An investigation into the aggressive aspects of narcissism. In: E. B. Spillius, ed., *Melanie Klein today: Developments in theory and practice, vol.1, mainly theory*. London: Routledge.

Rosenfeld, H. R. (1987). *Impasse and interpretation: Therapeutic and anti-therapeutic factors in the psychoanalytic treatment of psychotic, borderline and neurotic patients*. London: Brunner Routledge.

Roth, G. and Dicke, U. (2013). *Evolution of nervous systems and brains*, pp. 19–45 [Online]. Available at: www.researchgate.net/publication/278647746_Evolution_of_Nervous_Systems_and_Brains.

Rouchy, J. C. (1995). Identification and groups of belonging. *Group Analysis*, 28(2), pp. 129–141.

Sandler, A. M. (2004). Institutional responses to boundary violations: The case of Masud Khan. *International Journal of Psychoanalysis*, pp. 8527–8544.

Sartre, J. P. (1991). *The psychology of imagination*. New York: Carol Publishing Group.

Scanlon, C. (2012). The traumatised organisation-in-the-mind: Creating and maintaining spaces for difficult conversations in difficult places. In: J. Adlam, A. Aiyegbusi, P. Kleinot, A. Motz and C. Scanlon, eds., *The therapeutic milieu under fire: Security and insecurity in forensic mental health*. London: Jessica Kingsley, pp. 212–228.

Scanlon, C. (2015). On the perversity of *imagined* psychological solutions to very real social problems of unemployment (*work-lessness*) and social exclusion (*worth-lessness*): A group-analytic critique. *Group Analysis*, 48(1), pp. 31–45.

Scanlon, C. (2017). Working with dilemmas and dis-appointment in difficult places: Towards a psycho-social model for team-focussed reflective practice. In: A. Vaspe, ed., *Psychoanalysis, the NHS and mental health today: Understanding the needs of patients and staff*. London: Karnac.

Scanlon, C. and Adlam, J. (2008). Refusal, social exclusion and the cycle of rejection: A cynical analysis? *Critical Social Policy*, 28(4), pp. 529–549.

Scanlon, C. and Adlam, J. (2010). The *Recovery Model* or the modelling of a cover-up? On the creeping privatisation and individualisation of dis-ease and being-unwell-ness. *Groupwork: An Interdisciplinary Journal for Working with Groups*, 20(3), pp. 100–114.

Scanlon, C. and Adlam, J. (2011a). Cosmopolitan minds and metropolitan societies: Social exclusion and social refusal revisited. *Psychodynamic Practice*, 17(3), pp. 241–254.

Scanlon, C. and Adlam, J. (2011b). Who watches the watchers? Observing the dangerous liaisons between forensic patients and their carers in the 'perverse panopticon'. *Organizational and Social Dynamics*, 11(2), pp. 175–195.

Scanlon, C. and Adlam, J. (2012). Disorganised responses to refusal and spoiling in traumatised organisations. In: E. Hopper, ed., *Trauma and organisations*. London: Karnac.

Scanlon, C. and Adlam, J. (2013). On reflexive violence. *Psychoanalysis, Culture and Society*, 18(3), pp. 223–241.

Scanlon, C. and Adlam, J. (2018). Housing un-housed minds: Complex multiple exclusion and the cycle of rejection revisited. In: G. Brown, ed., *Psychoanalytic thinking on the unhoused mind*. London: Routledge.

Schermer, V. (2012a). Group-as-a-whole and complexity theories: Areas of convergence. Part I: Background and literature review. *Group Analysis*, 45(3), pp. 275–288.

Schermer, V. (2012b). Group-as-a-whole and complexity theories: Areas of convergence. Part II: Application to group relations, group analysis, and systems centered therapy. *Group Analysis*, 45(4), pp. 481–497.

Schlapobersky, J. and Pines, M. (2009). Gruppenanalyse und Analytische Gruppenpsychotherapie. In: G. Thieme, ed., *Herausgegaben von Volker Tschuschke*. New York: Verlag Stuittgart.

Schon, D. (1983). *The reflective practitioner: How professionals think in action*. New York: Basic Book.

Searles, H. F. (1955a). The informational value of the supervisor's emotional experiences. *Psychiatry*, 18(2), pp. 135–146.

Searles, H. F. (1955b). The informational value of the supervisor's emotional experiences. In: *Collected papers on schizophrenia and related subjects*. New York: International Universities Press, pp. 157–176.

Sennett, R. (1974). *The fall of public man*. London: W.W. Norton.

Shakespeare, W. (1994). *The merchant of Venice*. Harlow: Longman.

Silberstein, M. and Chemero, A. (2012). Complexity and extended phenomenological-cognitive systems. *Topics in Cognitive Science*, 4(1), pp. 35–50.

Simmel, G. (1950). *The sociology of Georg Simmel*. Trans K. Wolff. New York: Free Press.

Simpson, I. (2010). Containing the uncontainable: A role for staff support groups. In: J. Radcliffe, K. Hajek, J. Carson and O. Manor, eds., *Psychological groupwork with acute psychiatric inpatients*. London: Whiting and Birch.

Simpson, I. (2016). Containing anxiety in social care systems and neo-liberal management dogma. In: J. Lees, ed., *The future of psychological therapy: From managed care to transformational practice*. London: Routledge.

Simpson, I. (2017a). A reflection on reflective practice. In: C. Thornton and P. Zelaskowski, eds., *Special reflective practice edition: Group analytic contexts*. Vol. 75. Group Analytic Society, pp. 41–43. Available at: https://www.yumpu.com/en/embed/view/5ZKB6kOpqotlhRrX [Accessed 10 Feb. 2019].

Simpson, I. (2017b). What happens to us under neo-liberal conditions. In: E. Cotton, ed., *Surviving work in the UK* [eBook]. Available at: Middlesex University Research Repository.

Slavson, S. (1964). *A textbook in group analytic psychotherapy*. Oxford: International University Press.

Solomon, M. and Nashat, S. (2010). Offering a 'Therapeutic Presence' in schools and education settings. *Psychodynamic Practice*, 16(3), pp. 289–304.

Spero, M. A. (2003). Working conference on professional and managerial dilemmas working in and with organizations: Building bridges between group analysis and organizations. *Group Analysis*, 36(3), pp. 323–336.

Spillius, E. B. (1990). Asylum and society. *The Social Engagement of Social Science*, 1, pp. 586–612.

Stacey, R. D. (1992). *Managing the unknowable, strategic boundaries between order and chaos in organization*. San Francisco: Jossey-Bass-Inc.

Stacey, R. D. (1996). *Complexity and creativity in organisations*. San Francisco: Berrett-Koehler Publishers.

Stacey, R. (2001a). Complexity and the group matrix. *Group Analysis*, 34(2), pp. 221–239.

Stacey, R. (2001b). What can it mean to say that the individual is social through and through? *Group Analysis*, 34(4), pp. 457–472.

Stacey, R. (2005). Organizational identity: The paradox of continuity and potential transformation at the same time. *Group Analysis*, 38(4), pp. 477–494.

Stacey, R. (2012). *The tools and techniques of leadership and management: Meeting the challenge of complexity*. Hove: Routledge.

Stacey, R., Giffin, D. and Shaw, P. (2002). *Changing conversations in organisations: A complexity approach to change*. London: Routledge.

Stacey, R., Giffin, D. and Shaw, P. (2003). *Complexity and group process: A radically social understanding of individuals*. London: Routledge.

Steiner, J. (1993). *Psychic retreats: Pathological organisations in psychotic, neurotic and borderline patients*. London: Routledge.

Stern, D. (1985). *The interpersonal world of the infant*. New York: Basic Books.

Stewart, I. (1989). *Does God play dice? The mathematics of chaos*. Cambridge: Blackwell.

Storr, A. (1982). *Jung*. London: Fontana.

Thorndycraft, B. and McCabe, J. (2008). The challenge of working with staff groups in the caring professions: The importance of the 'Team Development and Reflective Practice Group'. *British Journal of Psychotherapy*, 24(2), pp. 167–183.

Thornton, C. (2004). Borrowing my self: An exploration of exchange as a group-specific therapeutic factor. *Group Analysis*, 37(2), pp. 305–320.

Thornton, C. (2010). *Group and team coaching: The essential guide*. Hove: Routledge.

Thornton, C. (2016). *Group and team coaching: The secret life of groups*. 2nd ed. Hove: Routledge.

Thornton, C. (2017a). Reflective practice and practical reflections: Linking thought and action in difficult places (Special Guest Editorial). *Group Analytic Contexts*, 75, pp. 5–11. Available at: https://www.yumpu.com/en/embed/view/5ZKB6kOpqotlhRrX [Accessed 10 Feb. 2019].

Thornton, C. (2017b). Towards a group analytic praxis for working with teams in organizations. *Group Analysis*, 50(4), pp. 519–536.

Thornton, C. (2019) Beyond the theory of everything: Conversation, group analysis and five questions to choose theory in action with teams. In: D. Clutterbuck, S. Hayes and K. Lowe, eds., *Practitioners' handbook of team coaching* Hove: Routledge.

Thornton, C. and Corbett, A. (2014). Hitting home: Irish identity and psychotherapy in the UK. *British Journal of Psychotherapy*, 30(3), pp. 286–304.

Toibin, C. (2009). *Brooklyn*. London: Penguin.

Tubert-Oklander, J. (2016). *Why a blog on field theory?* [Online]. Available at: www.internationalfieldtheoryassociation.com/blog-by-juan-tubert-oklander/why-a-blog-on-field-theory.

Turquet, P. (1975). Threats to identity in the large group. In: L. Kreeger, ed., *The large group, dynamics & therapy*. London: Constable, pp. 87–144.

Volkan, V. D. (2001). Transgenerational transmissions and chosen traumas: An aspect of large group identity. *Group Analysis*, 34(1), pp. 79–97.

Volkan, V. D. (2004). *Blind trust, large groups and their leaders in times of crisis and terror*. Charlottesville, VA: Pitchstone Publishing.

Volkan, V. D. (2009). Large-group identity: 'Us and them' polarizations in the international arena. *Psychoanalysis, Culture and Society*, 14(4), pp. 4–15.

Von Bertalanffy, L. (1951). General system theory: A new approach to unity of science. *Human Biology*, 23, pp. 303–361.

Von Friesen, A. and Wilke, G. (2016). *Generations-Wechsel: Normalität, Chance oder Konflikt?* Zürich: Lit Verlag.

Waldhoff, H. P. (2007). Unthinking the closed personality: Norbert Elias, group analysis and unconscious processes in a research group: Part I. *Group Analysis*, 40(3), pp. 323–343.

Waldhoff, H. P. (2007). Unthinking the closed personality: Norbert Elias, group analysis and unconscious processes in a research group: Part II. *Group Analysis*, 40(4), pp. 478–506.

Weintrobe, S. (2012). *Engaging with climate change: Psychoanalytic and interdisciplinary perspectives*. Hove: Routledge.

Whitaker, D. S. (1992). Transposing learnings from group psychotherapy to work groups. *Group Analysis*, 25(2), pp. 131–149.

Whiteley, J. S. (1986). Sociotherapy and psychotherapy in the treatment of personality disorder: A discussion paper. *Journal of the Royal Society of Medicine*, 79, pp. 721–725.

Whyte, D. (2015). *The solace, nourishment and underlying meaning of everyday words*. Washington: Many Rivers Press.

Wilke, G. (2002). The large group and its conductor. In: M. Pines and R. Lipgar, eds., *Building on bion*. London: Jessica Kingsley.

Wilke, G. (2005). Beyond Balint: A group-analytic support model for traumatized doctors. *Group Analysis*, 38(2), pp. 265–280.

Wilke, G. (2014). *The art of group analysis in organizations*. London: Karnac.

Wilke, G. (2016). Personal communication.

Wilkinson, R. and Pickett, K. (2009). *The spirit level: Why more equal societies almost always do better*. London: Allen Lane.

Wilkinson, R. and Pickett, K. (2017). *The inner level: How more equal societies reduce stress, restore sanity and improve everyone's wellbeing*. London: Allen Lane.

Winnicott, D. W. (1958). Transitional objects and transitional phenomena. In: D. Winnicott, ed., *Collective papers: Through paediatrics to psycho-analysis*. London: Tavistock Publications.

Winnicott, D. W. (1971). *Playing and reality*. London: Tavistock Publications.

Wojciechowska, E. (2009). Managing personal and professional Boundaries. In: P. Hartley and D. Kennard, eds., *Staff support groups in the helping professions: Principles, practice and pitfalls*. Hove: Routledge, pp. 147–160.

Zehr, H. (1990). *Changing lenses: Restorative justice for our times*. Harrisonburg, VA: Herald Press.

Zeldin, T. (1998). *Conversation: How talk can change our lives*. Mahwah, NJ: Hidden Springs.

Zinkin, L. (1989). The group as container and contained. *Group Analysis*, 22(3), pp. 227–234.

Žižek, S. (2001). *The fragile absolute: Or why is the Christian legacy worth fighting for*. New York: Verso Books.

Žižek, S. (2008). *Violence*. London: Profile Books.

Index

Printed in Great Britain
by Amazon